Before Command

Before Command

AN ECONOMIC HISTORY OF RUSSIA FROM EMANCIPATION TO THE FIRST FIVE-YEAR PLAN

Paul R. Gregory

PRINCETON UNIVERSITY PRESS

PRINCETON, NEW JERSEY

Library of Congress Cataloging-in-Publication Data

Gregory, Paul R.
    Before command : an economic history of Russia from emancipation
to the first five-year plan / Paul R. Gregory.
        p.   cm.
    Includes index.
    ISBN 0-691-04265-9 (cl.)
    1. Russia—Economic conditions—1861–1917. 2. Soviet Union—
Economic conditions—1918–1945. I. Title.
HC334.5.G74   1994   330.947—dc20   93-39139

This book has been composed in Sabon

Princeton University Press books are printed on acid-free paper
and meet the guidelines for permanence and durability of the
Committee on Production Guidelines for Book Longevity of the
Council on Library Resources

Printed in the United States of America
1 3 5 7 9 10 8 6 4 2

CONTENTS

PREFACE

THIS BOOK summarizes the research that I have done on the Russian and early Soviet economies over the past twenty-five years. As a graduate student working with Simon Kuznets, Abram Bergson, and Henry Rosovsky, I wrote my first paper on the level of Russian economic development—a paper that became my first publication. After this first effort, having discovered that I enjoyed doing empirical work, I set about for the next quarter of a century investigating the quantitative foundations of the late Russian and early Soviet economies.

The statistical raw material for each period was rich and largely unexplored. Moreover, much of the historical work done on these early periods resulted in grand theories or conclusions that were poorly or not at all grounded in the underlying data. Lenin wished to show that the Russian economy was the "weak link" in the capitalist chain. Alexander Gerschenkron used the Russian economy to develop his relative backwardness theory. Historians, without a serious investigation of the available data, became convinced that an agrarian crisis had occurred after emancipation.

I was fortunate to have the support of the National Science Foundation in the mid-1970s for my work on the tsarist period and again in the late 1980s and early 1990s for my work on the 1920s. The generous support of the Humboldt Foundation allowed me to do research in the best libraries of Europe in the late 1970s.

I wrote one monograph and quite a few articles during this period. Some found their way into economics journals, others into Russian studies journals, and yet others into collections and festschriften. Taken in their entirety, these publications present a picture of the Russian and early Soviet economies that is different from many of the standard versions of this period. It was for this reason that I concluded it would be useful to write a second monograph summarizing my findings and pointing out the ways in which they dispute previous findings.

With the turbulent events starting in 1985 and culminating in the coup of August 1991, I also thought it useful to look back to the distant past to determine how that period may guide decision makers as they seek an appropriate transition path.

Numerous scholars have contributed to the work on which this book is based. I have already named three of my professors. I would also like to mention Olga Crisp, Robert Davies, Peter Gatrell, Dietrich Geyer, and Arcadius Kahan as scholars who have provided valuable advice and assistance either through their own work or through discussion of my work. I have benefited from the writings and assistance of Russian scholars as well. In this regard, I mention Valery Bovykin, Ivan Kovalchenko, Genady Zoteev, Yury Bokarev, and Boris Mironov. The deepest intellectual debt is owed to the scholars who worked from the turn of the century to the early 1930s gathering and analyzing the statistics upon which this book is based—V. E. Varzar, A. L. Vainshtein, N. D. Kondratieff, and S. N. Prokopovich. My intellectual debt extends to many others too numerous to mention here.

Houston, Texas
August 1993

Before Command

Chapter 1

PERESTROIKA AND LESSONS OF THE PAST

THE COLLAPSE of the Soviet Union in late 1991 strengthened the resolve of the new leadership to create a market economy. The majority of the former Soviet republics favor both in word and in deed "radical reform." Radical reform, to date, has been pushed most rapidly in Russia and in the Baltic states. Although there is still disagreement about the pace of transition, there is little doubt that there is no way back to the old system. The transition formula has yet to be found, and the outcome of the political-economic battle over reform will not be known for a number of years.

Gorbachev's reform programs, begun in the second half of the 1980s, represented the first serious effort to replace the Stalinist command model with a more efficient economic system. The Soviet leadership, under Gorbachev, sought a middle ground between the failed Stalinist model and the market system of the industrialized West, which it viewed with suspicion. The major lesson of the Gorbachev experiment was the futility of half-measures. Whether this lesson will be duly noted by the new leaderships of the fragile Commonwealth of Independent States remains to be seen.

THE ROLE OF PRECEDENTS

Large-scale social experiments, such as fundamental reform of an entire socioeconomic system, should look to precedents and parallels for guidance. There are few to guide reform in the former Soviet Union. Reformers can look to the present for models—for example, to the industrialized market economies. In the late 1980s Sweden, with its high income, social safety net, and equal distribution of income, was often mentioned—without a strong sense of realism. The adaptation of the Swedish model to Soviet reality would obviously be difficult; Sweden has been a wealthy industrialized nation for over a century. It can better afford the efficiency losses associated with massive income redistributions.

Alternatively, reformers in the former Soviet Union can monitor the ongoing reforms in turbulent Eastern Europe and China hoping that someone somewhere has discovered how to dismantle successfully the Stalinist command model. This Eastern European parallel may be more relevant than the Swedish model because the Soviet Union and Eastern Europe have had a shared experience with the Stalinist economic model. Procedures for converting the command model may be the same, despite the vast social, cultural, and economic differences between the former Soviet Union and Eastern Europe. It is unclear how long we must wait before the Eastern European and Chinese experiments yield clear-cut successes or failures. The experiences to date, especially those of Poland and China, provide some comforting guidance.

The Soviet administrative-command system began directing resource allocation in the 1930s. Starting in 1928 Stalin eliminated private ownership in industry, trade, and agriculture; operated material balances through a planning commission and industrial ministries; forced requisitions from the collective farms that replaced peasant agriculture; and created a foreign trade monopoly that divorced producers and consumers from world markets. Administrative directives replaced private decision making throughout the economy.

The Stalinist model oversaw the rapid transformation of the Russian economy from an agricultural, rural, light-industry-oriented economy to an urbanized industrial economy. It created military power that, in the 1970s and 1980s, was purported to rival the military strength of the United States. The industrial transformation that took place between 1928 and 1940 required fifty to one hundred years in the industrialized West.[1]

The durability of the administrative-command economy does not mean that it worked well. Its weaknesses were apparent from the early 1930s. The Stalinist system did not operate at levels of efficiency anywhere near those of the industrialized West. It could neither create nor implement new technology; it could not produce the qualities and assortments of consumer goods desired by the population; and it created an inefficient and unproductive agriculture that did not share in the rest of the world's Green Revolution.

The task for reformers in the former Soviet Union is to make the transition to a new economic system that provides "acceptable" levels of efficiency and tolerable standards of living reasonably consistent with the underlying resource base. It would be unrealistic to expect them to find an ideal solution in the near future. If the reform leaderships can create a workable system, similar in efficiency to countries like contemporary Turkey or Israel, this would be a remarkable achievement.

THE PRECEDENTS OF THE PAST

The Soviet Union existed without capitalism for almost three quarters of a century. The civil war, which initiated the Soviet period, saw the introduction of "War Communism"—an abortive system that tried to direct resources administratively without the discipline of a developed administrative planning structure. It was during War Communism that the demolition of capitalist institutions began in earnest. The Land Decree of November 8,

1917, distributed the remaining large estates among the peasants. Industry and handicraft enterprises were nationalized down to those employing one or two workers. Private trade was declared illegal. The hyperinflation that accompanied the civil war changed the monetary economy into a barter economy. Peasant agriculture's "surpluses" were requisitioned by force.

Although War Communism did allow the Soviet leadership to emerge victorious from the civil war, its inconsistencies became increasingly apparent. Industry, agriculture, and transportation collapsed under the weight of War Communism's inefficiencies, and a new economic system was required for recovery. Lenin announced the "New Economic Policy," or NEP, in March 1921. It was a compromise blend of market and command.[2] The state continued to control the "commanding heights" sectors—heavy industry, banking, transportation, and wholesale trade—while markets directed agriculture, retail trade, and small-scale industry. A monetary reform, completed in 1923, reestablished a stable currency, the chervonets, which was the Soviet Union's last convertible currency. In agriculture, a proportional tax replaced forced requisitioning, and peasants were again allowed to sell in relatively free agricultural markets.

The NEP system prompted rapid recovery from the ravages of war, revolution, and civil war, but it was replaced in 1928 and 1929 with the administrative-command economy. Stalin cited the exhaustion of recovery opportunities and the unreliability of peasant agriculture as reasons for abandoning NEP. The NEP economy provided the Soviet population with a standard of living that remained unmatched for the next four decades. The NEP system saw a spectrum of private, cooperative, and state ownership arrangements, with private ownership dominating in agriculture, retail trade, and handicraft. Markets governed most resource allocations in small-scale manufacturing and agriculture. The New Economic Policy provided a number of bold experiments with foreign ownership and concessions.

It is no wonder that Soviet reformers refocused attention on NEP in the late 1980s. The parallels between the introduction of NEP in 1921 and Gorbachev's perestroika were striking. In both cases, the reform was proposed by the highest political authority (Lenin and Gorbachev). Both reforms represented a move from command allocation to market allocation; both sought to find an optimal mix of planned and market relations. Perestroika and NEP both faced strong ideological opposition from the Party orthodoxy.

Although some contemporary observers romanticized NEP as an ideal economic system, Soviet officialdom continued to represent it as a failed system.[3] It was pictured as a crisis-ridden economic system, particularly in agriculture, that failed to offer the Soviet leadership a viable alternative to collectivization and superindustrialization.

The Western historiographic assessment of NEP has been orchestrated to a remarkable extent by Stalin's interpretation of events.[4] The Soviet and Western literatures both characterized NEP as an unstable, crisis-ridden system the replacement of which was inevitable.

This book attacks NEP's undeserved reputation for failure. The NEP system spawned a remarkable recovery from the ravages of the civil war. The agricultural crisis of the early 1920s was the Soviet leadership's panicked response to market phenomena that they failed to understand. The "grain collection crises" at the end of the period were caused by inept state pricing policy, the obsession with government grain collections, and the ultimate desire to alter the social and political structure of the countryside. The recovery was far from complete at the end of NEP—contrary to the official depiction of NEP as having exhausted recovery possibilities.

The lessons of NEP are extremely important to current-day reform. The NEP economy reveals many of the problems that an economy combining market and plan inevitably will encounter. It demonstrates the uneasy coexistence of administrative decrees and market allocation. Many natural market phenomena—such as how much grain will be offered to the market or "speculative" behavior—tend to be interpreted as political rather than economic actions in such a setting. The greater flexibility of the private sector permits it to bid resources away from the state, thereby incurring the wrath of the state leadership. Moreover, there is a tendency not to trust market allocation during periods of shocks to the economy and hence to substitute administrative directives for market forces.

TSARIST ECONOMIC PERFORMANCE

If the reform leadership looks even farther back than NEP to the tsarist period, it encounters an economy shrouded in myths and stereotypes. Soviet historians were constrained by the research agenda set by Lenin in his *Development of Capitalism in Russia*.[5] This research agenda made it difficult, if not impossible, to obtain a clear picture of the tsarist economy in its last forty years.

Lenin was determined to prove that the socialist revolution would occur in Russia, the most economically backward European country. Lenin pictured Russia as a dual economy, combining backward semifeudal agriculture and handicraft with advanced enclaves of heavy industry. Lenin saw tsarist Russia as a semicolony of the capitalist West, whose investments created anomalous pockets of modern industry in a backward economy.

Lenin believed that industrial capitalism in Russia was more brutal and concentrated than in the West, where it was restrained by labor unions and social welfare legislation. Because it exploited the factory worker more, the Russian factory spawned a revolutionary proletariat more motivated to overthrow their capitalist bosses. Moreover, the Russian industrial worker had a natural revolutionary ally—the peasant burdened by the remnants of feudalism. In Lenin's model of socialist revolution, Russia, as the weak link in the capitalist chain, would be the host of the first socialist revolution.

The Leninist interpretation of Russian economic history captivated historians in both the East and the West. It painted a picture of capitalism in crisis—a capitalism bound to be overthrown by a superior economic system. Russian history as written in both the East and the West focused on revolution—on explaining in a logical manner why the Russian Revolution occurred.[6] If the Russian Revolution was to be consistent with the Marxian dialectic of inevitable socialist revolution, then internal contradictions (crises) must have characterized the final stages of capitalism. Historians have sought to find these contradictions. Russian economic history was, therefore, a history of perceived crises—agrarian crises, depressions, stock market busts, and political crises.

That the economic performance of the tsarist economy was unsatisfactory was a foregone conclusion dictated by the dominant research agenda. The Russian Revolution itself served as the ultimate proof of the failure of capitalism in Russia.

Soviet economic reformers initially paid scant attention to Russia's capitalist past; they simply assumed that capitalist Russia was a dismal failure. Why return to an unstable economic model that spawned crises and revolution?

The Soviet official presumption of economic failure was not based on objective factual information. In fact, the use of the theory of revolution to interpret Russian economic history is full of pitfalls. Just as economists are novices at explaining political phenomena, historians are novices in understanding economic history. The linkage between economics and politics has always been weak. Misinterpretations and misunderstandings are typically at their worst when economics is used to explain the dynamics of revolution.

QUANTITATIVE ANALYSIS

The failure to base the assessment of tsarist economic performance on factual information was not due to the lack of statistical material—information readily available to historians and policy makers. The numerous statistical offices of the Imperial Russian government filled libraries and government offices with statistics on agricultural output, industrial production, stock prices, consumer and producer price indexes, sown acreage, exports and imports. Moreover, because Russia was the world's largest debtor nation of the time, the world financial community took an intense interest in its economy. Hence, a massive volume of statistical information was generated both inside the Russian empire and in Europe. Moreover, the Russian empire produced more than its share of talented statisticians who ably processed and analyzed data.[7]

Despite the wealth of primary statistical information, the conclusion of tsarist economic failure was reached without investigation of even the most common indicators of economic performance, such as the growth of output or of productivity. The widely held conclusion that postemancipation Russia suffered a forty-year agrarian crisis was arrived at without a serious examination of per capita agricultural output. The numerous financial crises of the late tsarist era were heralded as signs of impending breakdown without serious analysis of trends in real business activity.

This book uses quantitative economic history to demonstrate that factual evidence does not support many of the stereotypes of Western and Soviet historiography. The rates of growth of output and productivity experienced by the tsarist economy in its last thirty years were comparable or even superior to those of Western Europe. The highly publicized Russian agrarian crisis was confined to the older regions of grain cultivation; Russian agriculture as a whole was achieving normal progress. The 1905 and 1917 revolutions did not follow economic downturns but rather periods of economic growth. The most serious cyclical downturn was caused by the civil unrest and disruptions that accompanied the 1905 revolution.[8]

In fact, the picture that emerges from the quantitative data is that of a Russian economy making substantial progress in overcoming its relative backwardness.

The Past as a Guide to the Present

Why is it important to reevaluate events, such as the economic development of tsarist Russia or of the NEP period, that took place in the distant past?

First, a society that is considering fundamentally restructuring its social, political, and economic institutions needs to know how well prior institutional arrangements worked. To prejudge the Russian capitalist economy or the NEP experiment as failures without dispassionate examination of the evidence limits the range of choice of institutional alternatives.

Second, the leadership cannot evaluate the success or failure of the administrative-command system without understanding the legacy of the previous system. The common stereotype is that the Stalinist model had to initiate economic development virtually from scratch. It was argued that the tsarist economy had failed to provide the necessary infrastructure, experience with sustained industrial and agricultural growth, and human capital. The "crises" of the NEP economy forced Stalin to embark on superindustrialization and forced collectivization in the late 1920s. Until the legacies of the tsarist and NEP economies are understood, the final chapter on the administrative-command system cannot be written. Moreover, it is easier to abandon a socioeconomic system that is retrospectively judged to have been unnecessary. If history does not justify the Stalinist model in terms of its social costs and benefits, arguments for its retention are weak.

Third, the social and economic behavior of a society is influenced by its past, especially when it confronts the choice of institutional arrangements. Macroeconomic policy in contemporary Germany continues to be influenced by the hyperinflation of seventy years earlier. The greater economic conservatism of the American South has been attributed to the Civil War hyperinflation that left a lasting imprint on public memory. Both the traumatic and the routine influence the collective memory of a society. Traumatic events, such as Stalin's terror, will haunt the Russian collective memory for centuries. The historical remoteness from market-economy experience affects both attitudes toward reform and its chances of success. The former Soviet Union can claim few citizens who have experienced the everyday routine of living and working in a market economy. There is virtually no collective understanding of buying, selling, producing, job searching, starting a business, or risk taking in a market setting. This lack of collective information hampers social reformers who may fail themselves to understand how markets work, and it hampers the creation of a base of public support for market-oriented reform.

The Pitfalls of Anecdotal Evidence

This book is about the quantitative economic history of Russia prior to the introduction of the administrative-command system. Quantitative analysis of historical events has had limited appeal because of its frequent use of economic theory and of statistical correlations and regressions. Moreover, quantitative analysis captures only a small part of the mosaic of the historical development of a nation. History is made up of more than output and productivity growth, stock market fluctuations, and changes in relative prices. Quantitative measures fail to pick up legislative initiatives, treaties, or changing moral and social values.

Much historical analysis rests on "anecdotal" evidence—the use of microeconomic evidence for historical analysis. Anecdotal evidence varies in its level of aggregation. At its lowest level of aggregation it includes travelers' accounts, accounting books from a single farm or factory, or fictional stories relating to life in a peasant village or factory. At its highest level of aggregation it includes the various budget studies of Russian peasant families conducted by local governmental bodies (the *zemstvos*) in late nineteenth century Russia.[9] When cumulated, these budget studies provide data on agricultural outputs and sales for entire regions.

Anecdotal evidence, at both its highest and lowest levels of aggregation, captures a segment of reality. Yet there are a number of dangers of generalizing from anecdotal evidence.

First, anecdotal evidence tends naturally to focus on extreme cases. For example, the assessment of nineteenth-century Russian peasant living standards varied by region, family, ownership forms, and a multitude of other factors. There was, in effect, a statistical distribution of Russian peasant living standards with associated means, modes, and standard distributions. The historian who uses anecdotal evidence would be more attracted to the extremes of the distribution than to its central tendency (the mean or mode). Contemporary newspaper or literary accounts of peasant life would be unlikely to focus on the mean or modal peasant family. Rather, such chroniclers would be attracted to the poorest peasant families.

Second, anecdotal evidence does not capture secular time trends well. Prominent or catastrophic events (such as famine) leave a more lasting impression on observers than do average events. The impact of the catastrophic event is so strong that it obscures secular trends that represent an averaging of periodic catastrophes with normal years. Just as people conclude that there is a long-term trend toward colder weather after the coldest winter of the century, so historians tend to generalize from unusual or catastrophic events.[10]

Third, it is easy to confound relative and absolute trends when using anecdotal evidence. Insofar as personal economic welfare tends to be judged in relative rather than absolute terms, individuals whose living standard is rising more slowly than that of others will likely conclude that their living standard has declined in absolute terms. Individuals are better judges of their relative than of their absolute economic position. If the Russian rural living standard was rising in the 1880s and 1890s but at a rate below the rest of the economy, peasant families could easily have concluded that their absolute living standard was declining.

Fourth, anecdotal evidence must be considered in the appropriate historical and geographic context. Modern users of anecdotal evidence must consider that the late nineteenth century was a brutal time in which to live—with its high rate of infant mortality, periodic famines, and crude transportation network. No one would deny the harshness of nineteenth-century Russian peasant and factory life as viewed from a modern perspective or even from the perspective of nineteenth-century western Europe. One must remember that some of Leo Tolstoy's children did not survive infancy despite his wealth and that many wealthy European entrepreneurs succumbed to plague and infection in Russia.[11]

Economic progress, however, is not measured in absolute terms but in terms of rates of change. When turn-of-the-century life is viewed relative to life a century earlier, it appears much less brutal. It is easy to overlook high rates of change, particularly from the vantage point of historical perspective.

Fifth, contemporary observers, even highly skilled ones, can be notoriously poor interpreters of economic events. David Ricardo, writing in the midst of England's industrial revolution, completely misread the importance of the technological advances surrounding him and predicted secular stagnation. It should therefore come as no surprise when less-skilled observers concluded that living standards were declining (when they were actually rising) or that a particular financial crisis was the most severe of the century (when it was not).

Anecdotal evidence does not easily reveal time series trends. Not only must the mean (mode) of the distribution be properly identified at one point in time (which is difficult due to the attraction of the extremes of the distribution), but the central tendency of the distribution at two distinct points in time must be identified and compared.

Anecdotal Evidence and Social Consensus

Despite its inherent unreliability in gauging aggregate trends, strong social consensuses have been based on anecdotal evidence. There was a remarkable degree of agreement among late nineteenth-century observers that the economic condition of the Russian peasant actually worsened after the emancipation. Among informed observers writing during this period, the deterioration of peasant living standards required no special demonstration. A quote from a member of a provincial agricultural committee is representative: "I suppose no one will require from me proof that our countryside is deteriorating. . . . We who live in the countryside can observe directly how, on the one hand, peasant agriculture is becoming impoverished and declining . . . and how, on the other hand, estate agriculture is also declining."[12]

The strength of the late nineteenth-century social consensus concerning the turn-of-the-century Russian agrarian "crisis" is remarkable, and it remains an important article of faith among historians. Careful thought, however, suggests that a long-term deterioration of rural living standards, especially during a period of rapid worldwide agricultural progress, would be unlikely. During this same period, Russian agricultural markets had been opened to world markets, there had been a dramatic expansion of the Russian agricultural frontier, and Russia had joined the United States to become one of the world's two leading grain exporters. Persuasive arguments would be required to demonstrate a long-term deterioration in this setting.[13]

The fact that anecdotal evidence, ranging from observations of a single economic unit (such as a peasant family or a gentry farm) to a single regional aggregation, provides unreliable information on macrovariables does not detract from its historical value. What contemporary decision makers thought was true at the time is more important than what statisticians, retrospectively reconstructing events, conclude was actually true. Political events, such as peasant uprisings and factory strikes, occur in specific locations. It is highly relevant to know that peasant living standards were declining in the region where unrest occurred, even if peasant living standards, on average, were improving throughout the economy. It would also be relevant to know the unemployment rate in the city in which the factory strikes occurred or the brutality of the owner, even if these factors differed significantly from average conditions.

LONG-TERM PERFORMANCE AND SYSTEM CHOICE

Historical evidence is used for different purposes. Economic historians are principally interested in long-term economic development—long-term growth rates and structural change in the economy. Short-term economic events are of less interest; they average out in the long run. Economic historians typically do not use their data to explain political events other than those that should be influenced by secular trends (such as shifting voting patterns due to urbanization). They are less interested in what people thought was going on at the time; rather, they wish to reconstruct events using statistical procedures that were often unavailable to decision makers at the time.

Historians typically have little interest in secular economic development. Rather, they are interested in explaining political and social events that were based on contemporary perceptions of reality.[14]

Historians tend to look for the unique and unusual; quantitative economic historians are more interested in the common and the general. The historian might view the monetary, fiscal, and tariff systems put in place in the second half of nineteenth-century Russia as creating economic outcomes that were unique to Russia (such as "hunger exports" or a "top heavy" industry). The quantitative economic historian, on the other hand, might look for the telltale signs of economic development. If individuals have common preferences and technology tends to be shared, all economies should follow similar paths of development.

The choice facing the reform leadership of the former Soviet Union is that of the economic and social system. Useful information and precedents in making this momentous decision are to be gained primarily from long-term information: How well did the tsarist economy perform under conditions of market-resource allocation? How well did the NEP system of mixed resource allocation work? Both economic systems are part of the region's collective memory and heritage. Their laws and institutions are still part of the collective record. The reactivization of a system that once was is easier for a society than the creation of a system that never was.

This book is about the quantitative economic history of the 1920s and of the late tsarist period. Both periods are relevant to the contemporary reform process in that they offer the leadership of the former Soviet Union historical alternatives to the administrative-command system. The Western and Soviet literatures presented both periods as economic failures: The tsarist economy did not grow, it experienced an agrarian crisis, and it suffered from periodic financial crises. Lenin's theory of revolution carried with it a strong presumption of failure. The socialist revolution occurred, according to Lenin, because Russia was the weak link in the capitalist chain.

The NEP period of the 1920s was also stereotyped as a failure. Once it had exhausted Russia's recovery possibilities, it no longer offered promise for further development. The continuation of NEP threatened reversal of the socialist revolution, and the periodic agricultural crises threatened the economic development of the Soviet Union.

The lack of attention to the quantitative analysis of these periods is striking. The presumption of failure was arrived at without serious analysis of the most common indicators of economic performance. This book will present counterevidence suggesting more favorable performance of both the tsarist and NEP economies.

Chapter 2

ECONOMIC GROWTH AND DEVELOPMENT
OF TSARIST RUSSIA

WE CANNOT reverse world history. We cannot reverse the Russian revolution of 1917; we cannot reverse Stalin's decision to collectivize agriculture in 1929 and to install the administrative-command economy in the early 1930s. If the leadership of the former Soviet Union were not standing today at a crossroad, the material presented in this chapter would be of considerable scholarly interest but of little practical import. But because it is standing at such a crossroad the leadership of the former Soviet Union should feel obliged to look backward almost one century to reexamine the remote legacy of its capitalist past. It should ask: Did we grow up believing in stereotypes and myths? Should we view our capitalist heritage in a different light?

It is time for a dispassionate review of the record of tsarist economic achievement or failure. This review will not be based on emotion or political rhetoric but on the statistical record.

WAS THE TSARIST ECONOMY A SUCCESS IN ITS LAST THIRTY YEARS?

There is no simple way to answer the question posed in the above heading. We have no magic standards for evaluating a country's economic performance, such as 4 percent per annum real growth or above constitutes "good" performance and 2 percent per annum growth or below constitutes "poor" performance. What we do know is that economic success, to the present day, remains limited to a small number of countries—the industrialized world—that account for no more than 20 percent of the world's population.

The economic performance of any country must be judged in appropriate historical context. The appropriate standard for evaluating the tsarist Russian economy is its performance in the late nineteenth and early twentieth centuries relative to the industrialized countries of the European continent and North America and to industrializing Japan. Did the Russian economy perform as well, better, or worse than the economies of the then industrialized West?

Nobel laureate Simon Kuznets delineated the patterns of modern economic growth of the nineteenth and early twentieth centuries.[1] Insofar as there were relatively few industrialized countries during this period (less than twenty) and their performance differed, we can only identify general trends and specify limits based on this relatively small sample of successful countries. To make comparisons of this sort, a large mass of historical data must be available, calculated according to common procedures. Several rich compilations of national historical series have been prepared and analyzed by Angus Maddison, Paul Bairoch, and B. R. Mitchell, as well as by Kuznets, and major studies of national income have been undertaken by Simon Kuznets and Robert Gallman (United States); Walther Hoffmann (Germany); Jan Marczewski and associates (France); Charles Feinstein, P. M. Dean, and W. A. Cole (Great Britain); O. J. Firestone (Canada); and Kazushi Ohkawa and Henry Rosovsky (Japan).[2] These studies describe the "Western" experience with economic development in the nineteenth and early twentieth centuries. The tsarist Russian economy of the late nineteenth and early twentieth centuries must be judged against these general trends and limits.

This appraisal of the Soviet Union's last full-fledged experience with market capitalism focuses on the last thirty years of the prerevolutionary era for two reasons. First, it makes little sense to examine Russia's premodern past. We date the "modern" era to the period after the 1861 serf emancipation and after the construction of the rail network. By the mid-1880s, both of these events had worked their way through the system. It was in the 1880s that industrialization began in earnest.[3] Second, reliable estimates of tsarist economic growth and performance prior to the 1880s are not available.

The cited estimates of Russian growth and structural change are primarily my own.[4] Appendix A provides a summary of calculation methods and biases and compares my estimates with those of other researchers. The general conclusions of this chapter hold irrespective of which set of estimates of Russian growth are used.

This chapter views the growth and structural change of the Russian economy during the late tsarist era in historical perspective. The Russian data are compared with those of industrialized countries during the nineteenth and early twentieth centuries.

We seek answers to two questions from such comparisons. First, we wish to determine whether the growth of the Russian economy was slow, average, or rapid relative to the then-industrialized countries over the same period. Second, we wish to determine whether the Russian industrialization experience differed in significant ways from the general Western pattern of economic development. Lenin argued in his writings that the Russian economy had unique characteristics that distinguished it from Western Europe and made it ripe for socialist revolution.[5] Alexander Gerschenkron proposed that tsarist Russia followed an "Asian model" of economic development that differed in substantive ways from the European model.[6]

The calculated Russian series, described in Appendix A, are based on methodology and primary data much like those of the historical series of the other industrialized countries. In fact, in some countries with a far more advanced level of economic development than Russia the raw statistics are much weaker (e.g., Great Britain).

Two Snapshots of the Russian Economy: 1861 and 1913

In the analysis of trends, the "big picture" is best seen by taking snapshots of the economy at two widely separated periods of time. Changes that are largely invisible over short periods cannot be overlooked over quarter centuries or half centuries. Moreover, errors and imprecisions in historical data tend to play a less important role when two widely separated benchmarks are used.

In the case of Russia, two appropriate benchmark years come readily to mind. The first is 1861, the year of the peasant emancipation. The second is 1913, the peak year of tsarist economic performance. The 1861 benchmark catches Russia on the eve of its major nineteenth-century experiment in social reform—the emancipation of the serfs—which ushered Russia into the modern era. It precedes the "railroadization" of the Russian empire—an event considered by some to be of equal importance to the emancipation.[7] Pushing the benchmark back to an even earlier date makes little sense. The data are too sparse. Moreover, our objective is to study the economic development of modern Russia, not the economic development of feudal Russia.

Two snapshots of the Russian economy almost fifty years apart bear witness to the amount of change that characterized the Russian economy from its entry into the modern era to the outbreak of World War I. Russian economic change must be judged in relative terms. The Russian economy was part of the nineteenth-century world economy and, more specifically, the European economy. Russia, on the eve of World War I, was the world's largest debtor nation. Europe's business cycles were felt in Russia. Russia hosted both Europe's capital exports and Europe's entrepreneurs, who set up shop in Russia in great numbers. European and American technology found its way into Russian industry and agriculture.

By the mid-nineteenth century western Europe and the United Kingdom had from fifty to one hundred years of experience with modern economic growth. Through sustained growth of per capita output, continental Europe and England had achieved unprecedented levels of affluence; the transformation from agrarian to industrial economies had been achieved. The average worker in the economy was no longer the peasant but rather the industrial worker. Both birth rates and death rates had declined in the process of demographic transition, freeing the industrialized countries from the Malthusian specters of overpopulation and subsistence wages. In 1861 the United States was poised to become the world's dominant economy. Its economy was already the world's largest in both absolute and per capita terms. Its affluence served as a magnet attracting European and Asian emigrants. America's vast frontiers remained to be opened.[8]

SIZE AND LEVEL OF DEVELOPMENT: THE RUSSIAN ECONOMY

Russia on the eve of World War I was one of the world's major economic powers (see Figure 2.1). Russia ranked as the world's fourth- or fifth-largest industrial power behind the United States, the United Kingdom, France, Germany, and perhaps Austria-Hungary.[9] The Russian empire produced about as much industrial output as did the Austro-Hungarian empire. Because of its size, the Russian empire was Europe's dominant producer of agricultural output.

The most striking difference between Russia as opposed to Europe and North America was the clear dichotomy between Russia's aggregate economic power, as dictated by the magnitude of the Russian empire, and its relative poverty on a per capita basis. Russia began its modern era with a population twice that of the next most populous country in Europe and North America (France) and ended the era with a population almost three times as large as its largest European neighbor (Germany). In 1913 the only country rivaling the Russian empire in size of population was the United States, with slightly more than half the population of Russia.

Given Russia's large population, exceptionally low per capita levels would be required to prevent Russia from being one of the world's major economic powers. This fact is reflected in national income rankings in 1861 and 1913. In 1861 Russian national output was roughly half that of the United States, about 80 percent that of the United Kingdom and Germany, and only slightly below that of France. By 1913 Russia's national output was well above that of France, roughly equal to that of the United Kingdom, about 80 percent that of Germany, and double that of Austria-Hungary. In relative terms, the only decline over this period was vis-à-vis the United States, an economy that grew rapidly in both population and per capita income between 1861 and 1913.

Russia's economic power was concentrated in the agricultural sector. In 1861 Russia produced more grain than any other country, and only the United States produced more grain in 1913. Yet in 1861 Russia was a minor producer of major industrial commodities (coal, pig iron, steel) and had only a rudimentary transportation system, despite its vast territory. By 1913 Russia's relative position had improved somewhat with regard to

A. Population
1861

Millions

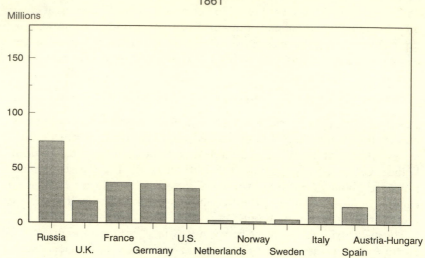

1913

Millions

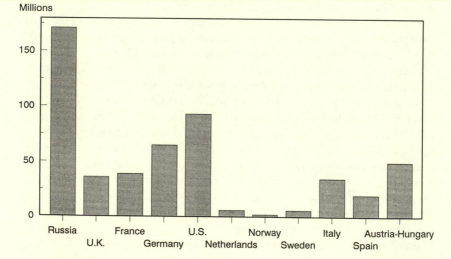

Figure 2.1: Selected economic and social indicators, Russia and other countries, 1861 and 1913

B. National Income (Million 1913 Rubles)
and Per Capita Income (1913 Rubles)
1861

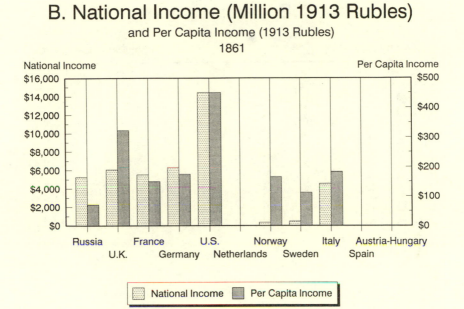

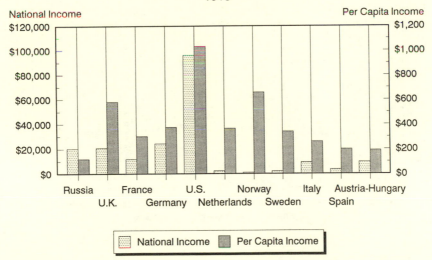

Fig. 2.1 (cont.)

C: Social Indicators

1861

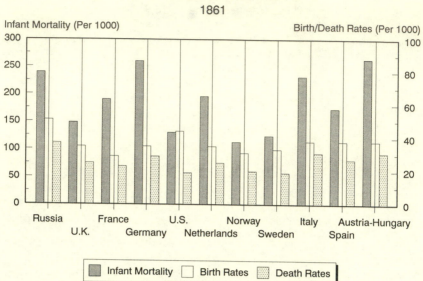

Infant Mortality (Per 1000)

Birth/Death Rates (Per 1000)

Russia   France   U.S.   Norway   Italy   Austria-Hungary

U.K.   Germany   Netherlands   Sweden   Spain

Infant Mortality   Birth Rates   Death Rates

1913

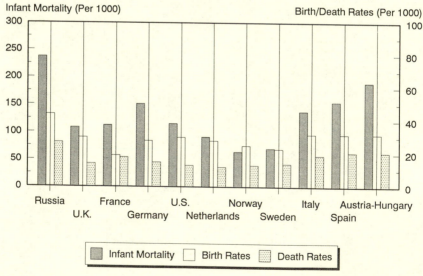

Infant Mortality (Per 1000)

Birth/Death Rates (Per 1000)

Russia   France   U.S.   Norway   Italy   Austria-Hungary

U.K.   Germany   Netherlands   Sweden   Spain

Infant Mortality   Birth Rates   Death Rates

Fig. 2.1 (cont.)

major industrial commodities (especially relative to France and Austria-Hungary), but Russia still lagged seriously behind the world's major industrial powers in industry. It was only in textiles that Russia occupied a position roughly equivalent to that of Germany, the continent's largest industrial producer.

The relative backwardness of the Russian economy is hidden by such aggregate figures but is evident in the per capita figures. Russia began its modern era with a per capita income roughly half that of France and Germany, one-fifth that of the United Kingdom, and 15 percent that of the United States. By 1913 Russia's relative position had deteriorated because of rapid population growth and relatively slow output growth until the 1880s. Russia's 1913 per capita output was less than 40 percent that of France and Germany, still one-fifth that of the United Kingdom, and one-tenth that of the United States. Of the major countries for which national income data are available for such an early period, Russia's per capita income in 1913 exceeded only that of Japan and was well below that of Spain, Italy, and Austria-Hungary.

The per capita figures reveal that Russia's imposing grain output was not the consequence of high output per worker. Some 75 percent of the labor force was engaged in agriculture, yet per capita grain output was well below that of France, Germany, and the United States in 1861 and was below that of Germany and the United States in 1913.[10] Yet Russia's per capita position was relatively more favorable in agriculture than in industry. For example, grain output per capita in Russia was roughly equal to that of Austria-Hungary in both 1861 and 1913; yet per capita output of

---

Sources for Fig. 2.1: The data in this figure have been collected from a number of sources. Most of the figures are from Mitchell, *European Historical Statistics*, Tables B.1, D.2, E.8, E.9, E.16, G.1, K.1. The U.S., Canadian, and Japanese data are drawn from Kuznets, *Capital in the American Economy*, Table R.22; Gallman, "Gross National Product in the United States, 26; Mendel'son, *Teoriia i istoriia ekonomicheskikh krizisov i tsiklov*, vol. 2, statistical apps.; Maddison, *Economic Growth in the West*, apps. A and B; Firestone, *Canada's Economic Development*, 74; Ohkawa and Rosovsky, *Japanese Economic Growth*, Table 3; U.S. Department of Commerce, *Historical Statistics of the United States*, Q284–312, Q321–8, B181–92, K502–16, K517–31, K532–7, P216–30.

The national income figures are calculated by applying 1913 exchange rates to the 1913 national income figures in current domestic prices. For those countries where only gross national product data are available, the United Kingdom 1913 ratio of net to gross product was applied. The exchange rates are given in Berlin, *Entsiklopediia russkogo eksporta*, 1:358.

The 1860 national income figures are calculated by applying real growth indexes of national income and population to the 1913 figures. In the Russian case, a 1.8 percent annual growth rate is taken between 1860 and 1885 from Gregory, "Economic Growth and Structural Change in Tsarist Russia," 433.

The Russian 1860 grain output figure is calculated by applying Goldsmith's index of grain output (including potatoes) for the fifty European provinces to the 1913 output figures. See Goldsmith, "The Economic Growth of Tsarist Russia," Table 1.

industrial products in 1913 was typically half that of Austria-Hungary. That Russia's comparative advantage lay in agriculture is clearly demonstrated by Russia's emphasis on agricultural exports.

Russia's most impressive relative improvement between 1861 and 1913 was the development of a rail network that was the largest on the European continent by 1913 (not unexpected given the vast territorial size of the Russian empire) and was comparable on a per capita basis to such countries as Italy and Austria-Hungary.

Russian infant mortality and death rates in 1861 were not much different from those of Germany, Italy, and Austria-Hungary a decade earlier. Forty years later, Russian infant mortality was virtually unchanged, whereas in the other countries it had declined significantly. The advances in public health services experienced in Europe were not shared by the masses in the Russian villages.

Russia was obviously backward relative to its major European competitors both at the beginning of its "modern period" (1861) and at the end of the tsarist era. This conclusion emerges unambiguously from the per capita figures and from social indicators. Russia's relative strength was in agriculture, where output per capita compared more favorably with the industrialized countries than in the industrial sphere. In industry, the most impressive per capita change was in textiles rather than in heavy industry.[11] Russia was indeed one of the world's major economic powers. In 1913 Russia's aggregate output was exceeded only by that of the United States, the United Kingdom, and Germany.

THE PACE OF CHANGE

Multiplication factors of changes in economic and social indicators can be seen from Figure 2.1. The 2.35 figure for Russian population shows that the 1913 Russian population was 2.35 times that of 1861. The 1913 Russian national income was 3.84 times that of 1861, and so on. The multiplication factors reveal the relative pace of Russian economic and demographic change between 1861 and 1913 against the backdrop of change in Europe and America. The multiplication factors reveal a pace of economic and social change for Russia that was generally consistent with that in Europe—although falling well behind the tempestuous changes occurring in the United States. Russian population growth was the most rapid in Europe and even came close to the emigration-driven high rates of the United States. Russia's growth of national income was equaled or exceeded only by that of Germany and Sweden. The combination of rapid output growth and exceptionally rapid population growth yielded a growth of output per capita that was relatively low by European standards.

Only the per capita output growth of Italy was less. Yet Russian per capita income growth after 1861 should not be written off as dismal; its multiplication rate was 85 percent of the European average.

The multiplication factor of Russian grain output (3.0) equaled that of Germany and was exceeded only by that of the United States, which experienced such rapid growth of grain output that it became the world's dominant producer, and by Sweden—a relatively minor grain producer. In the growth of pig iron production Russia was equaled or exceeded only by Germany, the United States, and Italy. The growth of the Russian rail network—which was initiated late relative to the industrialized European countries—was the highest in Europe and was four times that of the United States, a nation that also had a frontier to conquer.

Russia's most dismal failure was its inability to reduce infant mortality. The exceptionally high Russian infant mortality rate of 1913 was scarcely below that of some fifty years earlier. High Russian infant mortality shows that the Russian empire was an inhospitable place for newborns, with its harsh climate, high illiteracy rates, and poor provision of medical care. On the other hand, the pace of the demographic transition away from high birth and death rates was not significantly different from the European averages.

The multiplication factors of per capita output and population growth cast considerable doubt on previous conclusions about the failure of the tsarist economy. It should be emphasized that the period 1861–1913 includes a lengthy period of stagnant growth (1861–80); therefore, the growth rates of the "modern era" (the 1880s to 1913) should compare even more favorably with European performance.[12]

Russian Growth: 1885 to 1913

We turn now to an assessment of Russian economic growth during the industrialization era (1885–1913). How did it compare with the growth rates of other countries during the course of their industrialization? Historical growth rate series for Russia and for other countries are assembled in Table 2.1 for the purpose of comparison.

In comparisons of historical growth rates, one can never be sure that the individual series are comparable or that calculated differences are real in some statistical sense. One must, however, make do with the available series and hope that major distortions in the individual series will not affect the outcome.[13]

Table 2.1 presents series covering three periods of growth rates: "average period," "high period," and "early period." The average-period rate represents the average long-term growth rate between 1850 and 1913 (if a

TABLE 2.1
Average, High Period (HP) and Early Period (EP) Growth Rates: Late Nineteenth and Early
Twentieth Centuries, Russia and Industrialized Countries (% per annum)

	(A) Total Product	(B) Population	(C) Labor Force	(D) Per Capita Product	(E) Product Per Worker	(F) Incremental Net Capital- Output Ratios
1.						
Russia (1883–87	3.25			1.65	1.6	
to 1909–13)	(2.75)	1.6	1.65	(1.15)	(1.1)	3.1
HP: 1889–92 to 1901–4	4.7	1.3	—	3.4	—	—
EP: 1861–63 to 1881–83	1.8	1.1	—	0.7	—	—
2.						
Great Britain (1855–64						
to 1920–24)	2.1	1.0	0.8	1.1	1.6	3.3
HP: 1870–74 to 1890–99	3.0	1.2	0.8	1.8	2.2	—
EP: 1830–49	2.25	1.25	—	1.0	—	—
3.						
France (1860–70 to						
1900–1910)	1.5	0.2	0.7	1.3	0.8	—
EP: 1781–90 to 1835–44	1.25	0.6	—	1.65	—	—
4.						
Netherlands (1860–70						
to 1900–1910)	2.1	1.15	0.6	0.95	1.5	—
5.						
Germany (1850–59						
to 1910–13)	2.6	1.1	1.25	1.5	1.35	4.8
HP: 1886–95 to 1911–13	2.9	1.1	1.7	1.8	1.2	—
EP: 1850–70	2.4	1.1	—	1.3	—	—
6.						
United States (1880–89						
to 1910–14)	3.5	1.9	1.7	1.6	1.9	3.1
HP: 1869–78 to 1884–93	5.5	2.3	2.8	3.2	2.7	—
EP: 1834–43 to 1869–78	4.1	—	—	—	—	—
7.						
Canada (1870–74						
to 1920–24)	3.3	1.7	1.9	1.6	1.4	3.0
HP: 1891–1900 to 1911–20	4.1	1.6	2.4	2.4	1.6	—
8.						
Australia (1861–69						
to 1900–1904)	3.4	2.85	—	0.55	—	2.9
HP: 1861–65 to 1876–85	4.0	—	3.2	—	0.8	—
9.						
Japan (1885–94						
to 1905–14)	3.4	1.1	—	2.3	—	1.6
HP: 1920–24 to 1938						
10.						
Belgium (1970						
to 1913)	2.7	0.95	0.9	1.75	1.8	—

TABLE 2.1
(*Continued*)

	(A) Total Product	(B) Population	(C) Labor Force	(D) Per Capita Product	(E) Product Per Worker	(F) Incremental Net Capital-Output Ratios
11. Norway (1870 to 1913)	2.8	0.8	0.5	2.0	2.3	4.0
HP: 1915–to 24 to 1939	3.2	0.7	1.2	2.5	2.0	—
12. Sweden (1870 to 1913)	3.75	0.7	0.7	3.05	3.05	2.6
HP: 1926–35 to 1948–52	4.2	0.7	0.3	3.5	3.9	—
13. Italy (1870 to 1913)	1.45	0.65	0.35	0.8	1.1	—
HP: 1920–23 to 1938–40	2.4	1.1	0.1	1.3	2.3	—
14. Denmark (1870 to 1913)	3.2	1.1	0.9	2.1	2.3	2.4
HP: 1890–99 to 1914	3.7	1.1	1.2	2.6	2.5	—
15. Switzerland (1890 to 1913)	2.4	1.1	1.3	1.3	1.1	—

Source: Adapted from Paul R. Gregory, "Economic Growth and Structural Change in Czarist Russia and the Soviet Union: A Long-Term Comparison," in Steven Rosefielde (ed.), *Economic Welfare and the Economics of Soviet Socialism* (Cambridge: Cambridge University Press, 1981), 34.

Note: Dash indicates data not available. For figures in parentheses, see note 18.

series covering the entire time span is available). If such a long series is not available, then the average period covers the longest available time span prior to 1913.

The high-period rates are from Kuznets, who defines a high-period as the "one period among several distinguished (usually about 20 years in duration) with the highest growth rate in total product."[14] The high period in two cases (Italy and Japan) comes after 1913, but in most cases, it falls within the desired 1850–1913 time span. The early-period series represent the earliest available series for the few countries for which long statistical records are available. For Russia, the early period is defined as 1861 to 1883.

Table 2.1 reveals that the Russian growth rate of total product compares favorably with the average long-term rates of the industrialized countries between 1850 and 1914. In fact, Russian growth was equaled or surpassed by only the United States, Canada, Australia, and Sweden, and it equaled

or exceeded the growth of the two most important "follower" countries
(Japan and Italy) before World War I. With the exception of Sweden and
Denmark (with above average rates for Europe), Russian growth was similar to that of the European offshoots in North America and Australia,
countries that experienced rapid population growth through immigration
and high rates of natural increase. In the Russian case, however, rapid
population growth was entirely the consequence of high rates of natural
increase, since Russia experienced a net out-migration during this period.

The conclusion that Russian growth was high by international standards
is supported by Angus Maddison's figures for the period 1870–1913.[15]
Maddison calculates the average growth rate of "Western" output (Europe
and North America) at 2.7 percent per annum, as compared with the
Russian rate of 3.25 percent.

The high (by international standards) Russian growth of total product
was the consequence of rapid population (and thus labor force) growth.
However, on a per capita and per worker basis (columns D and E), Russian
growth is still respectable by the same international standards. The
average-period Russian per capita growth rate (1.65 percent) was surpassed or equaled by only Belgium, Norway, Sweden, the United States,
and Denmark. According to Maddison, the 1870–1913 average annual
growth rate of per capita output in the West of 1.6 percent was equal to the
Russian rate.

One must be cautious about the interpretation of the labor force growth
figures (column C) and the resulting output-per-worker growth rates (column E) because of conceptual and statistical differences in the measurement of labor force, particularly in the treatment of farm employment of
females. No adjustment can be made for differences in hours worked per
employed person, which likely fell during this time span but not at the same
rate for all countries. The Russian figures are themselves crude.[16]

Comparisons of the labor force and population growth rates fail to
reveal a consistent pattern. In some countries, labor force growth exceeded
measured population growth; in others it fell below population growth;
but only in the Italian and Dutch cases are population and labor force
growth rate discrepancies substantial. The conclusion follows that, as a
general rule, the population and the labor force grew at roughly equivalent
rates during this period. The long-term growth rates of product per worker
should, on the average, roughly equal those of product per capita, and this
is what Table 2.1 suggests when the countries are averaged.[17]

The Russian growth rate of output per worker (1.6 percent) was about
average for the countries surveyed. Average hours worked per employed
worker generally fell during this period, thus hours worked would rise at a
slower rate than population. One cannot, however, establish how Russian
average hours worked behaved relative to other countries. If anything, they
declined less than in the more advanced European countries.

Incremental net capital-output ratios (column F) are calculated by dividing the average ratio of net investment to output by the annual growth rate of output. Table 2.1 suggests that marginal capital productivity in Russia was average as judged by the experiences of the other countries in the sample. The exceptional cases appear to be Japan, with an exceptionally low (1.6), and Germany, with an exceptionally high (4.8), incremental capital-output ratio.

The surprising finding from the high-period comparisons is that the average growth of Russian output compared favorably with the high-period rates of the other countries. Russia grew as fast or faster than did Great Britain, Germany, Norway, and Italy, but notably slower than did countries such as the United States, Canada, Australia, Japan, Sweden, and Denmark, which experienced short periods of exceptionally rapid growth. On a per capita (per worker) basis, the Russian average growth rate is below the high-period rates of other countries.

The high-period growth rate of Russia covers a shorter time span than those of other countries (twelve years) and, hence, is not directly comparable to Kuznets's calculations of high-period growth. However, it may be noted that the Russian high-period rate (covering primarily the 1890s) exceeds all other high-period rates except that of the United States. On a per capita basis, the Russian high-period rate compares favorably with the highest high-period rates (United States, Japan, Sweden).

One cannot determine whether the growth rate differences of Table 2.1 are significant in a statistical sense. They use different total product concepts (Net National Product, national income, Gross National Product, Gross Domestic Product), and the labor force statistics are especially unreliable. Nevertheless, the conclusion is warranted that after 1885 the Russian economy grew at total per capita and per worker rates that are at least "average" relative to those of other major industrialized and industrializing countries. Surprisingly, this statement would remain valid for total output even if the most conservative estimate of Russian growth is used.[18]

We conclude that Russia had begun to experience modern economic growth after 1880, although this experience remained limited to less than thirty years. Accordingly, a long-term record is lacking in the Russian case. World War I and then the 1917 revolution interrupted this growth. Hence, it is difficult to know whether the growth would have persisted, accelerated, or decelerated in a capitalist Russia.

STRUCTURAL CHANGE

The course of structural change provides additional evidence on whether Russia underwent modern economic growth after 1885. Kuznets's estimates of the approximate dates of the initiation of modern economic growth in European and North American countries, as well as per capita

TABLE 2.2

Structural Change: The First Thirty Years of Modern Economic Growth, Russia and Other Countries

	Initial Date of Modern Economic Growth	National Income, 1965 $ at Initial Date	(A) Agriculture			(B) Industry			(C) Services		
			(1) Initial Date	(2) Initial Date + 30 Yrs.	(1 − 2)	(1) Initial Date	(2) Initial Date + 30 Yrs.	(1 − 2)	(1) Initial Date	(2) Initial Date + 30 Yrs.	(1 − 2)
1. Russia	1883–87	260	57	51	−6	24	32	+8	20	17	−3
2. United Kingdom	1780–85	227	45	32	−13	35	40	+5	20	28	+8
3. France	1831–40	242	50	45	−5	32	35	+3	18	20	+8
4. Germany	1850–59	302	32	23	−9	33	43	+10	35	24	−1
5. Netherlands	1865	492	25	20	−5	—	—	—	—	—	—
6. Denmark	1865–69	370	47	29	−18	—	—	—	—	—	—
7. Norway	1865–69	287	34	27	−7	32	35	+3	34	37	+3
8. Sweden	1861–69	215	39	36	−3	17	33	+16	44	31	−13
9. Italy	1895–99	271	47	36	−11	20	21	+1	25	28	+3
10. Japan	1874–79	74	63	39	−24	16	31	+15	21	31	+10
11. United States	1834–43	474	45	30	−14	24	39	+15	31	31	0
12. Canada	1870–74	508	50	36	−14	31	36	+5	19	28	+9
13. Australia	1861–69	760	18	21	+3	31	30	−1	51	48	−3

Source: Kuznets, Modern Economic Growth, 88–93, 131–32; Kuznets, The Economic Growth of Nations, 144–51, 24.

Note: Generally, the time spans covered by the Kuznets data exceed thirty years. In such cases the percentage changes are apportioned by the factor 30 divided by the number of years covered. Dash indicates data not available.

income at that date, are given in Table 2.2.[19] From additional data supplied by Kuznets, the approximate changes in the shares of major sectors (agriculture, industry, and services) during the first thirty years of modern economic growth can be compared with changes in Russia's industrial structure between 1885 and 1913.[20]

Russia began modern economic growth with a relatively high share of agriculture and a low share of industry, much like Japan. Unlike other countries beginning modern economic growth with high agricultural and low industrial shares (Japan, the United Kingdom, Denmark, Italy, the United States, and Canada), the decline in the agriculture share and the rise in the industry share were more gradual in Russia. In this respect, Russia parallels the French experience a half century earlier. Nevertheless, the amount of structural change, as measured by the changes in Russia's agriculture and industry shares between 1885 and 1913, was average or slightly below average when compared to the other countries surveyed.

Similar statistics could be cited for changes in the consumption, investment, and government shares of total product, but a casual examination of the data indicates that the Russian 1885–1913 experience was generally similar to that of other countries during the early stages of their modern economic growth.

RELATIVE AGRICULTURAL PRODUCTIVITY

Both Lenin and Gerschenkron pictured Russia as a "dual economy."[21] According to them, industry consisted of substantial pockets of modernity, fostered by foreign capital investment. Agriculture, on the other hand, was dominated by the vestiges of feudalism with cultivation techniques dating to the previous century. From Gerschenkron's and Lenin's description, one would expect to find abnormal divergences of agricultural from industrial labor productivity—a prime feature of their dual economy hypothesis.

The question of the productivity performance of Russian agriculture is of sufficient importance to investigate this matter despite the weak underlying statistics.[22] Table 2.3 demonstrates that Russian agricultural labor productivity grew at an annual rate of approximately 1.35 percent between 1883–87 and 1909–13. The industrial labor productivity growth rate was 1.8 percent, and the economywide productivity growth rate was 1.5 percent. In Russia, agricultural labor productivity failed to keep pace with industry and with the economy as a whole. The relative agricultural labor productivity ratio (agriculture to industry) was approximately three to four; that is, labor productivity in agriculture grew at three-quarters the pace of industry.

It is difficult to place these relative rates of growth in appropriate perspective because the relative rates of growth in the other countries during

TABLE 2.3
Composition of National Income, Russia, 1883–1913 (1913 prices)

Period	(1) Agriculture		2 Industry Construction, Transportation, Communication		(3) Trade and services		(4) National Income	
	(a) % of National Income	(b) Annual Growth Rate	(a) % of National Income	(b) Annual Growth Rate	(a) % of National Income	(b) Annual Growth Rate	(a) % of National Income	(b) Annual Growth Rate
A. Sector output, structure, and annual growth rates								
1883–87	57.4		23.4		19.2		100.00	
1883–87 to 1897–1901		2.55		5.45		2.5		3.4
1897–1901	51.3		30.6		18.1		100.00	
1897–1901 to 1909–13		3.0		3.6		2.75		3.1
1909–13	50.7		32.3		17.1		100.00	
1883–87 1909–13		2.8		4.5		2.7		3.3
B. Sector labor force growth rates								
1883–87 to 1897–1901		1.1		3.4		1.4		1.4
1897–1901 to 1909–13		1.7		2.0		2.0		1.8
1883–97 to 1909–13		1.4		2.7		1.7		1.6
C. Sector growth rates: output per worker								
1883–87 to 1887–1901		1.45		2.05		1.1		2.0
1897–1901 to 1909–13		1.3		1.6		0.75		1.3
1883–87 to 1909–13		1.4		1.8		1.0		1.7

Source: Gregory, *Russian National Income,* 133–34.

TABLE 2.4

The Growth of Agricultural Labor Productivity Divided by the Growth of
Industrial Labor Productivity, Russia and Selected Countries

Country	Period	Relative Growth Rate
Russia	1883–1913	0.75
Germany	1850–1909	0.67
France	1870–1911	0.99
United States	1870–1910	0.87
Japan	1880–1920	0.86
Norway	1875–1930	1.00
Canada	1880–1910	0.77
United Kingdom	1801–1901	0.74

Source: Gregory, Russian National Income, 169.

the same period vary substantially. According to Kuznets, in the course of
modern economic growth agricultural labor productivity grows at a pace
roughly equal to the economy as a whole, whereas industrial labor productivity grows more rapidly than the economywide average.[23] The Russian
experience is consistent with this pattern, but given the size of the agricultural sector both at the beginning and end of the period, it would not be
expected for the rate of growth of agricultural labor productivity to diverge
significantly from that of the economy as a whole.

Data on individual countries during the late nineteenth and early twentieth centuries are scarce. Table 2.4 summarizes the available evidence on
relative rates of growth of agricultural and industrial labor productivity.[24]

The most reasonable conclusion to be drawn from Tables 2.3 and 2.4 is
that Russian industrial and agricultural productivity does not appear to be
much different from that of other countries. The Russian relative agricultural productivity ratio was indeed in the lower group of countries
surveyed, but it did not diverge much from that of Germany, Canada, and
the United Kingdom, countries that no one could describe as "dual
economies."

Although these relative productivity calculations are only approximate, they are sensitive enough to reveal substantive Russian deviations.
Gerschenkron's and Lenin's depiction of Russia as a dual economy composed of a dynamic modern factory industry and a backward traditional
peasant agricultural sector does not appear to be accurate for the period
1885–1913.

DISTRIBUTION OF FINAL EXPENDITURES

The avowed objective of tsarist economic policy during the industrialization era was to raise the investment rate above rates that normally would

have prevailed in a low-income country by attracting foreign investment and increasing domestic savings.[25] According to the Gerschenkron model of Russian "Asian" development, high domestic savings were to be achieved largely by depressing rural living standards. An Asian pattern would be evidenced by high investment rates and low consumption rates at a low level of economic development.

Table 2.5 gives the breakdowns of total output by final expenditure category in Russia and in other countries for which data are available. The data are classified as "early" (the 1850s to the 1890s) and "late" (from the turn of the century to the early 1930s). We will examine whether the pattern of resource allocation in tsarist Russia differed from that of other countries.[26]

Definite signs of an Asian pattern are evident in both the early and late Russian figures. In the early (1885–89) period, the Russian net investment rate (7.8 percent) was exceeded only by that of Germany, the United States, and Australia—all countries with a per capita income dwarfing that of tsarist Russia (see Table 2.1). The other countries surveyed all had lower investment rates despite their much higher per capita income. The other country with an apparent Asian pattern was Japan, with a net investment rate roughly equal to that of Russia despite lower per capita income. Yet in the Japanese case, a portion (15 percent) of net investment was financed out of foreign savings, whereas in Russia it was financed during this early period entirely from domestic savings.

The early Russian domestic savings rate was thus high for a low income-country, exceeded only by that of the United Kingdom (1870–74), Germany, France (1850–59), and the United States. Russia's early personal consumption rate was exceptionally low for a low-income country. Whereas higher per capita income countries in this early period typically had consumption rates slightly below 90 percent, the Russian rate (84 percent) was more like those of the highest income countries (United Kingdom, Germany, and the United States).

Another distinguishing Asian feature of this early period was the large share of government final expenditures. The Russian government share of final expenditures (8 percent) was the highest of the countries for which data are available. Because Russian government expenditures were devoted primarily to defense and administration (and not to health and education), they reflect the heavy burden of military competition with the more advanced European countries and the considerable size of the Russian bureaucracy.

The Asian features of the early period became more pronounced by the eve of World War I. The Russian investment rate was now exceeded only by that of Germany and was roughly equal to that of the United States. Russia's domestic savings rate, however, was exceeded by several countries,

TABLE 2.5
Distribution of NNP, Russia and Other Countries, Current Prices (% share of NNP)

		(1) Private Consumption	(2) Government Consumption	(3) Net Domestic Capital Formation	(4) Net Foreign Investment	(5) Net National Savings
A. Early Period						
Russia	1885–89	83.7	8.2	7.8	0.3	8.4
U.K.	1870–74	85.2	4.5	4.0	6.5	10.5
	1885–89	85.9	5.9	2.2	5.5	7.7
Germany	1871–74	90.3		11.8	2.1	13.9
	1885–89	78.4	6.8	12.1	2.7	14.8
France	1850–59			6.8	2.9	9.7
	1880–89	82.1		7.2	0.7	7.9
U.S.	1869–88	83.6	3.9	13.5	−1.0	12.5
Denmark	1870–89	96.8		5.1	−1.9	3.2
Norway	1865–74	87.9	4.0	6.9	1.3	8.2
	1875–94	89.4	5.1	7.0	−1.5	5.5
Sweden	1861–80	89.3	4.6	6.6	−0.5	6.1
	1881–90	89.2	5.7	6.8	−1.7	5.1
Italy	1861–80	92.4	4.4	4.6	−1.6	3.2
	1881–90	88.6	5.0	6.4	0.0	6.4
Canada	1870–90	94.0	6.1	7.6	−7.9	−0.3
Japan	1885–89	85.8	7.7	7.6	−1.0	6.6
Australia	1861–80	92.8		12.3	−5.1	7.2
B. Late Period						
Russia	1909–13	79.6	9.7	12.2	−1.4	10.8
U.K.	1909–13	82.7	7.9	2.6	8.2	10.8
Germany	1909–13	75.5	8.4	15.2	0.9	16.1
France	1910–13	87.8		8.9	3.3	12.2
U.S.	1889–1908	81.9	4.9	12.5	0.6	13.1
Denmark	1890–1909	93.9		8.6	−2.4	6.2
Norway	1885–1914	88.7	7.0	9.5	−5.2	4.3
Sweden	1901–20	86.4	6.1	8.0	−0.5	7.5
Italy	1901–10	84.3	4.5	9.6	1.5	11.1
Canada	1890, 1910 1913	91.2	8.2	9.2	−8.8	0.4
Japan	1909–13	87.5	8.8	5.3	−1.6	3.7
Australia	1900–1901 to 1919–20	92.3		9.6	−1.9	7.7

Source: Gregory, *Russian National Income,* 172–73.

for Russia had become by this late period a significant foreign borrower. During the early period (the period of preparation for the gold standard), Russia financed investment entirely out of domestic savings. By the end of the period, domestic investment came to be financed out of both domestic and foreign savings.

At the end of the tsarist era, the share of Russian government final expenditures was the highest of the countries surveyed, but the differences between the Russian share and that of other countries had become smaller. Japan came to have Asian features much like Russia, namely, an exceptionally high share of government spending for a low-income country.

It is difficult to establish whether foreign capital played an exceptional role in Russian development, because "normal" patterns of foreign capital are not that well known. As judged by the experiences of smaller capital-importing countries (the Scandinavian countries, Canada, Australia, Japan, and the United States during its earlier period of debtor status), the Russian experience (net foreign investment accounting for up to 20 percent of domestic investment) is not unusual. We are not able to define what a "normal" capital flow is, and foreign saving as a percentage of total output appears to be inversely correlated with country size.[27] The Russian economy was very large; so perhaps the flow of foreign investment into Russia was indeed exceptionally large.

Resource allocation in tsarist Russia exhibited Asian features in terms of relatively high domestic investment and domestic savings rates, high government spending shares, and low personal consumption shares for a low-income country. In this regard, Russia resembled Japan. The puzzle is the mechanism by which Russia achieved its Asian distribution, for in Japan almost half of capital formation was from public investment, whereas in Russia public investment (except in railroad construction) played a relatively minor role.[28]

THE PERSONAL DISTRIBUTION OF INCOME

That income was distributed more unequally in Russia than in the advanced European countries is a fairly safe proposition. Russia's highly unequal distribution of income is commonly cited as a major cause of the revolutions of 1905 and 1917. It therefore comes as a major surprise that the Russian distribution of income calculated by the Ministry of Finance for 1905 and 1909–10 was not more unequal than that of the United States and was likely more equal than that of the United Kingdom (see Table 2.6).

In light of this unexpected result, one must question the validity of the Finance Ministry study. A casual examination of the Finance Ministry study does reveal a counterintuitive finding, namely, that income from land accounted for only 17 percent of income over one thousand rubles.[29] In a

TABLE 2.6
Shares in National Income of Ordinal Groups,
Russia and Selected Countries

	Top 1%	Top 5%
Russia		
1905	15	—
United Kingdom		
1880	—	48
1913	—	43
Prussia		
1854	—	21
1913	—	30
Denmark		
1870	—	37
1908	—	30
Norway		
1907	—	27–32
United States		
1913	14	24

Source: Gregory, *Russian National Income,* Table 6.4;
Kuznets, *Modern Economic Growth,* 208–11.
Note: Dash indicates data not available.

country that was still largely agricultural with a highly unequal distribution of land, such a low percentage seems implausible. It appears that the calculated distribution well understates the degree of inequality in Russia. Until a major reevaluation of the Finance Ministry study is undertaken, the Russian figures must be treated with skepticism.

LESSONS FOR PERESTROIKA

The Russian economy, on the eve of the October Revolution, was the most backward of the major European countries. This backwardness developed as a consequence of Russia's failure to participate early in the process of modern economic growth that began in England in the mid-eighteenth century and then spread to western Europe and to North America. The Russian empire began to experience modern economic growth in the 1880s, and from the 1880s to 1913 was able to keep pace with the industrialized economies of Europe in per capita terms and even catch up in terms of total product.

During the last thirty years of the Russian empire, Russia's economic growth was more rapid than western Europe's, but its rapid population growth held per capita growth to the west European average. The structural changes that occurred in the thirty years preceding World War I were in line with the first thirty years of modern economic growth elsewhere. Russia definitely had begun the process of modern economic growth by the outbreak of the First World War I.

Russian modern economic growth began under unfavorable circumstances. Long-term property rights had not been established in agriculture; onerous tariff barriers protected the domestic economy from competition; political instability had begun to grow, and the government bureaucracy was rife with corruption. Yet fundamental economic forces dictated sustained economic growth and profound structural changes. Because barriers to growth would have continued to disappear, Russian growth would likely have accelerated. If this insight is correct, Russian growth over the next half century (1913–1963) would have exceeded the rates recorded for the period 1885–1913.

We have no way of knowing for sure what would have happened had there been no world war, no October Revolution, and no Russian civil war. What we can say is that the Russian economy had begun the process of overcoming its relative backwardness and was on the way to sharing the affluence of western Europe and North America. The branding of the Russian economy as a failure is a consequence of the Leninist desire to show the ripeness of Russia for socialist revolution. It is not supported by the empirical facts. In fact, a remarkable feature of the debate over the state of the Russian economy prior to the Revolution is the failure to use empirical data. The empirical data, as we have shown, present a fairly clear picture of an economy taking the first steps toward affluence.

Chapter 3

THE AGRARIAN CRISIS

THE WESTERN and Marxist literatures explain that the Russian revolution was caused, in no small part, by the agrarian crises that plagued Russian agriculture from the 1870s to the early twentieth century. This chapter explores the sources of the so-called agrarian crisis and presents empirical evidence that refutes its existence.

AGRARIAN CRISIS AND REVOLUTION

The notion of an agrarian crisis features prominently in Lenin's writings on prerevolutionary Russia: The 1905 revolution was a reaction by exploited peasants and downtrodden industrial workers to growing immizerization. Symptoms of the agrarian crisis were rising land prices, growing peasant tax arrears, the famine of the early 1890s, declining peasant per capita landholdings, peasant impoverishment in grain-deficit provinces, and most significant, declining per capita rural incomes. The 1905 uprising was the peasants' way of reacting to their deteriorating economic situation.

Western economic historians such as Alexander Gerschenkron, Lazar Volin, and Alec Nove have largely accepted the existence of an agrarian crisis. They draw parallels between tsarist and Stalinist agrarian policies.[1] In both cases, industrial capital formation was financed by forced reductions in peasant living standards. Agriculture was starved to pay for the tsars' ambitious industrial programs.

Most historians believe that postemancipation Russian agriculture experienced an agrarian crisis.[2] To quote a typical conclusion: "Heavy taxes had exhausted the peasant population's ability to pay and had driven all of Russian agriculture into an endemic crisis."[3] Lazar Volin emphasizes the remarkable agreement among late nineteenth-century observers that the condition of the Russian peasant had actually worsened since the peasant emancipation of 1861. The deterioration of peasant living standards over the final quarter of a century "required no special demonstration."[4] Few social and economic writers felt that Russian agriculture was progressing on a promising course. Soviet students of prerevolutionary agriculture took the existence of an agrarian crisis as a confirmed fact.[5]

Sources of the Social Consensus

The Western literature has always been ambivalent in its view of tsarist Russian agriculture. On the one hand, Russia's prominent role in the world grain market has been cited as evidence of the vitality of prerevolutionary Russian agriculture and of the subsequent decline of Soviet agriculture.

On the other hand, writers of the period were convinced that conditions in agriculture were deteriorating. In fact, a remarkable social consensus existed among observers of rural conditions concerning the growing destitution of the village. Numerous sources—both literary and statistical—were cited to support the view of deteriorating living conditions in the countryside. Censuses of livestock in the Kromskoi district of Orel province in central Russia taken in both 1887 and 1901 showed a substantial decline in livestock holdings per family. *Zemstvo* commissions graphically documented the epidemics, the unsanitary conditions under which peasants lived, the malnutrition of peasants in many districts, and the high rate of infant mortality among peasant families.

Literature played an influential role in forming a social consensus about growing rural poverty. As Volin writes: "In belles-lettres, which always reflected accurately the pulse of social thought in pre-Soviet Russia, the theme of rural distress was taken up by outstanding writers of the period, such as Gleb Uspenskyy and Zlatovarskii, and later Chekhov. Perhaps the best portrayal came from the pen of A. N. Engelhardt who in the late seventies depicted rural poverty in his celebrated 'From the Countryside.'"[6]

There were indeed appalling cases of rural poverty in Russia. The existence of rural poverty in a particular time and place, however, does not necessarily yield accurate evidence about its trend over time or about its spatial distribution. According to the statistical evidence, agricultural decline was especially prominent in the populous central black earth region, whereas agriculture was expanding in other regions, especially on the periphery.[7] But since the central black earth region was populous and politically important, there was a tendency to generalize about the rest of Russian agriculture based on its experience.

In the course of any economic development, there will be rising and declining regional economic fortunes. The declining agricultural fortunes of the central black earth region were being offset by the rising fortunes of western Siberia and the Baltic provinces.

Aggregate data show how agriculture as a whole is performing. Averaging across families and regions smooths out differences at the extremes. Government commissions are usually organized to study problems, not to record successes. Literary accounts focus on the most downtrodden peasant family, not on the average family.

Defining an Agrarian Crisis

The literature has suggested a number of ways to determine whether Russia was indeed suffering an agrarian crisis in the decades after the peasant emancipation—for example, rising land rents, falling per capita landholdings, and tax arrears. There is no ready-made definition of an agrarian crisis, so we must craft one that fits the objective of this study. We must ask: Were organizational arrangements and state policy so structured in Russian agriculture after the emancipation to prevent the agricultural economy from achieving rates of growth of output, productivity, and consumption sufficient to sustain modern economic growth? If the answer is yes, then Russian agriculture was indeed in the throes of an agrarian crisis.

If we accept this definition, the appropriate test for the existence of an agrarian crisis would be the aggregate growth of Russian agriculture's output, productivity, and living standards. Although, as noted above, regional differences would be of considerable importance in explaining political and social actions, the major concern must be the aggregate performance of agriculture.

DOUBTS ABOUT THE AGRARIAN CRISIS

Russian agriculture had for centuries developed in an extensive manner.[8] The opening of the Russian frontier via military conquest, expansion into low-density areas inside the periphery, and later railway-led expansion were major sources of growth of agricultural output. Russian agriculture had grown largely through the expansion of cultivated areas, not through improvements in productivity. Even the central black earth zone was regarded as a relatively empty agricultural area in which rapid population growth was encouraged in the early nineteenth century.

Russian agricultural development followed the typical pattern of an economy with a vast frontier. Russia was able to expand agriculture's cultivated area by pushing out the frontier. As expansive areas were opened, older agricultural areas tended to decline.

The proponents of the agrarian crisis do not suggest that there was a crisis on Russia's agricultural frontiers. The institutional impediments to rational land cultivation were less prominent in the frontier areas. The agricultural development of western Siberia, for example, proceeded largely on the basis of land freeholdings much like in western Europe.

Long-term deterioration of peasant living standards, especially during a time of substantial agricultural progress in other countries, would be a rare historical phenomenon, requiring a convincing explanation. The agrarian crisis was purportedly characterized by an actual decline in real peasant incomes over a thirty-year period. As such, it would have to be caused by fundamental long-term forces, not by the natural fluctuations in agricultural prices and output. Moreover, the Russian agrarian crisis was manifesting itself at the very time when the fruits of railroad construction were being felt, transportation costs were being lowered, world technological progress in agriculture was rapid, and Russian agriculture was being integrated into world markets. It was during this very period that Russia and the United States emerged as the major suppliers of grain to the rest of the world.[9]

Russian peasant emancipation was compelled by the political foreboding over a restless enserfed peasantry and the growing conviction that serf agriculture was in a sorry state. To assert that peasant living standards deteriorated even further from the very low starting point of 1861 requires a convincing explanation.

Gerschenkron's Explanation

Alexander Gerschenkron sought to supply a theoretical explanation for the long-term decline in Russian peasant living standards that he believed took place after the emancipation. Gerschenkron contended that the agrarian crisis was caused by the emancipators' economic and political decision to retain communal agriculture.[10] The emancipation handed land over to the commune, not to individual peasant households. Moreover, the commune was made responsible for the mortgaged value of the land that was ceded to the commune and for making mortgage (redemption) payments, which it had to collect from individual peasant families.

Political authorities wanted continuation of the policing and tax-collection services of the commune, and the gentry wanted cheap labor, which was to be guaranteed by inadequate land allotments to the commune.

A heavy tax burden, by itself, would not be expected to cause a general decline in rural living standards. If land allotments had gone directly to peasant families and the communal form had been dropped, those peasants with the best farming skills would eventually have bought out other peasants. A private agriculture based on medium-scale units would have emerged along with the more viable estates. Labor would have naturally sought out its highest return, and for many peasants this would have meant giving up their land and working as farmhands, in the factory, or in rural artisan activities.

The retention of communal agriculture, according to Gerschenkron, made western-European-type agricultural development impossible. The restrictive features of the commune were too strong. The Emancipation Act of 1861 required that peasant families pay off fully their mortgage responsibilities before withdrawing their land from the commune. The Emancipation Act failed to create a viable capital market for peasant land purchases, which would have allowed peasants to pay off their mortgages. Even if a capital market had existed, the peasants' debt initially exceeded the capitalized value of the land. Paying off principal was not a viable option for the peasants in the first decades after the emancipation, nor would it have made much business sense.

The formal rules of the commune did not encourage productivity improvements. If a peasant family made land improvements, its investment might benefit another family at the next periodic redistribution. Joint responsibility for debts created a giant "free rider" problem. The more industrious peasant families, theoretically, had to pay the debts of laggards.

Key cultivation decisions, such as when to plant and when to start joint improvement projects, were left up to village elders, who often won election by offering vodka to their supporters. The peasant families who sent adult members to the city stood to lose land. Periodic redistributions were based on the number of adult family members, so the migration of a family member to the city would reduce the family's claim to land.

Because of natural differences in productivity and location, the equity-minded commune could not consolidate landholdings. Instead, peasant holdings were composed of strips of land located in different areas of the commune. Strip farming held down productivity.

According to Gerschenkron, the retention of a communal form of agriculture, overburdened by debt, caused the growth of agricultural output to fall short of the growth of agricultural population. Gerschenkron calculated that per capita wheat and rye available for domestic consumption in the late 1890s was lower than in the early 1870s.[11] Other indicators of the agrarian crisis were the growth in peasant tax arrears and rising land prices and rental rates.

The strongest and apparently most compelling evidence of an agrarian crisis was the well-documented existence of rural poverty in Russia. Rural poverty was chronicled by the Valuev Commission in the 1870s and by the numerous *zemstvo* studies of peasant consumption and wealth holdings. The terrible famine of the early 1890s was followed by famines in 1897 and 1901.

In the Gerschenkron model, communal agriculture eventually strangled industrialization. Restrictions on labor mobility starved industry of labor and forced Russian industry to use capital-intensive factor proportions. The exhaustion of the peasantry created political instability. Communal agriculture depressed agricultural productivity and deprived the Russian economy of agricultural raw materials. The agrarian crisis kept the peasant consumer from the market, forcing the Russian state to be the main purchaser of industrial goods.[12]

The civil unrest of 1905 forced the Russian leadership to introduce meaningful reform, in the form of the Stolypin reforms. These reforms cancelled peasant indebtedness and gave peasant families the right to withdraw their land from the commune. The Stolypin reforms came too late. The outbreak of World War I was followed by the October Revolution, which ended the chances of a prosperous private agriculture in Russia.

AGRICULTURAL PERFORMANCE AND THE AGRARIAN CRISIS

The neatness and convenience of Gerschenkron's agrarian crisis hypothesis have made it a part of the received doctrine on prerevolutionary Russia. It provides an apparently logical explanation of the major political event prior to October 1917—the 1905 revolution. It is a point of view that can draw support from Marxist and Western scholars alike. For this reason, the agrarian crisis hypothesis remains firmly entrenched in most standard histories of prerevolutionary Russia.

Much of the discussion of the agrarian crisis has not been based on direct evidence of rural living standards. Instead, indirect evidence such as peasant tax arrears, excise tax payments, rising land rents, and accounts of rising poverty have been cited to prove the existence of an agrarian crisis.[13]

The most compelling evidence of an agrarian crisis would be country-wide declining rural living standards. If real per capita rural income was indeed dropping or stagnant over the decades preceding the 1905 revolution, the agrarian crisis hypothesis would appear justified.

It is impossible to estimate a comprehensive index of rural real per capita income for the period 1860–1905. The conceptual difficulties and data problems are simply too great. In the end, one must rely on more partial indicators of rural living standards.

The best available data are for grain production and technical crops.[14] Reliable livestock, dairy, hunting, fishing, and vegetable production statistics are scarce as are data on peasant purchases in retail markets. Moreover, data on peasant earnings in nonagricultural pursuits is sketchy.

The available data allow three approaches to test the agrarian crisis hypothesis. The first is to use aggregate data (agricultural output, consumer goods output). Second, the wealth of data on grain production, sales, and exports can be used to draw inferences concerning peasant living standards.[15] The major drawback is that grain products accounted for only 50 percent of retained farm consumption at the end of this period.[16] The third approach is to use data on the real wages of hired agricultural workers.[17] Presumably, real wage trends would reflect trends in rural living standards.

Aggregate Output

The national income figures cited in Chapter 2 provide some insights on the agrarian crisis. Agriculture accounted for 85 percent of the Russian population and for 75 percent of the Russian labor force at the turn of the century. It is therefore unlikely that trends in rural real incomes would differ substantially from the economy as a whole. For urban incomes to grow much faster than rural incomes in the long run, severe restrictions on rural-urban migration would have to be present to prevent a narrowing of wage differentials.[18]

As noted in Chapter 2, the growth of real per capita income in Russia was comparable to that in other countries over the period 1861–1913. If one concentrates on the "industrialization era" (the 1880s and 1890s), Russia's growth of per capita output was comparable to western Europe's during the supposed peak of the agrarian crisis. In a predominantly agricultural country, any secular decline in rural per capita income would almost inevitably show up as a decline in per capita national income. If the national income figures of the previous chapters are to be believed, they provide no evidence of a countrywide agrarian crisis prior to the turn of the century.

Agricultural Production

The most comprehensive study of Russian agricultural production over the 1861–1913 period was done by Raymond Goldsmith in 1961.[19] Goldsmith used data from the fifty European provinces of Russia and hence omitted the faster growing periphery areas. Moreover, the Goldsmith series were for gross agricultural production rather than net production. Insofar as Russia began this era with exceedingly high ratios of seed grain to grain output, net growth would have been higher than growth of gross agricultural production.[20] Accordingly, the Goldsmith series represent a conservative estimate of Russian agricultural output.

The Goldsmith series (Table 3.1) reveal that per capita agricultural output was probably stagnant between the early 1870s and early 1880s, but grew substantially on a per capita basis from the onset of the industrialization era in the 1880s through the first five years of the twentieth century and resumed its growth after the unrest of 1905.

Goldsmith fails to provide support for the agrarian crisis hypothesis. Both agricultural and factory production were growing faster than the population from the 1880s to 1904, albeit with considerable annual fluctuations.

As aggregate figures, the Goldsmith data tell us little about regional trends or about the distribution of this output between the estates and peasant households. It is unlikely for an agriculture that was growing on a per capita basis not to have this growth shared by the majority of the rural population. Peasant agriculture was the dominant form of agricultural production during the late tsarist period. Between 1885 and 1913 estate agriculture's share of cultivated land fell from 30 to 25 percent, while the shares of peasant allotments and privately held peasant land rose from 60

TABLE 3.1

Indexes of Agricultural Production, Factory Production, and Population, Fifty
European Provinces, 1870–74

Period	Crops	Factory Production	Total Population	Rural Population
1870–74	100	100	100	100
1883–87	117	217	120	117
1900–1904	185	588	156	151

Source: Goldsmith, "The Economic Growth of Tsarist Russia."

to 66 percent.[21] These percentages probably understate the relative shares
of peasant households because a large portion of gentry land was leased to
peasant families.[22]

The alternate agricultural production series for the 1885–1913 period
that I present in Table 3.2 corrects for the two major deficiencies in the
Goldsmith series.[23] Table 3.2 includes the non-European provinces and
adjusts for the decline in the seed-output ratio.[24] For these two reasons, it
yields agricultural growth rates higher than Goldsmith's.

The author's results confirm Goldsmith's basic result: that there was
substantial per capita growth during the two decades preceding the 1905
revolution. From 1883 to 1901 agricultural output grew at 2.55 percent
per annum—a rate double the 1.3 population growth rate.

A third source of aggregate evidence for the twenty years leading up to
the 1905 revolution is an index of per capita output of consumption goods,
prepared but never published by the prominent Russian statistician V. E.
Varzar.[25]

Varzar's index consists of physical output series weighted by 1913 prices
(see Table 3.3). It includes consumer goods such as grains, animal products, and textiles, and some producer goods such as pig iron and copper.

TABLE 3.2

Growth of Russian National Income, 1883–1913 (annual growth rates)

Period	Agriculture	Industry	Trade and Services	National Income
1883–87 to 1897–1901	2.55	5.45	2.50	3.4
1897–1901 to 1909–13	3.0	3.6	2.8	3.1

Source: Gregory, *Russian National Income,* Table 6.3.

TABLE 3.3
Varzer's Index of Output of Consumption Goods
(1913 prices)

Period	Value of Production (in millions of rubles)	Per Capita Output
1887	4298	48.0
1904	7057	60.6

Source: Maslov, Kriticheski analiz burzhauznykh statisticheskikh publikatsii, 459.

The Varzar index shows a 26 percent increase in the real per capita output of consumer goods between 1887 and 1904 (a 1 percent annual rate of increase). Insofar as the rural population accounted for 85 percent of the total population, simple arithmetic rules out the possibility that these increases in real per capita consumption would have been restricted to the urban population alone.

In sum, the available agricultural production series suggest that agricultural production grew more rapidly than the rural population did between the 1880s and 1905. Both series grew at circa 2.5 percent per annum. According to both series, agricultural output was growing at around 1 percent per capita. The available agricultural output series do not suggest declining output per capita in agriculture. Instead, they point to a substantial growth of per capita agricultural output when cumulated over twenty years. Extraordinary upward biases would be required to yield declining per capita output.[26]

Agricultural Exports

The forcing of "hunger exports" from the rural population has been cited as another indicator of the agrarian crisis. The "hunger exports" proposition argues that an increase in agriculture's output per capita could still have been consistent with declining rural living standards. The increase in grain exports recorded during this period was a sign not of rising prosperity but of the peasants' scramble to meet tax obligations.

Grain export statistics (which are the most reliable statistics cited in this chapter) reveal that grain exports did indeed grow more rapidly than grain output during this period. Between 1884 and 1904 grain exports grew at an annual rate of 3.5 percent, as compared to a growth rate of grain output of 2.5 percent.[27] The ratio of grain exports to grain output therefore rose at an annual rate of around 1 percent over these two decades.

Do increasing grain exports mean that peasants were being "forced" by oppressive taxes to part involuntarily with their grain production and thereby suffer declines in their standards of living? By marketing grain, peasants were more likely exchanging cash crops for manufactured goods and other farm products. Such exchanges, if voluntary, raise, rather than lower, standards of well-being. The question is therefore: Were such exchanges voluntary?

It is doubtful that the Russian state possessed sufficient power in the countryside to force peasants to part involuntarily with their output. The evidence on tax arrears suggests that peasants treated direct tax obligations rather casually. "Fixed" tax payments were positively correlated with agricultural incomes. When harvests were good and prices were high, the peasants paid their taxes. When harvests were bad and prices were low, they did not.

It is hard to imagine the peasant community marketing grain in face of hunger in order to meet direct tax obligations. The state's reliance on indirect taxes supports the proposition that peasants could not be forced by direct taxes to market output against their wishes.

Agricultural Wealth

A further indicator of rural living standards is the capital wealth of the agricultural population. The real capital stock of a farm population consists of its livestock herds, farm equipment, inventories, and farm structures. Unfortunately, the simplest indicator of rural wealth—livestock—is subject to a wide margin of error in tsarist statistics. The official series on livestock gathered by veterinary authorities and the Ministry of Agriculture are considered unreliable, and hence we cannot determine conclusively whether per capita livestock holdings were rising between the 1880s and 1904.

Two studies that have been undertaken of livestock herds come to very different conclusions.[28] Depending on which one we use, livestock herds could have fallen slightly or remained constant on a per capita basis between 1885 and 1905.

We have better data on other forms of real capital wealth in Russian agriculture. Available estimates of the agricultural capital stock are provided in Table 3.4. They show that the agricultural capital stock was growing more rapidly than farm population between 1890 and 1904. This conclusion holds irrespective of which series is used for livestock herds.

RURAL LIVING STANDARDS

National income, agricultural production, and agricultural capital stock all point to per capita increases between the 1880s and 1904. Such series,

TABLE 3.4
Annual Growth Rate of Agricultural Capital Stock, Russia
(1890–1914, 1913 prices)

1. Equipment and structures	2.7%
2. Equipment, structures, and livestock (Kahan)	1.8%
3. Equipment, structures, and livestock (Gregory)	2.0%

Sources: Line 2 is from Kahan, "Capital Formation," 300. Line 3 is from Gregory, *Russian National Income,* apps. 8 and 9. Column 1 is from the Gregory series on farm structures and Kahan's series on farm equipment.

however, do not shed light on regional and household distributions. It is possible, for example, for one agricultural region to experience declining per capita output while the aggregate series is growing per capita. It is also possible for one agricultural group, say small landholders, to experience declining per capita output while the aggregate series grows.

We cannot break down the agricultural series between the estates and peasant farms. It is important to the agrarian crisis debate, however, to demonstrate that capita growth was shared by peasant farmers and was not limited to estate agriculture.

Grain retained by peasants for their own consumption (given Adam Smith's adage about the demand for food being limited by the capacity of the stomach) should roughly indicate the farm population's consumption of grain products. Peasant budget studies show that grain made up a substantial portion of the peasant family's budget and, hence, grain consumption serves as a key indicator of peasant real income.

Figures on food grains retained (consumed) by the farm population are recorded in Table 3.5. Between 1885–89 and 1897–1901, the constant-price value of grain products retained by the farm population rose by 51 percent, while the rural population increased by 17 percent. Grain consumption on the farm grew three times faster than the rural population.

Table 3.5 shows a changing composition of retained grain products in favor of the "luxury" grain, wheat. In the 1880s wheat was primarily produced for the market, and rye was consumed by the peasant family. By

TABLE 3.5
Retained Grain Products, Russia (1913 prices in millions of rubles)

Year	Wheat		Rye		Ale		Potatoes		Total	
1885–89	154	(100)	551	(100)	113	(100)	65	(100)	883	(100)
1897–1901	44	(223)	649	(118)	168	(149)	171	(263)	1332	(151)

Source: Gregory, "Grain Marketings," 147.

the turn of the century peasant families were consuming significant portions of their wheat crops—a fairly clear sign of rising per capita income.

RURAL WAGES

Tsarist statistical authorities compiled considerable data on the wages of hired agricultural workers. Much of this data has been summarized by S. G. Strumilin.[29] Agricultural wages adjusted for inflation also provide evidence on the existence of an agrarian crisis. It would be highly unlikely for real agricultural wages to rise while rural real incomes generally fell.

The Strumilin wage data apply to the average wages of hired farmhands for the fifty European provinces. Hence, they are averages that cover most hired agricultural workers. After adjustment for inflation, Strumilin finds that the average daily real wage of hired farm workers rose by 14 percent between 1885–87 and 1903–5. Again, we find no evidence of an economywide decline in agriculture. Strumilin, as a prominent Gosplan economist, would have had no vested interest in producing such a result.

An impressive array of evidence thus supports the proposition that postemancipation Russian agriculture was not deteriorating. Both agricultural output and grain consumption point to the fact that the output and consumption of agricultural goods rose faster than did rural population from the early 1880s to 1905. Varzar's data on per capita consumption fail to support the view of declining rural living standards. Real agricultural wages were rising from the early 1880s to 1905. In fact, none of the cited series supports the basic propositions of the agrarian crisis.

A DUAL ECONOMY?

Postemancipation agriculture grew on a per capita basis. Perhaps its growth was so slow compared to industrial growth that, in relative terms, it gave the impression of crisis. Perhaps postemancipation agriculture could be characterized as a dual economy, consisting of a backward and primitive peasant agriculture and an advanced industrial economy.

For such a dual economy to exist, there would have to be a strong mechanism for limiting the flows between the two sectors, particularly flows of population and labor force. The dual economy thesis is based, in part, on the notion that the emancipation placed such severe restrictions on mobility that large income differentials could emerge between agriculture and industry.[30] In this way, the farm population would be forced to shoulder the burden of industrial investment.

To find evidence of a dual Russian economy one can look at urban and rural living standards and relative agricultural-industrial productivity. In Table 3.6, data are assembled on growth indexes of "urban" and "rural"

TABLE 3.6
Urban and Rural Consumption Expenditures (annual growth rates)

Year	Urban Consumption	Rural Consumption	Government
1885–89 to 1889–93	1.2	0.4	0.4
1889–93 to 1893–97	5.7	5.9	11.9
1893–97 to 1897–1901	5.7	1.6	3.4
1897–1901 to 1901–1905	2.9	3.1	2.9
1885–89 to 1897–1901	3.2	2.7	4.5

Source: Gregory, Russian National Income, Table 6.2.

real consumption. Needless to say, these two indexes are inexact. The urban index assumes that all retail sales were to urban residents, and the rural component includes only retained farm products and rural housing services.

The two indexes on urban and rural real expenditures fail to reveal a significant divergence between urban and rural real consumption trends. Real rural consumption growth is likely underestimated due to the allocation of all retail sales to the urban population. Accordingly, the growth of per capita consumption was not limited to the urban population alone. As noted above, in a country dominated by rural population, arithmetic rules out the possibility of substantial per capita increases that exclude the rural population.

The relative rate of growth of agricultural labor productivity in Russia and other countries was discussed in Chapter 2. A dual Russian economy would be revealed by low relative rates of growth of agricultural labor productivity vis-à-vis other countries. As Table 2.4 showed, Russian *relative* agricultural labor productivity growth did not stand out as being extraordinarily low relative to other countries. Although Russian agricultural productivity lagged behind industrial productivity, this phenomenon is characteristic of modern economic growth. The extent of the Russian lag appears not to have been exceptional by western European standards.

How Did Communal Agriculture Actually Work?

The aggregate evidence suggests that Gerschenkron underestimated the vitality of post-emancipation Russian agriculture.[31] Gerschenkron, however, makes a convincing case of the nonviability of Russian communal agriculture in the postemancipation period. The postemancipation commune restricted labor mobility, dampened incentives, and created inefficient strip farming.

The Flexibility of the Commune

In its legal form, the Russian commune, both before and after the emancipation, could not have been set up in a worse form for raising productivity. Periodic redistribution, strong equity principles, and collective responsibility, if strictly observed, should have strongly impeded productivity improvements. The real issue, however, is not the formal rules of the commune, but its actual operating arrangements. Scholars who believe that the commune operated according to its legal rules implicitly accept the populist arguments of A. V. Chayanov that Russian peasants did not act as rational economic agents. Chayanov believed that they operated according to an unusual set of rules that caused them to satisfice and to give priority to equity considerations within the family and commune.[32]

The alternative approach would be to assume that Russian peasants operated according to "rational" neoclassical economic rules. They sought out profit opportunities and acted as utility maximizers. If this assumption is correct, then the neoclassical model would predict that many of the formal rules of the commune would have been overridden by considerations of economic rationality.

If the commune indeed distributed land in a manner uncorrelated with peasant farming skills (such as the initial emancipation distribution), there would have been pressure for redistribution among peasant households based on informal agreements and side payments. The more able farmer would have offered terms to cultivate the less able peasant's land that would increase the welfare of both parties. A mutually beneficial exchange would have given less able farmers the opportunity to employ their labor elsewhere. Side payments could have varied from the use of draft animals to a share of the crop to a money payment.

With a profit-minded peasantry, it would be difficult to envision Russian agriculture not taking advantage of these opportunities. The initial distribution of land, therefore, would have had a much stronger effect on the distribution of income within peasant agriculture than on its productivity. In effect, an equal distribution of land would have resulted in the eventual redistribution of income from the more able to the less able peasants.

The historical literature has yet to offer the necessary case studies of the actual operation of the Russian commune. A close analysis of the commune might show a strong pattern of informal land and wealth redistributions based on mutually beneficial side payments. A land distribution based on equity rather than productivity need not detract significantly from long-run productivity as long as a system of informal side payments redistributes land to its most productive use.

The restrictive feature of the commune emphasized strongly in the Gerschenkron model was the inability (and unwillingness) of adult members of the commune to leave their land for alternate employment. A permanent departure of an adult family member would have reduced the family's claim to land at the next redistribution. The neoclassical model, however, predicts that the decision to leave the commune would require a comparison of lifetime family earnings (assuming the maximizing unit is the peasant family) with or without the permanent departure of an adult family member from the commune.

The decision to leave would depend positively on the discounted value of the lifetime earnings outside the commune and negatively on the discounted value of the extra earnings from an eventual higher land allotment. If earnings outside the commune were relatively high, the time between redistributions long, or the link between adult family size and the redistribution weak, then the hold of the commune on departing family members would be limited.

Studies of internal passports, the finding of weak rural ties of the urban labor force, the rapid growth of the industrial labor force, and the vast internal migration of the Russian population after 1861 prove that the commune's hold on departing family members was weak.[33] In fact, the growth of Russia's industrial labor force (based on flows from the countryside) was rapid by international standards during this period.[34]

One surprising feature of the commune's limited hold on departing members was that this weakness was already apparent in the eighteenth century.[35] The notion of a permanent attachment to the commune by those who had left was more romanticized than real.

If indeed a peasant family's long-run landholdings depended on family size, then fertility might be higher in those areas in which land was periodically redistributed. This question would have to be studied empirically by relating regional fertility and marital rates to chronicled land redistribution practices. The empirical evidence is mixed because the direction of causation between per capita landholdings and marriage is uncertain and because patterns were dictated by longstanding customs and practices that vary by region of the country (for example, the more Western pattern of demographic behavior occurred in the Baltic provinces).

In a neoclassical framework, the relationship between completed family size and land redistribution practices is complex. The rearing of a child would have its costs and the payoff in terms of a larger family allotment would be delayed until the child became an adult. It is also unclear whether the peasant family would maximize per capita family output or total output. If the desire was to maximize per capita output, the calculation would become very complex because the family would have to determine whether the eventual marginal product of the new family member would be greater than the average product, hence raising per capita family output.

Another open question is the extent to which the postemancipation

Russian commune actually implemented its formal egalitarian principles. If indeed a peasant family could be deprived of its improved land, this would have placed a damper on productivity improvements. Neoclassical theory would predict that redistributions would be spaced far apart (giving the proprietor a de facto long-term lease), and that when they took place they would not seriously disrupt the existing distribution of land wealth.

If the existing distribution was based on side payments, then the informal side payment could be continued after the redistribution. Presumably, the elected village elders would be chosen from the more experienced and successful farmers, and these elders would be unlikely to penalize a family who had done well and carried a disproportional burden of the commune's tax obligations. A rational commune government, pressured to meet its tax obligations, would recognize the free rider problem fostered by egalitarian redistributions.

Analysis of these issues requires being able to look inside the governance of the commune to see how these matters were dealt with in practice. One indirect indicator of the commune's adherence to a purely egalitarian policy is the extent to which the tax burden was distributed equally among commune members. Some evidence suggests a distribution of the tax burden according to ability to pay.[36] The acceptance of this principle would have made it difficult to pursue a purely egalitarian redistribution policy.

The Russian commune was probably much more flexible in its actual working arrangements than its formal rules suggest. Throughout its history, Russian serf and communal agriculture proved to be a relatively flexible institution. In the eighteenth century it was flexible enough to allow serf-owning serfs and serf industrialists, and it did not prevent the settlement of a vast frontier. The emancipation's removal of feudal obligations should have increased rather than reduced this natural flexibility.

The Tax Burden

The inflexibility of Russian communal agriculture is not the only cause of the purported agrarian crisis. A second argument is that the peasant's tax burden destroyed incentives and deprived peasants of the opportunity to accumulate capital. The origin of the unmanageable tax burden was the overvaluation at the time of the emancipation of peasant land values relative to the capitalized value of net income. The resulting debt burden strapped the tax-paying capacity of the peasantry.

Left with less land than before the emancipation, peasants scrambled to acquire additional land. This scramble for land drove up land prices (creating a "land hunger"), which made it even more difficult for peasants to meet their tax obligations.

The first point to note is that long-run land prices should equal the present value of anticipated earnings net of taxes from the land. For land prices to rise, either farm prices or productivity would have to rise, raising present values of income from land after payment of tax obligations. Rising land prices are typically taken not as a sign of declining farm income but of rising farm income.

At a microeconomic level, rising land prices and rents would, of course, be perceived by individual peasants as an unpleasant rise in the cost of doing business, and peasants with less farming skills and less accumulated capital would find themselves priced out of land markets. Yet, on average, rising land values mean a rising effective demand for farmland that was being exercised by one segment of the peasant population. The distribution of land between peasant and gentry shifted in favor of peasants during this period.[37] Therefore, a considerable portion of the effective demand for land was being exercised by the peasant population.

The massive research of Kovalchenko and Milov confirms the theoretically expected relationship among agricultural prices, land prices, and land rents during the 1861–1900 period.[38] The Kovalchenko and Milov data underscore the dangers of generalizing from isolated regional data. The enormous regional disparities in output prices, land prices, and rents throughout this period make it possible to draw virtually any conclusion simply by selecting a particular region that confirms the desired picture.

Kovalchenko and Milov avoid these pitfalls by estimating the general functional relationships that emerge from the regional data. They confirm that land prices depended positively on agricultural prices and that land rents were correlated with land prices. Thus land prices rose rapidly when agricultural prices were rising rapidly, and land prices fell (or failed to rise rapidly) when agricultural prices were falling (or not rising rapidly).

The Kovalchenko and Milov study also reveals that land prices had risen by 1879 to a level generally higher than the above-market prices on which the redemption payments were based. Although Russian peasants entered the emancipation era saddled with debt based on overvalued land prices, this disadvantage was wiped out within less than twenty years.

According to Anfinov's study, direct taxes accounted for about 6 percent of peasant income in 1901.[39] It would be hard to argue that direct taxes averaging 6 percent of peasant income represented ruinous taxation. Data from the state bank also show that peasant tax arrears rose substantially between 1866 and 1881.[40] It appears that peasants tended to adjust their tax payments to trends in grain prices, raising their arrears during periods of falling prices and becoming more conscientious debtors during periods of rising prices. This is not an unexpected pattern in a world in which debt payments are fixed in nominal terms and prices are subject to radical fluctuations.

The most important fact arguing against the ruinous taxation theory is that the secular trend in land prices was upward. As long as land prices represented the present discounted value of the earnings stream from the land, rising prices indicate that rising productivity and expected future prices more than compensate for the tax burden. Another important point to emphasize is that land taxes should not affect agricultural output and productivity. As Henry George taught, land taxes affect only the distribution of income by redistributing land rents from land owners to the state. In this sense, land taxes should not affect agricultural output and productivity.

LESSONS FOR THE PRESENT

Property rights in agriculture remain one of the most sensitive questions for the present leadership of the former Soviet Union. This leadership continues to cite two reasons for not returning to private peasant agriculture. The first is the failure of private agriculture under the tsars. The Soviet literature continued to emphasize the deep agrarian crisis that characterized Russian postemancipation agriculture. The second reason is the failure of private peasant agriculture during the NEP period of the 1920s—a matter that will be discussed in Chapter 6.

This chapter shows that, despite its institutional problems, Russian agriculture was progressing at normal or even above normal rates (as judged by the experiences of western Europe) in its last thirty years. The empirical evidence does not support the notion of a deep agrarian crisis. In fact, on an economywide basis, Russian agriculture was growing per capita, peasant living standards and real wages were rising, and exports were booming. The agrarian crises that did exist were limited to the eroding traditional agricultural regions.

The experiences of the tsarist period, therefore, do not provide ammunition for the anti-private-agriculture arguments of the present. The levels of agricultural output and affluence achieved by 1913 probably were not achieved again until after World War II.

Chapter 4

STATE POLICY, THE GOLD STANDARD, AND FOREIGN CAPITAL

THIS CHAPTER is about the Russian state and Russia's integration into the world economy prior to the revolution. As the leaders of the former Soviet Union look to the outside world for capital and technical assistance, it is timely to review the role of the world economy in Russia's economic development. And as Russia develops a new commercial legislative framework and a tax system, it is also timely to consider the framework that was in place on Russian territory in 1917.

On the eve of the World War I, Russia was the world's largest debtor. Its currency was backed by gold; the gold ruble exchanged at a fixed and stable rate with the currencies of the other industrialized countries. The stocks and bonds of Russian corporations, state governments, and the imperial government traded actively in financial centers not only in Moscow and Saint Petersburg but also in London, Paris, and Amsterdam. The multinational companies of the late nineteenth and early twentieth centuries—the Singer Company, Siemens, and Krupp—had branches in Russia. Although foreign companies operating in Russia complained about corruption and the difficulty of obtaining necessary government licenses, the commercial laws of Russia appeared to provide sufficient stability to attract direct investment into Russia.

In international markets, Russia exchanged its timber, wheat, oil, and textiles for machinery, garments, and automobiles. Financial crises in Paris and London affected financial markets in Moscow and Saint Petersburg. Well-heeled Russians were no strangers to the capitals of western Europe, spending their time not only in commerce but in recreation at the famous spas of Europe.

THE STATE, INDUSTRIALIZATION, AND THE WORLD ECONOMY

Just as Alexander Gerschenkron set the Western research agenda for Russian postemancipation agriculture, so he dictated the course of research on the Russian state. The Russian state's industrialization policy, often called the Witte system after Sergei Witte, the minister of finance from 1892 to 1903, played a prominent role in determining the course of Russian industrialization and its opening to the West.[1]

According to Gerschenkron, an about-face in Russian state policy in the 1850s led to a substantial acceleration in industrial growth beginning in the mid-1880s, persisting to 1900, and reaccelerating after 1905. Russian industrial growth during this period exceeded by a significant margin industrial growth in the advanced European countries during their own industrial revolutions. Prior to the 1880s Russian industrial growth had been unimpressive, with the exception of the significant but narrow growth of cotton textiles between 1830 and 1860.[2]

The spurt in Russian industrial growth starting in the 1880s served as a cornerstone of Gerschenkron's theory of relative backwardness, which he used to explain why late industrializers industrialize at more rapid rates.

Gerschenkron wrote that the Russian state sought to impede economic development prior to its about-face in the 1850s.[3] In the Russian feudal autocracy, power was exercised by the tsar through advisers, relatives, and ministers. The affairs of state were entrusted to a bureaucracy that was large for a relatively backward country but often lacking in professional competence.[4] Russian bureaucrats issued patents and licenses, collected sales and excise taxes, managed the affairs of the court, supervised state and crown lands, ran the legal system, levied tariffs, collected statistics, and managed state enterprises.

The ruling elite remained convinced of the virtue of feudal agriculture in the first half of the nineteenth century. The feudal nobility used the village commune to police the unruly peasantry, restrict peasant mobility, collect agricultural taxes, and provide military recruits. Prior to the about-face, the Russian state feared that industrialization and modernization would concentrate revolution-minded workers in cities, railways would give them mobility, and education would create opposition to the monarchy.

Russia's backward feudal system served the ruling elite well until the 1850s, despite a long history of peasant uprisings. Russia's manpower advantage and vast territories had repelled Napoleon. The lack of railroads made it difficult for foreign invaders to penetrate the Russian heartland, and Russia's artillery was not notably inferior to western Europe's at the turn of the nineteenth century.

Gerschenkron dates the about-face in Russian state attitudes to the loss of the Crimean war (1853–56) to France, England, Turkey, and Sardinia. The accession of Tsar Alexander II in 1855 and the capture of Sevastopol led to the Treaty of Paris, which ended the dominant role of Russia in southeast Europe. The Crimean War confronted the Russian leadership for the first time with its economic inferiority vis-à-vis France, Germany, and England.

The shock of relative backwardness forced the state to turn its attention to catching up with western Europe before Russia became a second-rate power in Europe. According to Gerschenkron, the about-face of state policy represented a key turning point. With a powerful state bureaucracy dedicated, rather than opposed, to industrialization, Russia had—for the first time—a real opportunity to deal with its relative backwardness.

Gerschenkron identified three types of state actions that were employed to overcome Russia's relative backwardness: first, constitutional changes to provide appropriate property rights and incentives for economic development; second, monetary and fiscal actions to create an appropriate financial climate for economic development; third, state entrepreneurial actions to substitute for missing entrepreneurship.[5] He concluded that the Russian state failed in the area of agrarian property rights, whereas it achieved notable successes in the other two areas. It was the failure in the constitutional area that caused Russian development to be halted by revolution and recession at the turn of the century, at which time more appropriate constitutional changes were adopted.

Property Rights in Agriculture

England's head start in modern economic growth was aided by the early creation of a legal and constitutional framework that supported private property rights and sanctity of contract. Prior to the about-face of the 1850s, Russia's constitutional framework actively inhibited economic development. The vast majority of Russia's population lacked juridical freedom. Serfs could be bought and sold; they lacked the basic personal and economic rights that were taken for granted in western Europe. Russian serfdom was based on compulsory labor obligations in the richer agricultural regions and on quitrents in the steppes. The Russian village was run by a village self-government that handled matters of policing, tax collection, land distribution, family disputes, and military recruitment. The three major owners of land—the gentry, the church, and the crown—all relied on serf labor to farm their lands. Private small-scale agriculture was lacking except on the periphery.

The about-face of the 1850s forced the Russian leadership to conclude that constitutional changes in agriculture were necessary. The tsar concluded that the initiative had to come from above (in view of the strength of gentry opposition to emancipation) before the peasants took matters into their own hands.

The Emancipation Mistake

Gerschenkron felt that if serfdom had been replaced by private farming in Russia, the major obstacle to Russia's long-term economic development would have been removed, and Russian history would have been altered. It was the failure to create private peasant property rights in 1861 that doomed the state's other actions to overcome relative backwardness. In fact, compensatory state actions in the two other areas were required to compensate for the failure to create private farming in Russia.

In an autocracy dominated by landed interests, serf emancipation had to compensate not only for the land ceded to former serfs but also for lost labor services or quitrents. Indeed, the 1861 emancipation granted the gentry an implicit payment for lost labor services in the form of overvalued land prices. The peasants, who had expected outright ownership, were saddled with redemption payments that were to amortize the land over nearly a half century. Moreover, the peasants ended up with less land, on average, than they had cultivated under feudal arrangements.

The 1861 emancipation act decreed that land be distributed to the village commune, not to individual peasant families. The emancipation retained the village commune to manage land allocation and redistribution, policing, and tax collection. Peasant families were made collectively responsible for the debts of the commune. Responsible households had to step in to cover for free riders.

The peasants received their juridical freedom but not their economic freedom. They could not withdraw their land from the commune without paying off their share of the debt, and as long as their land remained within the commune, peasants could not make their own resource allocation decisions. Moreover, with periodic redistributions of land, adult family members had to stay in agriculture to ensure the peasant family's share of communal land. Furthermore, periodic redistributions penalized families that had made capital improvements on their land.

The formal provisions of the Emancipation Act of 1861 were not promising from an economic point of view. Gerschenkron concluded that the 1861 emancipation made balanced growth of the Russian economy an impossibility. The commune tied labor to agriculture and created the paradox of a labor-rich country starved for industrial labor. The inadequate land distribution of the emancipation left peasant families with inefficiently scaled plots. The retention of communal agriculture—and the lack of development of private farming—meant that productivity advances in agriculture would be minimal. The debt burden placed on the peasantry by the overstated land prices meant that there would be insufficient private demand to support industrialization.

In Chapter 3, I claimed that Gerschenkron overestimated the negative effects of the emancipation on Russian agricultural development, and I showed that agricultural performance was superior to that acknowledged by Gerschenkron. The basic argument of Chapter 3 is that Russian communal agriculture attained the necessary flexibility by informal means to achieve satisfactory agricultural growth. It should be noted, however, that the constitutional framework established by the emancipation created obstacles that had to be overcome by innovative actions. How rapid agricultural progress would have been without these obstacles is unclear.

Monetary and Fiscal Policy

Just as all states must determine a constitutional and legal framework, so must all states make government expenditures, collect taxes, and regulate the money supply. Russia's monetary and fiscal policies were to a great extent dictated by the desire to join the international gold standard. In Russia's case, a remarkable series of influential finance ministers pursued a consistent fiscal policy of budgetary surpluses and limited monetary growth to create a stable currency on international currency markets. After more than two decades of stringency, the Russian credit ruble was trading at a fixed rate of exchange to the gold ruble by 1895, and Russia officially went on the gold standard in 1897.

The Russian state was not alone in directing its monetary and fiscal policies to the international gold standard. It appeared to be what respectable countries did in the second half of the nineteenth century.[6] The peculiar significance Gerschenkron attaches to Russian monetary and fiscal policies of the last quarter of the nineteenth century was that monetary stability was deliberately pursued to attract foreign capital. In a famous policy paper, Finance Minister Witte spelled out the importance of foreign capital in light of Russia's deficient domestic saving capacity.[7] Unlike other countries that pursued monetary stability and accumulated gold reserves to achieve fixed exchange rates, Russia did so expressly to substitute for a missing precondition—the lack of domestic saving.

According to Gerschenkron's assessment, Russia's monetary and fiscal conservatism paid off handsomely. Prior to the turn of the century, considerable direct foreign investment was attracted, bonds were floated in European money markets to finance railroad construction, and foreign entrepreneurs were attracted to Russia in large numbers. The Russian investment rate was pushed up by foreign saving and also by public saving from the state budget.

The State of Entrepreneur

Constitutional and monetary and fiscal policy actions are common to all states. They do not involve an unusual substitution of the state for missing preconditions. Gerschenkron saw the unique role of the Russian case to be the substitution of the state bureaucracy for a missing entrepreneurial class.

According to Gerschenkron, the Russian state followed what would now be called an enlightened "industrial policy," which contributed significantly to Russian industrialization. The state managed construction of state-owned railroad lines and guaranteed loans to private railways. The state assisted in floating foreign-currency loans in European money capitals. The state reserved steel, military, and railway equipment contracts for domestic industry. The state erected tariff barriers that increased the demand for domestic goods and attracted foreign direct investment behind Russian tariff walls. Moreover, the state engaged in a massive campaign to attract Western entrepreneurs and craftsmen to Russia. The state granted licenses to foreign companies that wished to do business in Russia. The state suppressed the formation of trade unions.

Gerschenkron contended that the Russian state had to substitute its own demand for private demand. The backwardness imposed on Russia by communal agriculture meant that domestic demand was deficient. By directing state purchases to domestic producers, the Russian state substituted state demand for private domestic demand. By placing a heavy fiscal burden on the peasantry and by generating surpluses from state-owned monopolies, the state budgetary surpluses compensated for deficient private saving. Finally, by creating a stable environment for foreign investment, state monetary and fiscal policies attracted foreign saving to serve as a further substitute for deficient domestic saving.

The Gerschenkron model of the state as ersatz entrepreneur has been challenged by a number of scholars. Arcadius Kahan, in his analysis of Russian state budgets, pointed out that there was a notable lack of industrial subsidies in Russian state budgets.[8] An active industrial policy calls for subsidies of industries selected by the state for development. In the Russian budget, the only items that show up in the state budget were loan guarantees for private railway construction and some minor expenditures on ports and military equipment. State expenditures for military hardware made up such a small proportion of the total that the military budget could not have served as a significant vehicle for hidden subsidization.[9]

State enterprises, which could have served as vehicles for state entrepreneurship, did not appear to play an important role in Russian industrialization. State-owned railroads, the postal and telegraph systems, some munitions plants, and the state spirits monopoly were the only significant state enterprises. Although railroads played a key role in Russian industrialization, the state's role was no more prominent in Russia than elsewhere.[10] With the exception of national railroads, Russian state enterprises were either those that were typically state owned or those, such as the spirits monopoly, that were not the advanced technology industries associated with enlightened industrial policy.

Moreover, there is a consensus that Russian tariff policy was dictated by revenue needs rather than by a coherent industrial policy. There is no evidence of discretionary tariffs to favor specific industries or to encourage foreign industries to locate behind Russian tariff walls.[11] Manufacturing inputs were taxed at the same rates as manufactures. In fact, foreign manufacturers, seeking to penetrate Russian markets, paid remarkably little attention to lobbying for tariff reductions on the grounds that the state's revenue requirements made changes impossible. Foreign manufacturers appeared to be more interested in gaining monopoly power in Russian markets, which would allow them to pass tariffs on to the Russian consumer.[12]

The role of state officials in attracting foreign capital was another entrepreneurial function emphasized by Gerschenkron. The image of political and financial stability engendered by Russian officialdom was indeed important to attracting foreign capital, but there is disagreement on its effect on foreign capital. McKay demonstrated that foreign capital was attracted primarily by higher rates of return, not by lobbying efforts of Russian bureaucrats.[13] Interest rate differentials do indeed appear to explain capital movements into Russia, as will be noted later in this chapter.[14] Russia in the late nineteenth century was regarded as a land of unlimited economic opportunity, albeit a market with considerable risks.

Case studies of foreign investments in Russia demonstrate that the Russian state was regarded more as an impediment than as a source of assistance.[15] Foreign concerns had to learn how to deal with the byzantine Russian bureaucracy. Bureaucrats had to be bribed as a matter of course, and learning how to deal effectively with the bureaucracy and to find important patrons could take years of effort. In the German case, few companies earned quick and easy profits.[16] The companies that made long-term investments were primarily the ones that earned long-term profits in Russian markets.

In defense of the Russian state bureaucracy, it should be noted that the bribes paid to Russian officials were not very significant. Moreover, the Russian bureaucracy granted licenses primarily on the basis of merit. Companies that were the world leaders in their industries were typically licensed by the Russian bureaucracy, which may simply have been making conservative choices by going with proven concerns. A listing of foreign companies licensed to operate in Russian markets included an honor roll of the best European and American firms of the day. It does appear, however, that the Russian bureaucracy failed to engender competition by restricting licensing to single companies rather than permitting competition.

The Russian system was slow in fostering the limited liability corporation. Many private fortunes were lost prior to limited liability, and risks to Russian entrepreneurs were exceptional in the eighteenth and early nineteenth centuries. Thomas Owen has chronicled the gradual changes in

Russian commercial law and the ambivalent attitude of the Russian bureaucracy toward the corporation.[17] The late development of the corporate
legal form definitely had a dampening effect on Russian industrialization.

THE COSTS AND BENEFITS OF THE WITTE SYSTEM

Gerschenkron and others have accorded high marks to Russian state industrialization policy. Although the extent and effectiveness of state entrepreneurial activities may have been exaggerated, the financial stability
associated with Russian monetary and fiscal policies appears to have been
a strong asset of Russian commercial policy.

Critics of Russian industrial policy have argued that the costs of the
Witte System may have been excessive relative to its benefits and that
similar rates (or perhaps higher rates) of industrial growth could have been
attained with different fiscal and monetary policies. Russian macroeconomic policies of the late nineteenth century are not without their
detractors.

Arcadius Kahan argued that the costs of the Witte System, attributable
to improper fiscal measures, were largely understated and unrecognized:
Heavy taxation retarded the domestic market; state activity in the capital
market siphoned funds from private investors; and protective tariffs imposed consumption costs in excess of fiscal benefits.[18] Kahan also maintained that the costs of the gold standard in the form of foregone interest
earnings (a consequence of accumulating "excessive" gold reserves to support the gold-backed ruble) retarded Russian industrialization.

Haim Barkai criticized state macroeconomic policy from a different
perspective.[19] Barkai argued that the deflationary monetary policy required to achieve a favorable balance of trade and, accordingly, a stable
Russian currency resulted in costs that outweighed the benefits. The slow
growth of the money supply until 1890 held the rate of growth of industry
below its potential. According to Barkai, the fact that the industrialization
spurt began in the 1890s was the consequence of relaxing monetary policy
after the tight money of the previous two decades. The industrialization
drive of the 1890s was not the payoff of the state policies emphasized by
Gerschenkron. According to Barkai, Russia could have experienced industrialization much earlier: "The contrast between the depressed 1880's and
the 'booming industrialization decade' of the 1890's is undoubtedly related to this significant difference in monetary developments. The annual
growth rate of more than 4 percent in the stock of money during the 1890's
acted as a stimulant that allowed the latent forces of expansion to come
into their own."[20]

Barkai asked whether the cumulative loss of potential industrial output
during the years of scarce money was offset by the gains of foreign capital

from the gold standard. Using balance-of-payments figures calculated in the 1920s, Barkai concluded that the gain in foreign capital from introducing the gold standard was patently small for the deflationary output loss.[21]

AN EVALUATION OF THE WITTE SYSTEM

The late nineteenth century was a crucial period in Russia's industrial history. An acceleration of industrial growth took place starting in the mid-1880s, Russia joined the international gold standard in 1897, and the Russian empire became the world's largest debtor nation. Critics have questioned whether the Russian state's macroeconomic policies were worth their costs. Perhaps the deflationary policies pursued to join the gold standard were too costly. Critics also ask whether the gold standard "paid off" by attracting foreign capital to Russia.

To examine the contention that the tight money that enabled Russia to join the gold standard cost Russia considerable output we must first resort to some elementary theory. Macroeconomic theory teaches that deflationary policies will not reduce real output if prices are flexible and the deflation is anticipated. Under these conditions, money is said to be "neutral," or a "veil" that affects only the price level, not real output.[22] With rigid prices, however, output losses can indeed result from persistent excess demand for money. If people chronically wish to hold more money than has been made available, real output losses could occur if prices fail to adjust.

When prices are flexible, the supply of money should not affect real output. Tight money simply causes prices to drop. With lower prices, people require less money, and money demand and supply balance. Price flexibility keeps the economy at full employment. Restrictive monetary policies lower nominal national income without affecting real national income.

Accordingly, the degree of flexibility of Russian prices is critical to the issue of the deflationary costs of achieving the gold standard. The period from the mid-nineteenth century to World War I was an era of considerable domestic and international economic competition, such that domestic and world prices were generally flexible both downward and upward. Figure 4.1, on U.S., U.K., French, Swedish, and German prices from 1885 to 1913, shows the considerable price flexibility that existed in the late nineteenth and early twentieth centuries. Moreover, Figure 4.1 underscores the interrelatedness of prices. The price levels of the major countries tended to move together with the international business cycle.

The price flexibility of the nineteenth and early twentieth centuries smoothed economic adjustments to disruptive economic forces such as monetary and fiscal shocks; therefore a "correct" monetary policy was

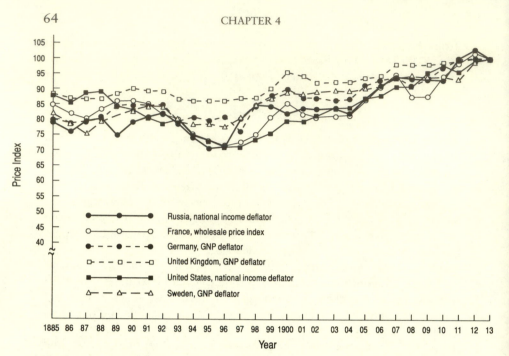

Figure 4.1: Price Indexes for Russia, France, Germany, United Kingdom, United States, and Sweden, 1885–1913.
Source: Gregory, *Russian National Income*, 141.

much less important between 1850 and 1914 than in modern times, which are characterized more by price rigidities.

Figure 4.2, which gives longer-term Russian price series (1867–1913), provides strong evidence of price flexibility, substantial variability in inflation (deflation) rates during specific subperiods, and a general conformity to the pattern of world prices. The classical mechanism of adjustment

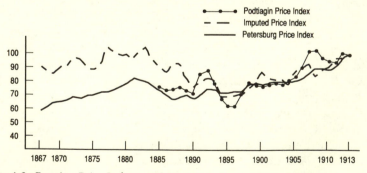

Figure 4.2: Russian Price Indexes, 1867–1913; Base: 1913 = 100
Source: Gregory and Sailors, "Russian Monetary Policy and Industrialization," 841.

toward monetary equilibrium through price-level adjustments is a valid approximation of Russian nineteenth-century reality, based on the evidence in Figures 4.1 and 4.2.

Rather than rely exclusively on evidence of Russian price flexibility to rule out substantial costs of restrictive monetary policies, we can look for direct evidence of disequilibrium of money demand and supply. If the 1880s were indeed characterized by chronic excess demand for money (which was not eliminated by deflation), while the 1890s were characterized by a balance between money demand and supply, the case could be made that tight money had indeed restrained output growth in the 1880s.

Even in modern times, it is difficult to determine money demand and money supply. We have alternate definitions of the money supply, some narrow and some broad. Moreover, we can only approximate the demand for money because of the public's tendency to change its money-holding habits.

Table 4.1 contains approximate data on the annual growth rates of the Russian money supply, prices, real national income, and money demand during the 1880s, 1890s, and 1900–1913. The latter two periods were characterized by rapid growth of real national income and by positive growth of the money supply; the first period was characterized by slow growth of real national income and by a decline in the money supply. The table raises the question: Was Russian growth delayed by one decade by the highly restrictive monetary policy of the 1880s? Was the acceleration of the 1890s caused by a loosening of monetary policy, rather than by state investment and international capital flows?

We have reasonably consistent estimates of the Russian money supply

TABLE 4.1

Annual Growth Rates of Money Supply, Real National Income, Prices, and Money Demand, Russia, 1880–1913

	(1)	(2)	(3)	(4)	(5)	(6)	(7)
		Currency Plus Current Account Deposits	Price Level	Real National Income	Money Demand $(3+4)$	Money Demand Minus Currency $(5-1)$	Money Demand Minus Currency & Deposits $(5-2)$
	Currency						
1880–90	−1.9	−1.6	−2.5	1.7	−.8	1.1	0.8
1890–1900	3.5	4.4	1.5	4.5	6.0	2.5	1.4
1900–1913	4.4	7.0	1.1	3.3	4.4	0	−2.6

Sources: Columns 1 and 2 are from Drummond, "The Russian Gold Standard," Table 1. To obtain a consistent current account series, we define current accounts as the sum of nontreasury current accounts in Gosbank and current accounts in joint stock banks. Column 3 is an average of the inferred and direct price indexes. In column 4, the real national income index is from Gregory, *Russian National Income*, Table 3.1. The 1880–85 segment is estimated from Goldsmith, "The Economic Growth of Tsarist Russia."

for the period 1875–1914.[23] The money supply can be defined broadly or narrowly.[24] We use two money stock series: a narrow currency-plus-coin series and a broad series that also includes current account deposit series (see Table 4.1). Prior to 1900 the narrow and broad money stocks grew at similar rates. After 1900, broad money grew much more rapidly than narrow money.

Both money stock figures show an acceleration of monetary growth over the period 1880–1913, beginning with negative growth in the 1880s (−1.9 to −1.6 percent per annum), positive rates in the 1890s (3.5 to 4.4 percent), and accelerating to even higher rates of growth after 1900 (4.4 to 7.4 percent). Barkai rests his criticism of tsarist monetary policy on the negative monetary growth of the 1880s.

Tight money can depress real output if money supply growth falls chronically short of money demand growth. With circulation constant, the growth of money demand should equal the sum of real output growth (which determines the volume of real transactions) and the growth of the price level. The growth of money demand is given in column 5 of Table 4.1. The growth of money supply is given in column 1 for narrow money and column 2 for broad money.

Some conclusions can be drawn from comparing money demand and money supply during these three periods. The 1880s was a period of slow growth of money demand. Real output was growing slowly and prices were falling; hence the demand for money was falling at slightly less than 1 percent per year. The money supply, however, was falling at 1.6 to 1.9 percent per year. According to these calculations, the state was falling short of supplying enough money to accommodate the money demand. During the rapid economic growth of the 1890s, money demand was growing at 6 percent per annum, while the money supply was growing between 3.5 and 4.4 percent per annum. If anything, the state was falling even farther short of meeting money demand in the 1890s than in the 1880s. If excess money demand was going to restrain real output, it would have more likely depressed output in the 1890s than in the 1880s.

The period 1900–1913 saw the money supply growing as fast (narrow concept) or faster (broad concept) than money demand. If anything, the state was supplying too much money during this period. Yet real output growth slowed during this period, which included the disruptions of the 1905 revolution.[25]

The calculated rates of growth of money demand and money supply show that demand growth exceeded supply growth in both the 1880s and 1890s, while supply growth may have exceeded demand growth in the period 1900–1913. The measured monetary disequilibrium in the 1890s was greater than that of the 1880s. If deficient money supply depressed real growth, the period 1900–1913 should have had the most growth, and the period 1890–1900 should have had the least growth. This obviously was not the case. We therefore find no evidence that the elimination of excess monetary demand in the 1890s sparked the industrialization of that decade.

The Russian money stock series is sensitive to the definition of the money supply; the broader the definition, the faster the rate of growth. For example, if total state bank deposits, including treasury deposits, are considered part of the money supply, there is virtually no decline in the money supply during the 1880s.[26] The growth of the money supply is very sensitive to the definition given it; hence comparisons of money demand and supply of this sort are prone to measurement errors.

We must choose between inexact calculations of money demand and supply, which suggest the presence of some monetary disequilibriums, and a theoretical model of adjustment through price level changes, buttressed by evidence of flexible prices. We fail to find from either source evidence that money was tighter in the 1880s relative to demand than in the 1890s. We fail to find evidence that the tight money policies required to achieve the gold standard created substantial real output losses.

FOREIGN CAPITAL IN RUSSIA

When Russia joined the gold standard in 1897,[27] it gained prestige and enhanced standing in the world financial community. The Russian state also hoped to attract significant foreign capital as a consequence of gold standard membership. By the end of the tsarist period, Russia had become the world's largest international debtor, with substantial investments from France, Germany, and England. This point alone demonstrates the success of the strategy.

We have no way of knowing whether an influx of foreign capital of this magnitude would have occurred in the absence of the gold standard or whether the Russian capital market would have been sufficiently attractive to foreign capital if the credit ruble had not had a fixed rate of conversion into gold? We can only compare foreign capital inflows before and after the gold standard and form some judgment on whether the empirical differences are attributable to the gold standard.

Table 4.2 summarizes net foreign investment in Russia for the period 1881–1913.[28] Because the gold standard was introduced in 1897, we have sixteen years from the period leading up to the gold standard and sixteen years from the gold-standard era. The pre-gold-standard years capture the lengthy preparations for the gold standard, namely, the gradual reduction of fiat money (credit rubles) in circulation, the introduction of tariffs to be paid in gold, the raising of tariff rates, the balancing of the state budget, and the subsidizing of freight rates. It should be obvious from a listing of these

TABLE 4.2
Net Foreign Investment (Balance on Current Account), Russia, 1881–1913 (millions of credit rubles in current year prices)

Year	(1) Merchandise Account	(2) Interest Payments on Public Debt Abroad	(3) Interest and Dividend Payments Abroad, Corporations	(4) Repatriated Profits of Foreign-Owned Nonincorporated Enterprises and Interest Paid Abroad by Cities	(5) Net Tourist Expenditures	(6) Miscellaneous Items[a]	(7) Net Foreign Investment (1 − 6)
1881	−12	(−99)[b]	−8	(−4)	(−26)	(−5)	(−154)
1882	+51	(−120)	−9	(−4)	(−27)	(−5)	(−114)
1883	+78	(−102)	−10	(−5)	(−28)	(−6)	(−73)
1884	+53	(−107)	−10	(−5)	(−29)	(−6)	(−104)
1885	+102	−134	−11	−6	−33	−7	−89
1886	+54	−136	−13	−6	−29	−9	−139
1887	+216	−137	−13	−8	−25	−9	+24
1888	+395	−141	−14	−7	−28	−8	+197
1889	+313	−143	−15	−8	−47	−1	+99
1890	+282	−140	−15	−7	−39	+3	+84
1891	+329	−132	−15	−8	−55	−4	+115
1892	+71	−136	−17	−8	−54	−7	−151
1893	+138	−146	−19	−9	−54	−11	−101
1894	+100	−145	−21	−11	−46	−14	−137

1895	+150	−155	−27	−12	−58	−10	−112
1896	+72	−141	−31	−12	−63	−12	−187
1897	+125	−153	−35	−12	−75	−11	−161
1898	+91	−153	−46	−13	−76	−8	−205
1899	−56	−153	−51	−12	−80	−9	−361
1900	+71	−156	−53	−11	−106	−13	−268
1901	+164	−153	−48	−10	−107	−13	−167
1902	+261	−160	−50	−10	−98	−1	−58
1903	+314	−174	−53	−10	−104	−13	−30
1904	+371	−165	−53	−12	−117	−9	+15
1905	+425	−177	−54	−12	−130	−13	+39
1906	+285	−163	−56	−13	−175	−16	−138
1907	+198	−213	−63	−14	−155	−12	−259
1908	+77	−227	−66	−16	−137	−12	−381
1909	+510	−225	−78	−19	−147	−12	+29
1910	+353	−229	−93	−23	−195	−16	−203
1911	+416	−226	−114	−27	−220	−12	−183
1912	+329	−221	−139	−34	−257	−10	−332
1913	+128	−221	−150	−30	−292	−13	−578

Source: Gregory, "The Russian Balance of Payments."

[a]Interest receipts, insurance, freight, foreign military equipment, and reparations.

[b]The figures in parentheses are guesses and extrapolations.

measures that the eventual conversion to the gold standard must have been, to some extent, anticipated.

Whether the gold standard was anticipated is not certain. The tsarist government had attempted before, without success, to introduce a stable, gold-backed currency. Whether a stable gold-backed currency was generally anticipated well before 1897 is important to an evaluation of the success of the gold standard, for if it was, the benefits would have begun to accrue before full convertibility.[29]

Table 4.2 shows that the annual fluctuations in Russia's net foreign investment account were considerable. Although the account was typically passive (that is, foreign capital was flowing into Russia) during this period, the years 1888 through 1891 witnessed a significant outflow of savings. The remainder of the period was characterized either by inflows of foreign investment or virtually zero net foreign investment (1905, 1906, and 1909).

The sources of these annual fluctuations are not difficult to detect. In general, the significant annual fluctuations of both imports and exports around a rising time trend (with a low correlation between the two) explain the fluctuations. The other major accounts (interest and dividend payments, net tourist expenditures) rose steadily with only small fluctuations. From this we can conclude that contemporary financial authorities were generally correct in paying attention to the merchandise balance as an indicator of fluctuations in the balance of payments.[30]

Some movements in net foreign investment can be related to specific political and economic events. The positive balances between 1887 and 1891 were most likely the consequence of policy moves to restrict imports and promote exports (the gold tariff, the tariff rate increases of 1890 and 1891, and the subsidization of internal grain freight rates). The negative balances after 1892 were the consequences of poor harvests and growing interest and dividend obligations from earlier foreign investments. In any case, from 1891 on export surpluses were not large enough to meet both interest and dividend obligations and net tourist expenditures, except in years of extraordinary export surpluses (1904, 1905, and 1909).[31]

The large annual fluctuations in net foreign investment make it difficult to generalize about the flows of foreign investment into Russia by looking at short periods of time. We therefore average the annual data into pre- and post-gold-standard periods.

Average annual foreign investment in Russia for the period 1885–97 was 43 million rubles; for the period 1897–1913 the corresponding figure was 191 million rubles—an increase by a factor of 4.4. As a ratio of national income, for the pre-gold-standard era, the ratio of foreign investment to national income was slightly over 0.5 percent (or 5.5 percent of net investment); for the gold-standard era, it was about 1.5 percent (11 percent of net investment). The annual growth rate of the share of foreign investment of national income was about 7 percent between the two periods.

If we make the heroic assumption that the increase in the foreign investment share after 1897 was due *entirely* to the introduction of the gold standard, the annual growth rate of output after 1897 would have been 0.5 percentage points lower on an annual basis. With an actual growth rate of 4 percent per annum during this period, the growth rate without the gold standard would have been 3.5 percent.[32]

Although this calculation is based on a heroic assumption, it nevertheless suggests a possible upper limit of the impact of the gold standard on the growth rate, namely, to raise it by some 11–14 percent (or slightly less than 0.5 percent per year). Applying this growth rate differential to the post-1897 period, we obtain a 1913 NNP of 18,881 million rubles without the gold standard and 20,266 million with the gold standard, a gain of 1,385 million rubles. This calculation illustrates the danger of assuming that small changes in annual growth rates are unimportant, for with compounding over a long period (in this case sixteen years) the end effect will be large.[33]

Just how heroic is the assumption that the increase in the share of foreign investment after 1897 was due entirely to the gold standard? On the one hand, there may have been natural forces (improvements in transportation and communications, higher rates of return) that would have increased foreign investment in Russia without the gold standard. On the other hand, the assumption may even be conservative. Table 4.2 shows that the civil unrest of 1904 and 1905 caused foreign capital to dry up immediately. Yet there was a substantial rebound of foreign investment in the period 1906–8, despite the decline in real output that persisted from 1904 to 1907.[34] The rebound in foreign confidence after 1905, might not have taken place without the assurance of the gold standard. The fact that the Russian economy attracted so much capital after 1897 despite the tumultuous events of 1904–7 suggests a substantial payoff of the gold standard.

THE FINANCING OF FOREIGN INVESTMENT

By definition, net foreign investment equals the net increase in private and public debt owned by foreigners plus the net decrease in official reserves of gold and foreign currencies.[35] Foreign investment shows up in the form of increased liabilities to foreigners. Accordingly, foreign investment can be calculated either as the increase in indebtedness to foreigners (see Table 4.3) or as the net flow of goods and services from the rest of the world to Russia (see Table 4.2). In fact, one method can be used to check the accuracy of the other.[36]

TABLE 4.3

Net Foreign Investment and Changes in Official Gold Reserves and Foreign Indebtedness, Russia, 1885–97 and 1897–1913
(millions of credit rubles)

	(1) Change in Official Gold Reserves Minus Domestic Gold Production Net of Industrial Uses	(2) Change in Corporate Foreign Debt	(3) Change in Government Foreign Debt	(4) Change in Foreign Debt of Unincorporated Enterprises and Cities	(5) Net Foreign Investment (Direct Method) (2 + 3 + 4 − 1)	(6) Net Foreign Investment (Indirect Method)	(7) Statistical Discrepancy
1885–97 Total	+425	+404	+635	+70	684	558	+126
Annual (÷13)	+33	+31	+49	+5	53	43	+10
1897–1913 Total	−113	+1683	+1280	+315	3391	3241	+150
Annual (÷17)	−7	+99	+75	+19	199	191	+8

Sources: Gregory, "The Russian Balance of Payments."

Russian foreign investment was financed by reduced gold reserves, increases in corporate foreign debt, or increases in unincorporated debt to foreigners.[37] It is instructive to compare financing methods used before and after 1897. For the period 1885–97, receipts from official borrowing abroad were used to a great extent between 1885 and 1897 to build up official reserves of gold and convertible currencies. Between 1885 and 1897 the tsarist government borrowed abroad annually some 49 million rubles (about 60 percent of all imperial government borrowing). Of these 49 million, 33 million rubles were used annually to acquire gold and convertible currencies, leaving an annual figure of 16 million rubles (plus domestic borrowings of about 36 million rubles) to finance railroad construction and general government outlays.

These numbers confirm the contemporary suspicion that a significant portion of foreign borrowing was employed to build up official reserves in preparation for convertibility; the surprising feature is the magnitude of these acquisitions.[38] Between 1885 and 1897 Russian gold reserves (including convertible currencies) held both at home and abroad increased by 860 million rubles. Of this figure, approximately half (425 million) was acquired through the proceeds of official foreign borrowing and the remainder through domestic gold production.[39]

The relevant criterion for judging whether Russian total monetary reserves were excessive is to compare Russian reserves with those of other countries at the turn of the twentieth century. Bloomfield, in his definitive study of the international gold standard, provides calculations of the reserve ratios of the gold-standard countries.[40] His figures show the Russian reserve ratio (gold, silver, and foreign exchange divided by total sight liabilities) was in the range of the mid-sixties to high seventies, close to that of France (the country with which Russia shared the strongest economic ties) and not very different from the other countries with the exceptions of Finland, Belgium, and England.

The composition of external assets reveals some important differences. For seven countries gold was the most important reserve asset, while for three countries foreign exchange constituted the dominant reserve asset. For Russia foreign exchange was a substantial portion of the total. Compared to other gold standard countries, Russia did not have an excess of gold compared to commitments. In fact, Russia had a relative shortage of gold reserves after 1900. At that time, other countries perceived their shortages of gold reserves, which resulted in intense international competition for additional gold reserves.[41]

Once Russia's gold reserve was acquired and convertibility was achieved, official foreign borrowing was no longer used to acquire gold reserves. Official reserves rose by 600 million rubles between 1897 and 1913, but domestic gold production net of industrial uses equaled 713 million rubles during the same period. The gold standard era saw Russia drawing lightly on official reserves (7 million rubles annually) to finance foreign transactions, quite unlike the pre-1897 period, when foreign borrowing was used to acquire gold.

The 33 million rubles out of foreign borrowing devoted annually to acquire reserves represents the most significant opportunity cost of attaining convertibility. If one makes the extreme assumption that the entire sum used to acquire gold would have otherwise been devoted to productive investment (in reality about a quarter was devoted to railroad construction, the remainder to general government), then this represents an investment loss of approximately 0.5 percent of national income between 1885 and 1897. The loss of these investment resources could have depressed annual growth by 0.2 percent. The 0.2 percent reduction in the 1885–97 growth rate is grossly exaggerated because it assumes that all of the increase would have gone into capital investment.

We calculated that the increase in annual growth after 1897 resulting from the gold standard was 0.5 percent per year. If the loss of growth prior to 1897 was less than 0.2 percent per annum, the growth rate gain after 1897 far outweighed the loss associated with building gold reserves.

Prior to 1897, the prime source of investment finance was government borrowing. After 1897, private borrowing outweighed government borrowing as a source of foreign capital, and increases in corporate debt to foreigners became the most important means of financing foreign investment.

THE CAUSES OF THE CAPITAL FLOW INTO RUSSIA

The portfolio theory of capital flows among countries provides a convenient explanation of why foreign capital entered Russia: With an initial distribution of world capital among countries, the marginal productivities of capital (and hence real returns to capital) vary among countries.[42] If capital is mobile, it will flow from nations where the marginal productivity of capital is relatively low to those where it is relatively high. Exogenous forces (wars, capital export controls) can disrupt this flow, but in general capital will respond to profitability differentials. The flow of capital will cause a redistribution of world capital and bring about a gradual equalization of rates of return among countries.

Real interest rate differentials, adjusted for risk and maturity, measure the profitability differentials among countries. Most empirical work demonstrates that foreign capital does flow to those countries with higher rates of return. McKay, in his study of foreign capital in Russia, argued most convincingly that portfolio choice explains much of the capital flow into Russia.[43]

TABLE 4.4
Official Discount Rates, St. Petersburg, Berlin, and Paris (twelve-month notes)

Years	St. Petersburg	Berlin	Paris
1885–90	6.1	3.72	3.0
1890–95	5.95	3.63	2.63
1895–1900	7.8	3.3	3.0
1900–1905	5.9	3.9	3.0
1908–12	5.1	4.8	3.2

Sources: *Ezhegodnik ministerstva finansov*, sec. "Birzhy"; *Russki denezhny rynok*; Gindin, *Russkie kommercheskie banki*, 260; Homer, *A History of Interest Rates*, 230, 231, 264, 265.

In the Russian case, where German and French portfolio capital dominated, the relevant interest rates are the Russian, French, and German rates. Table 4.4 provides average official discount rates on two-month notes quoted in St. Petersburg, Paris, and Berlin for five-year intervals for the period 1881–1913. Between 1885 and 1890 the Russian interest rate was higher than the unweighted average of the French and German rates by a factor of almost 2.5. This factor remained steady until the mid-1890s, when it rose, and then fell steadily to a factor of about 1.3 at the end of the period.

Russia's interest rate experience, therefore, is consistent with portfolio theory: It shows that foreign capital was initially attracted by higher interest rates. The resulting inflow of capital served to reduce interest rate differentials by the end of the period. Insofar as Russian prices generally moved with European prices during this period, nominal interest rate movements tended to be representative of real interest rate movements.

To help analyze the impact of exchange risk on foreign investment and the impact of foreign investment on the ruble exchange rate, Table 4.5 provides data on foreign investment, the ruble exchange rate, the variance in the exchange rate, the supply of rubles, and nominal national income. Table 4.5 shows that foreign capital was entering the country (the minus numbers in column 1) during periods when exchange risks, as measured by the standard deviation of exchange rates, were low (1881–85 and 1891–95). Foreign capital left the country when exchange risks were high (1886–90). These figures are consistent with the hypothesis that increased risk reduces foreign portfolio capital.

What was the relationship between foreign capital, the money supply, and the credit ruble exchange rate? Presumably, the ruble exchange rate would rise with an increase in foreign capital as more rubles are demanded in international money exchanges. From Table 4.5, however, we see that the ruble exchange rate fell during the period 1881–85, when capital was

TABLE 4.5
Net Foreign Investment and the Supply of Credit Rubles, 1881–95

Year	(1) Net Foreign Investment (annual avg.)	(2) Change in Credit Ruble Exchange Rate (%)	(3) Standard Deviation of Ruble Exchange Rate	(4) Change in Supply of Credit Rubles (%)	(5) Change in Nominal NNP (%)
					a decline greater than
1881–85	−107	37.0	1.3	−57.0	−5.7
1886–90	+53	+21.0	59.0	0.0	+15.0
1891–95	−77	+1.0	1.6	+7.0	+8.0

Source: Column 1 is from Table 4.2, Columns 2–4 are from Sobolev, *Tamozhennaia politika Rossii vo vtoroi polovine XIX veka*, 412. Column 5 is from Gregory, *Russian National Income.*

[a] This figure is a rough guess, but most likely true. According to the index of St. Petersburg consumer prices, prices declined by 1.6 percent between 1881 and 1885. Assuming a real NNP growth rate of 3 percent, this would mean a decline well above the decline in the supply of credit rubles.

flowing in, and rose during the period 1886–90, when capital was flowing out.[44]

The data in columns 4 and 5 provide a more likely explanation of the ruble exchange rate. During the 1881–85 period the supply of credit rubles was falling more slowly than the demand (as measured by nominal national income). Between 1886 and 1890 the demand for credit rubles was rising much more rapidly than the supply, thereby pushing up the exchange rate. The stability of the exchange rate between 1891 and 1895 is explained by the equivalent rates of growth of money demand and money supply.

DID RUSSIA HAVE A CHOICE?

Could Russia have opted to stay off the gold standard without sacrifice of international trade volume? The discovery of silver in Nevada drastically altered relative gold-silver prices and eventually forced silver-standard countries, including Russia, off a silver standard and onto paper or gold standards.[45] It thus appears that Russia would have had to move to a paper or gold standard like other countries.

The great expansion of trade and international capital flows after 1879 has been attributed to the stability offered by the international gold stan-

dard to both merchandise and capital flows, and for Russia to have remained apart from this standard would have meant its partial isolation
from world commodity and capital markets. Moreover, private preferences
for gold among bankers and traders of the major trading nations meant
that balances were being cleared in gold anyway; therefore conversion to
the gold standard represented official and perhaps inevitable recognition of
private business practices.

Russia actually had little choice but to adopt the gold standard in order
to benefit from the expansion of world trade and investment. Russia would
have found it difficult to trade and receive foreign investments on a currency standard radically different from that of the rest of the world.

Integration into the World Economy

The Russian economy's susceptibility to external disturbances during the
late nineteenth and early twentieth centuries was an important ingredient
in political-economic discussions in tsarist Russia during this period. The
point under debate was whether fluctuations in the tsarist economy were
caused by external forces—for example, by international business
cycles—or by agricultural disturbances.[46] This debate had widespread
policy implications: Should Russia follow a "noncapitalist" agrarian pattern or emulate the capitalist industrialization model of the West?

The susceptibility of the Russian economy to short-term fluctuations in
the world economy indicates the extent to which the Russian economy was
integrated into world product and capital markets. A well-integrated Russian economy meant that the tsarist economy would be subject to the same
international forces affecting both short and long swings in growth
throughout the capitalist world. Moreover, the impact of political events
on the Russian economy can be studied by investigating the Russian business cycle. In particular, the effect of the civil disorders of 1905 and 1906
on aggregate output is an important historical issue in its own right.

The subject of the correspondence of the Russian business cycle to cycles
in other countries has been analyzed in the Soviet literature. In fact, the
Russian business cycle has received more attention in Soviet and tsarist
literature than in Western literature.[47] The impact of the world economic
crisis at the turn of the century does, however, play a prominent role in the
writings of Western scholars, who regard it as an important turning point
in Russian economic history.

Figures 4.3 and 4.4 compare the Russian output and investment series
with the corresponding series of the world's major economic powers: England, France, Germany, the United Kingdom, and the United States.
Sweden is included to round out the group. Of this group, only Sweden and

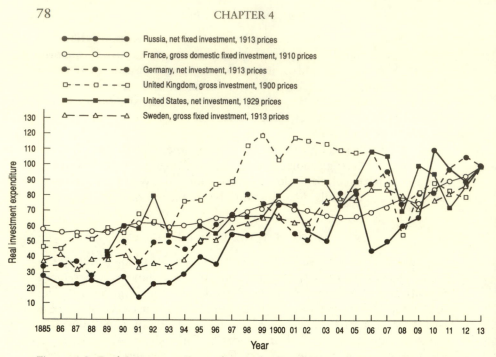

Figure 4.3: Real Investment Expenditures for Russia, France, Germany, United Kingdom, United States, and Sweden, 1885–1913.
Source: Gregory, *Russian National Income*, 142.

Russia were capital importers. The other countries were capital exporters, with the United Kingdom and France serving as the most significant suppliers of capital to foreign countries.

Investment cycles are difficult to analyze visually, because relationships are very complicated. In fact, the data presented in Figure 4.3 could easily be the subject of a substantial scientific investigation. The matter of leading and lagging countries is an especially interesting issue because the German investment cycle generally appears to lead the Russian investment cycle.

Several general statements can be made, however, concerning the Russian investment cycle. First, Russian investment cycles are generally related to investment cycles in other countries: Russia participated in the general upswing in investment spending during the 1890s, in the general decline near the turn of the century, and in the upswing in investment spending between 1908 and 1913. Second, the Russian investment cycle seems most closely related to the German and Swedish cycles. Third, the turning points occur first in the larger economies (the United Kingdom, France, and Germany) and then are transmitted to the smaller economies (Sweden and Russia).

The major distinguishing feature of the Russian investment cycle was the

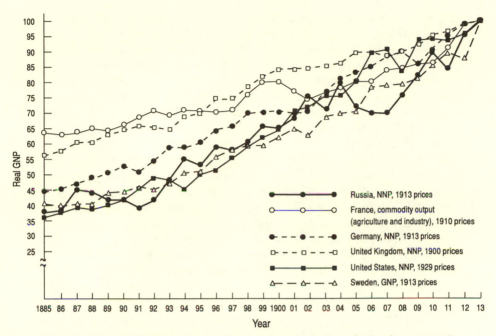

Figure 4.4: Real GNP for Russia, France, Germany, United Kingdom, United States, and Sweden, 1885–1913.
Source: Gregory, *Russian National Income*, 143.

impact of the civil unrest of 1905 on Russian investment. A significant decline in Russian investment spending occurred in 1906 following the 1905 revolution, despite generally rising investment expenditures in other countries. Russia avoided the significant drop in investment spending experienced by other countries in 1908 and 1909. During these years, it was recovering from the earlier drop in investment spending. The decline in investment spending that accompanied the crop failure of 1891 fails to distinguish the Russian investment cycle significantly from that of other countries because it appears to have been shared by other agricultural countries (Germany, Sweden, and to some extent the United States).

One can only conclude that the Russian investment cycle, like the Russian price level (see Figure 4.1), was strongly linked to cycles in other countries. The exact nature of the linkage is difficult to establish due to the complex nature of leads and lags. The only strong distinguishing feature in the Russian case is the significant impact of the 1905 revolution on Russian investment spending—this political event caused Russia to fall out of step with the world investment cycle.

In Figure 4.4, indexes of total output for Russia and the five other industrialized countries are plotted. Again, as in the case of investment, the picture is a complicated one, and it is difficult to establish leads and lags among countries. A major independent inquiry would be required to untangle these relationships. As a general rule, however, one can say that prior to 1900 distinct similarities between the Russian business cycle and that of the United Kingdom, France, and Germany can be discerned. The Russian series, in general, appears to be subject to larger annual fluctuations, and these may be traceable to agricultural disturbances (e.g., in the years 1890 and 1891). After 1900, the Russian business cycle appears to be more independent of the European business cycle. The Russian economy did not turn down immediately in response to the slowdown in world economic activity around the turn of the century (except during a short episode between 1902 and 1903), but it did turn down significantly in response to the civil unrest of 1905 and 1906; whereas the other European countries were generally recovering from the slow (and sometimes negative) growth at the turn of the century. The striking feature of the period 1905–7 is the significant loss in output that accompanied the 1905 revolution and its aftermath (three years of negative growth). Without this three-year episode, the growth of Russian national income after 1900 would have taken on a quite different perspective. In fact, the slower growth recorded for the period 1900–1913 appears to be the sole consequence of the 1905 revolution and its aftermath.

Lessons for the Present

As contemporary Russia navigates the difficult transition from a planned to a market economy, it may benefit from a backward look to the late nineteenth and early twentieth centuries. During this period, tsarist Russia was confronting many of the same problems that the contemporary Russian leadership faces: how to modernize the legal framework of the economy, whether to become a part of the prevailing international monetary system, how much to integrate the domestic economy into the world economy.

This chapter emphasizes the benefits that inured to Russia when it became an integral part of the world economy. It also emphasizes the discipline and costs required to join the world economic community. The discipline required to join the gold standard may be analogous to that required of modern Russia to achieve a convertible currency and become a member in good standing of the International Monetary Fund.

Perhaps bold steps were easier to take in this early period. Persistent and bold finance ministers needed to convince the tsar of the wisdom of their policies. The current Russian leadership must convince a conservative and distrusting Parliament and populace to endorse steps that are politically difficult.

Chapter 5

THE LAST MARKET ECONOMY

THE FORMER leaders of the Soviet Union and the new leaders of the successor republics to the former Soviet Union are in agreement that their administrative-command economies must be transformed into market economies. How to effect this transformation is the major puzzle of remaining years of the twentieth century.

Expert and popular opinion differ on the dating of the region's last experience with a market economy. Some look back to the New Economic Policy of the 1920s as a period of market-resource allocation. Others claim that we must go even farther back to the late tsarist period to find a market economy in what was to become the Soviet Union. A surprising number of experts and laypeople are convinced that Russia never had a market economy. Completely lacking in the experience of markets, it is argued, Russia will have a hard time giving birth to a market economy.

This chapter addresses the question of Russia's (and the Soviet Union's) previous experiences with market capitalism.

DID RUSSIA EVER HAVE A MARKET ECONOMY?

Chapters 3 and 4 touched on the institutional arrangements of the late tsarist economy. Historians and social thinkers have been divided on the issue of whether one can legitimately describe the Russian economy of the period 1880–1913 as a market economy. The anti-Western Slavophiles promoted the idea that Russia was somehow unique—that its economic and social institutions were significantly different from Western institutions. Russian rural life, with its communal institutions, was an exception to the rule of market agriculture. The Russian "factories in the field," described by M. Tugan-Baranovsky, distinguished Russian manufacturing from that of Europe.[1] The Slavophiles wished to keep Russian economic and social life distinct from the corrupting influences of the capitalist West.

Lenin described Russia as a unique blend of backwardness and modernity with a "dual economy" composed of backward agriculture and handicraft and of modern factory industry. Although Lenin recognized isolated elements of advanced capitalism in Russian industry, he believed that most resource-allocation decisions were based on custom and tradition.

The Case for a Nonmarket Russian Economy

The case that Russia was not a market economy rests on two pillars. The first is that Russian agriculture was feudal in nature. Resource-allocation decisions were not based on normal market principles but rather on customs and tradition. The most influential purveyor of this opinion was A. V. Chayanov, who argued that the Russian peasant household's economic decision processes were basically different from those of a capitalist farm.[2] The peasant household operated without hired labor and made its production, consumption, and leisure choices differently from the capitalist farm. The second pillar was provided by Alexander Gerschenkron, who argued that the Russian state replaced so many of the functions of the market that the Russian economy was no longer a "market economy" in the normal sense of the term.[3] State officials served as entrepreneurs; government orders replaced private markets; and state industrial policy dictated the direction of economic activity. Gerschenkron also joined Chayanov in stressing the unique noncapitalist features of Russian agriculture, which were the consequence of the Russian state's option for communal agriculture at the time of the 1861 emancipation.

The Tsarist Economy as a Market Economy

Despite the formidable writings of Chayanov and Gerschenkron, there is abundant evidence that the tsarist economy in its last thirty to forty years was indeed a market economy.

As was pointed out in Chapter 4, the economic role of the Russian state was much less pervasive than Gerschenkron thought. State enterprises were no more prevalent in Russia than in western Europe. Significant budgetary subsidies, which would have formed the backbone of a state industrial policy, cannot be found in state budget data. Tariffs and indirect taxes were levied strictly for the revenue needs of the state and played no industrial policy role. The Russian state did play a significant role in railroad construction, but state financing of railroads does not make a case for nonmarket-resource allocation in Russia.[4]

The Russian state did not engage in economic planning, and product prices and factor prices were set by markets. Russia had active commodity markets and participated actively in world capital markets. Substantial flows of foreign investment came into Russia (as the world's largest debtor nation of the period) in response to normal profit incentives, and the stocks of Russian corporations were listed in both domestic and foreign stock exchanges. As John McKay has ably demonstrated, foreign investment flowed into Russia because Russia—as a newly industrializing economy—offered sufficiently high rates of return to compensate for the greater risk.[5]

Although Russia developed the institutions of modern capitalism later than western Europe, by the last quarter of the nineteenth century Russia had its corporate laws in place and had developed its own commodity and capital markets.[6] The student of Russian economic history can thumb through the elaborate records of Russian stock market and commodity market quotations to obtain a feel for the vibrant commercial life of Moscow and Saint Petersburg. Accounts by foreign entrepreneurs show the perceived wealth of economic opportunities in Russia at the turn of the century.

Although Russian industry came to be increasingly dominated by trusts in its last thirty years, the existence of trusts does not mean nonmarket-resource allocation. It simply means that trusts may have engaged in monopoly pricing; but even this conclusion is questionable. We do not know enough about the pricing policies of Russian trusts, and those trusts that produced raw materials—oil, metals—would have had to charge world market prices.

Chapter 3 looked at Russian agriculture. Although the Emancipation Act of 1861 called for the retention of communal agriculture, evidence was presented that Russian peasants found ways to circumvent those features of feudal agriculture that depressed agricultural output. The emancipation provisions were supposed to freeze rural labor, but there is ample evidence of considerable peasant mobility, which allowed the rapid growth of the industrial labor force and the regional redistribution of labor.

The most convincing evidence that Russian agriculture was, by and large, operating according to market principles was the striking performance of Russian agriculture after railroad construction was completed in the 1880s. Russia became the world's largest exporter of grain, and the econometric studies of Soviet economic historians showed that regional price dispersion fell as transportation costs were lowered and that agricultural marketings and land rents were dictated by "normal" market principles.[7]

Macroeconomic evidence also demonstrates that the Russian economy was a market economy integrated into the world economy. The Russian business cycle was dictated by the European business cycle (see Chapter 4). Moreover, the structure of the Russian economy on the eve of the revolution was like that of other market economies at that level of economic development.[8] The statistical profile of the Russian economy was that of a market economy taking the first decisive steps toward modern economic growth.

The above evidence convincingly establishes that Russia had developed a market economy by the eve of World War I. Those who wish to dispute this conclusion must provide counterevidence that industrial, agricultural, labor, and capital resources were being allocated by some yet-to-be-identified nonmarket mechanism. The major test of a market economy—prices being set by market forces free of government intervention—was being met.

FROM REVOLUTION TO FIVE-YEAR PLAN

The period from 1917 to 1928–29 saw two experiments with new economic systems. The first experiment, called War Communism, dated from 1918 to 1921. War Communism was a transitional economic system, dictated in large part by the civil war emergency. The second experiment, called the New Economic Policy (NEP), dated from March 1921 to the adoption of the administrative-command economy at the very end of the 1920s.[9] This section is mainly about the NEP period.[10]

The roots of War Communism can be traced to the October Revolution. One of the first actions of the fledgling Bolshevik regime was to nationalize the remaining large estates through the Land Decree of November 8, 1917. The change in land tenure was to have a far-reaching impact on economic policy throughout the 1920s. In their enhanced capacity as proprietors, the peasants were no longer obligated to deliver a prescribed portion of their output either to the landlord (as a rental payment) or to the state (as a tax or principal payment). Now they, not the state or the landlord, made the basic decisions about how much to produce and what portion of this output would be sold. Thus, the total agricultural output and the marketed portion of this output became dependent on the Russian peasant. Moreover, the 1917 revolution essentially did away with large farm production units. Before the revolution, 4 percent of the farm households farmed more than thirteen dessiatines of land and another 13 percent were landless. By 1922 virtually no farm families had landholdings of more than thirteen dessiatines, and only 5 percent were without land.

There was a revival of the mir during and after the revolution. The mir was the institution that had confiscated and redistributed the land of the gentry, and it remained the principal voice of legal and administrative authority within the village during the early years of Soviet rule.[11] The village assembly settled most of the questions of interest to the peasants and was able to steer a course independent of the local administrative arms of the Bolshevik government. However, as M. Lewin writes, one should not overemphasize the socialist instincts of the peasants.[12] The peasants remained attached to their village communities, and in their eyes the purpose of the revolution was to give them their own farms. That the land was nationalized and belonged to the mir did not detract from the peasants' conviction that the land was theirs to farm and manage as they saw fit.

The initial Bolshevik attitude toward private industry was cautious and restrained, since an uneasy truce between Bolshevik and capitalist was required to prevent a drop in industrial output. Trade unions were formed after the October Revolution—two thousand in the first two months. Workers' Committees in privately owned enterprises were given the right to supervise management, but at the same time the proprietor had the executive right to give orders that could not be countermanded by the Workers' Committees. Also, the Workers' Committees were denied the right to take over enterprises without the permission of higher authorities. Only enterprises of key importance—such as banking, grain purchasing and storage, transportation, oil, and war industries—were nationalized, establishing a form of state capitalism based on state control of key positions in the economy; mixed management of enterprises; and private ownership of agriculture, retail trade, and small-scale industry.

WAR COMMUNISM, 1918–21

The uneasy truce between the Bolsheviks, capitalists, and peasants did not last long. By 1918 the Bolsheviks were locked in a struggle for survival with the White Russian forces supported in part by foreign powers. The Germans were in possession of the Ukraine, while the White Russian armies occupied the Urals, Siberia, and North Caucasus. Poland invaded in May 1920. At the low point, the Bolsheviks retained only 10 percent of the coal supplies, 25 percent of the iron foundries, less than 50 percent of the grain area, and less than 10 percent of the sugar beet sources of the former Russian empire.[13] At one point, 75 percent of USSR territory was occupied by opposing forces.

The Bolsheviks resorted to printing money to finance the civil war. Rapid monetary expansion, combined with shrinking supplies of consumer goods, created hyperinflation. On November 1, 1917, the amount of money in circulation was 20 billion rubles. By July 1, 1921, 2.5 trillion rubles were in circulation. In the spring of 1919 printing presses could no longer print money at a fast enough pace. Supplies of consumer goods dwindled as materials were diverted to military uses, and prices rose more rapidly than the rate of growth of the money supply. Between 1917 and 1921 prices increased eight thousandfold.[14]

Hyperinflation destroyed the market exchange economy. Peasants were reluctant to exchange their products for depreciating money. The economy increasingly used barter transactions, leading to the "naturalization" (demonetization) of the economy. Naturalization was welcomed by the left wing of the Bolshevik party, which termed the government printing press "that machine gun which attacked the bourgeois regime in its rear, namely, through its monetary system."[15] Demonetization created, however, an immediate crisis. The central government found itself powerless to obtain through the market the goods, especially food supplies, they needed to fight the war.

The Bolshevik government resorted to requisitioning of agricultural products. Police and military were sent to the countryside to confiscate agricultural surpluses—a policy creating enormous resentment on the part of the peasants against Soviet power. To limit private sale, private trade was declared illegal. Virtually all businesses, both large and small, were nationalized.

The Soviet regime had succeeded in solidifying its position by the end of 1920. A peace treaty had been signed with Poland, and the White Russian army had been driven out of crucial industrial and agricultural regions. The crisis under which War Communism had come into existence had been overcome, and the dangers of continuing that economic policy were growing more apparent. The still powerful trade unions were revolting against the crippling centralization of industry and the conscription of labor. Alienated peasants called for abolition of the state grain monopoly. Industrial workers were restive, the military was in a rebellious mood, and the Soviet regime was in danger of falling victim to internal discontent. Factory output had fallen to less than 15 percent of its prewar level. Table 5.1 shows the extent of the drops in industrial and agricultural output, the decline in transportation services, and the USSR's virtual withdrawal from world trade. At the end of 1920 and the beginning of 1921 there were peasant uprisings in the countryside against requisitioning. Supplies to Moscow and Petrograd collapsed. The final blow was the Kronstadt Uprising of March 1921, when the sailors of the Kronstadt naval base revolted in support of the Petrograd workers. The Soviet leadership moved quickly to dispel popular discontent by replacing War Communism with the New Economic Policy in March 1921.

The New Economic Policy, 1921–28

Just as War Communism may have been thrust upon the Soviet regime by the civil war in 1918, the New Economic Policy was forced upon the Soviet leadership by the excesses of War Communism. For whatever its reasons, the Soviet leadership at the time took pains to stress the temporary nature of both periods. Lenin declared that "War Communism was thrust upon us by war and ruin. It was not, nor could it be, a policy that corresponded to the economic tasks of the proletariat. It was a temporary measure."[16] In the same vein, Lenin described NEP as a temporary step backward (away from socialism) in order to take two steps forward later. From the viewpoint of the Bolshevik leadership, NEP was a transitional step backward because of the important roles that "antisocialist" institutions—such as private ownership, private initiative, and capitalist markets—were allowed to play during this period.

The most striking feature of NEP was its attempt to combine market and socialism: Agriculture remained in the hands of the peasant, and industry (with the exception of the "commanding heights") was decentralized. Market links between industry and agriculture and between industry and consumer replaced attempts at state control. Most industrial enterprises were denationalized. The largest enterprises, which produced three-quarters of industrial output—the so-called commanding heights—remained nationalized. It was hoped that the state could provide general guidance by retaining direct control of the commanding heights of the economy—heavy industry, transportation, banking, and foreign trade—while allowing the remainder of the economy to make its own decisions.

The political basis of NEP was the *smychka*, or alliance, between the Soviet regime and the peasant. The political objective of NEP was to regain the support of the peasant. The War Communism policy of requisitioning agricultural output had to be abandoned, for the peasants would never ally themselves with a regime that confiscated their surpluses. Market agriculture had to be reestablished, freeing the peasant both to sell and buy their products freely.

Smychka represented a significant concession from the Bolshevik leaders. The policy of conciliation placed them in the tenuous position of choosing between the support of the peasantry and the attainment of party objectives. The reestablishment of market agriculture would serve to create a commercially minded peasantry. The very success of NEP would require increasing economic differentiation and the emergence of relatively prosperous peasants, who would produce the critical market surpluses. Marx had condemned the wealthy and middle peasant as adamant opponents of socialism, but NEP would serve to promote this class. The ideological concession of NEP was great.

The cornerstone of NEP was the proportional agricultural tax (the *prodnalog*) introduced in March 1921 to replace requisitions. First paid in kind, and by 1924 in money, it was a single tax based on a fixed proportion of each peasant's net produce. The state took a fixed proportion of production, and the peasant again had an incentive to aim for as large a surplus as possible. The *prodnalog* was differentiated according to income level and family size. In 1923, for example, the *prodnalog* varied from 5 percent (for landholdings less than one-quarter of a hectare) to 17 percent (more than three hectares) of annual income. Throughout the NEP period the burden of the *prodnalog* was shifted increasingly to the middle and upper peasants, and it accounted for about a quarter of state revenues. According to studies conducted in the mid-1920s, the average tax was below 10 percent of income. Studies by Western historians find that the tax burden during NEP was about the same as in 1913 when all types of taxes are considered.[17]

The agriculture tax, the first step in reestablishing a market economy, necessitated further measures. Unless the peasants could freely dispose of their after-tax surplus, they would have little incentive to produce above subsistence levels. Therefore, the state granted the peasants commercial autonomy to sell their output, whether to the state, a cooperative, or a private dealer. Accordingly, private trade was again permitted to compete with state and cooperative trade organizations. Peasants could market their after-tax surplus at terms dictated by market forces, not by a state monopoly. Finally, peasants were allowed to lease land and hire farm workers, both of which had been forbidden under War Communism.

Within one year, private activity dominated Soviet retail trade and restored the market link between consumer and producer. By the end of 1922 nine-tenths of all retail trading outlets were private, and they handled about three-quarters of retail trade turnover, with state and cooperative outlets handling the balance.[18] The private trader, or "Nepman," was less strongly entrenched in wholesale trade, which remained dominated by state and cooperative organizations.

The New Economic Policy also brought about significant changes in industry. The majority of industrial enterprises were permitted to make their own contracts for materials and supplies and for the sale of their output; during War Communism, the state had attempted to perform these functions. Small enterprises employing twenty persons or less were denationalized, and some were returned to their former owners. Others were leased to new entrepreneurs, thereby re-creating a class of small-scale capitalists. The Bolsheviks even granted a limited number of foreign concessions. (The lessee typically signed a six-year contract obligating the enterprise to sell a prescribed portion of its output to the state.)

Denationalization was limited to small-scale enterprises, and the overwhelming portion of industrial production during NEP was turned out by nationalized enterprises. The industrial census of 1923 showed that private enterprises accounted for only 12.5 percent of total employment in "census" establishment. In addition, only 2 percent of the output of large-scale industry was produced by the private sector in 1924–25.[19]

While much of large-scale industry remained nationalized, decision making throughout industry was largely decentralized. Nationalized enterprises were divided into two categories. The commanding heights—fuel, metallurgy, war industries, transportation, banking, and foreign trade—were part of the state budget and remained dependent on centralized allocations of state supplies. The remaining nationalized enterprises were granted substantial financial and commercial autonomy from the state budget. They were instructed to operate commercially and sell to the highest bidder, whether to state or private trade. They were not obligated to deliver output according to production quotas to the state.

The nationalized enterprises were allowed to federate into trusts, which soon became the dominant industrial form. By 1923 the 478 chartered trusts accounted for 75 percent of all workers employed in nationalized industry.[20] These trusts were given the legal authority to enter into independent contracts. They were supervised loosely either by the Supreme Economic Council (VSNKh) or by the *sovnarkhozy* (the regional economic councils), but their commercial independence from the state was protected. The most powerful trusts remained under the direct administration of VSNKh. About 25 percent of industrial production (mainly light industry) was under *sovnarkhoz* supervision. The profits of trusts were subject to property and income taxation in the same manner as private enterprises. The monopoly state bank controlled trust commercial credit. Although the commanding heights enterprises remained within the state budget, they also were instructed to operate as profitably as possible to eliminate reliance on subsidies. Emphasis on capitalist-type cost accounting was the order of the day.

NEP: A MARKET OR COMMAND ECONOMY?

The New Economic Policy combined elements of market and plan. Large-scale industry was owned by the state. Other areas of the economy were characterized by private or private-communal ownership. State-owned enterprises, with the exception of the few budget-financed enterprises, had to cover their own costs and presumably had an incentive to earn profits.

The amalgamation of enterprises into trusts was done to simplify control and coordination. The amalgamation of trusts into syndicates was initially done to coordinate industry sales. Trusts and syndicates were favored by the Soviet leadership's ideological preference for large-scale industry.[21] By the late NEP period, the syndicates came to dominate the sales of state industry, accounting for 82 percent of state industry sales in 1927–28 and for all sales of ferrous metal. The trusts and syndicates acquired considerable commercial autonomy. Syndicates were allowed to enter directly into foreign trade agreements (without permission of the state foreign trade monopoly) and had the right to receive credit from domestic credit institutions and from foreign banks. The growing autonomy of trusts and syndicates had its disadvantages, particularly when the trusts attempted to charge monopoly prices for their products.

Use of money had been virtually eliminated during War Communism as a result of hyperinflation, and money had been replaced by a system of barter and physical allocation. Such a system was too clumsy for NEP. Soviet authorities reintroduced the use of money with the reopening of the state bank in 1921. Both public and private enterprises were encouraged to deposit their savings in the state bank; limitations on private bank deposits were removed, and safeguards protected deposits from state confiscation. A new stabilized currency, the chervonets, was issued by the state bank in 1921, a balanced budget was achieved in 1923–24, a surplus in 1924–25, and the old depreciated paper ruble was gradually withdrawn from circulation in the currency reform of May 1924. A relatively stable Soviet currency was created, which for a time was even quoted on international exchanges. Money transactions between state enterprises replaced earlier barter transactions. The chervonets was the last freely convertible currency of the Soviet Union.

During NEP there was also an attempt to reestablish relatively normal trading relations with the outside world.[22] A state monopoly over foreign trade had been established shortly after the Bolshevik takeover, and foreign trade virtually disappeared during the civil war. During NEP the Soviet leadership was reluctant to become dependent on capitalist markets. Rather, the NEP strategy was enunciated in Lenin's dictum of "learning from the enemy as quickly as possible." Thus, the trading monopoly aimed at importing capitalist technology and equipment that could not be produced at home. With this strategy in mind, foreign concessions were granted and credits from the capitalist world were sought. It was hoped that in their scramble for Russian markets, the capitalist countries would mute their political hostility to the Soviet regime, which had repudiated tsarist Russia's foreign debt.

The volume of foreign trade grew rapidly during NEP, from 8 percent of the prewar level in 1921 to 44 percent in 1928. Yet unlike the production figures, which showed a recovery to prewar levels, the volume of foreign trade throughout NEP remained well below half of the prewar level. Credits from the capitalist nations were not forthcoming, and foreign policy failures made them even less likely. The concessions program never got off the ground; at the end of NEP, there were only fifty-nine foreign concessions, accounting for less than 1 percent of the output of state industry.

Economic Recovery

Just as War Communism provided the means for waging the civil war, NEP provided the means for recovery from the war. In this sense, it was an important strategic success. The economic recovery during NEP was impressive.

Production statistics for 1920 in Table 5.1 indicate the low level of economic activity at the end of War Communism. Industrial production and transportation were both only at one-fifth of the prewar level. The shortage of fuel threatened to paralyze industry and transportation, and industry was living on dwindling reserves of pig iron. The food shortage led to the exhaustion and demoralization of the labor force. Agricultural production was 64 percent of the prewar level. Foreign trade had virtually disappeared.

TABLE 5.1
Production and Trade Indexes, USSR, 1913–20 (1913 = 100)

	Industry	Agriculture	Transportation	Exports	Imports
1913[a]	100	100	100	100.0	100.0
1920	20	64	22	0.1	2.1

Sources: Nutter, "The Soviet Economy," 165; Kaser, "A Volume Index of Soviet Foreign Trade," 523–26.

[a]The 1913 figures refer to interwar territory of the USSR.

In 1928, on the eve of the First Five-Year Plan and at the end of NEP, the official statistics provide a striking contrast: Both industry and agriculture had surpassed their prewar levels. Foreign trade remained well below prewar levels but had recovered substantially from War Communism lows.

More recent calculations suggest that official Soviet figures may have overstated the extent of recovery during NEP and that Soviet national income in 1928 was still below 1913 levels. (See Appendix B for a discussion of the estimates of recovery.) The recovery from the economic devastation demonstrated by the figures for 1920 was impressive irrespective of which set of statistics one uses (see Table 5.2). Although the NEP recovery was impressive, particularly as judged by official statistics, high rates of growth during recovery periods are common once a suitable economic environment is established. The NEP policies provided this suitable framework for recovery.

TABLE 5.2
Selected Indicators of Soviet Output Levels in 1928 Relative to 1913
(1913 = 100)

National income		Selected physical production series	
1913 prices	117	Grain production	87
1926–27 prices	119	Pig iron	79
		Steel	102
		Coal	122
Industrial production		Cotton cloth	104
1913 prices	129	Freight turnover	104
1926–27 prices	139–43	Electric power	203
		Foreign trade	
Agriculture production		Exports	38
1926–27 prices	111	Imports	49

Source: Gregory and Stuart, Soviet Economic Structure and Performance, 63.

THE END OF NEP

According to Soviet statistics, the highest level of NEP is usually dated to 1926, when prewar production levels were generally surpassed. The absolute growth of the nonagricultural private sector stopped in 1926.[23] At that time, all seemed to be going well; yet two years later, NEP was abandoned in favor of the radically different system of central planning by the state, collectivization of agriculture, and nationalization of industry and trade. This radical turn of events seems puzzling in view of the impressive NEP successes. Why was NEP abandoned?

First, leftist party members viewed NEP as a temporary and unwelcome compromise with class enemies. Now that the state was stronger, they argued, the offensive against class enemies could be resumed.[24]

Second, Soviet authorities feared that economic policy had become dominated by prosperous peasants and Nepmen. Increasingly, policies were being dictated to suit the needs of the peasants, not the objectives of the state. A prime example was the "Scissors Crisis" of 1923, which forced the Soviet regime into the paradoxical stance of favoring private agriculture over socialist industry.

According to Soviet figures, the total marketed surplus of agriculture in 1923 was 60 percent of the prewar level, with grain marketings falling even below this figure. On the other hand, industrial production was only 35 percent of the prewar level.[25] The more rapid recovery of agriculture placed pressure on industrial prices relative to agricultural prices. Moreover, the already limited output of industry was being withheld by the industrial trust and syndicates, who were using their monopoly power to restrict trust sales to raise prices. The relative price movements between early 1922 and late 1923 (see Figure 5.1) took on the shape of an open pair of scissors, hence the term Scissors Crisis.

Soviet authorities viewed the opening price scissors with alarm, for they expected the peasants to react by refusing to market their surpluses as their terms of trade with the city fell. Soviet authorities were sensitive to signs of peasant unrest. In August 1924 there was an uprising of Georgian peasants. There was also a ground swell of public opinion favoring formation of a peasant association that would represent peasant interests against the Party, and in the elections to the Soviets in fall of 1924, the peasant turnout was under 30 percent (despite Party efforts to have mass peasant participation).[26] During the prewar period, Russian peasants marketed on the average 30 percent of their output outside of the village. In early 1923, before the price scissors had opened sharply, they marketed about 25 percent, and Soviet authorities feared a further drop. It is uncertain what actually happened to peasant marketings as the scissors opened, because statistics for this early period are difficult to interpret. James Millar suggests that the

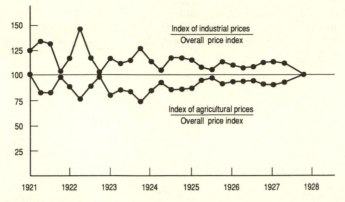

Figure 5.1: The Scissors Crisis
Source: Gregory and Stuart, *Soviet Economic Structure and Performance*, 65.

Bolsheviks mistakenly expected peasant marketings to decline as agricultural prices fell in relative terms.[27] In fact, Millar argues, the peasants had traditionally responded to a decline in the terms of trade by selling more in order to maintain their standard of living. The Millar argument is supported by evidence showing that prewar grain marketings were not significantly affected by the terms of trade.[28] Grain marketing statistics for the Ukraine do, however, suggest a reduction in peasant marketings between 1923 and 1925, but such evidence is fragmentary.[29]

Right or wrong, the Soviet government viewed the Scissors Crisis as a threat to economic recovery, for the industrial worker had to be fed and light industry required agricultural raw materials.

A third source of dissatisfaction with NEP was the conviction that economic recovery had reached its limits. The NEP statistics revealed that much capacity had been lost as a result of World War I and the civil war: The capital stock of heavy industry as of 1924 was estimated to be 23 percent below its 1917 peak, and this capital equipment was on the whole old and outmoded. In 1924 the output of steel, a principal component of investment equipment, was 23 percent of 1913 output. Little had been done to replace industrial capital, although the building of socialism and the expansion of military capacity were priority objectives. After eight years of Soviet rule, investment and military commodities accounted for the same proportion of industrial output as they had prior to the revolution.[30] To a regime already committed to the ideological primacy of large-scale heavy industry, this was an unacceptable outcome.

The high unemployment rate of the mid- and late 1920s was a fourth reason for official dissatisfaction. Rising unemployment was supposed to trouble only capitalist societies; yet rural underemployment was estimated to be between 8 and 9 million, and there were well over a million unemployed in the cities.[31] The existence of such high unemployment was not only ideologically embarrassing, but the social unrest it engendered represented a real political threat.

A final source of dissatisfaction related to national security problems. The fear of imperialist conspiracies, England's breaking off of diplomatic relations in 1927, and concern over Japanese activities in the Far East prompted the Soviet leaders to realize that rapid industrialization would be required for security purposes and that NEP was not well suited for rapid industrialization. The leadership in 1927 expected a war with the capitalist West, and panic purchases by the population worsened the supply situation.[32]

In spite of their dissatisfaction with the course of industrial development during the 1920s, the Soviet leaders considered their hands tied as long as NEP continued. They feared that a drive to increase heavy industry would reduce the availability and raise the prices of light industry. The terms of trade would turn further against agriculture and threaten an additional agricultural supply crisis.

The New Economic Policy was not a command economy. Planning authorities generally provided trusts with "control figures," which were to be used as forecasts and guides for investment decisions. Mandatory output plans were drawn up only for a few key heavy industries. The limited physical planning and distribution were carried out through the Committee of State Orders, which placed orders through VSNKh and negotiated the orders with the producer trusts. During NEP, the most important force of economic control and regulation was the Peoples Commissariat of Finance (Narkomfin), which exerted its influence through the budget and credit system (the so-called "dictatorship of finance"). Planning during the NEP period was carried out by a variety of organizations—VSNKh, the State Planning Committee (Gosplan, established in 1921), the commissariats, and local authorities. Until the late 1920s planners limited themselves to forecasting trends as dictated by market conditions. There was also a notable lack of coordination among the various planning agencies until Gosplan established itself as the dominant coordinating planning body after 1927.[33] The lack of a planning system to coordinate economic activity suggests that most decisions were based on profit-loss motivations or were directed by state budget decision making.

Misunderstanding Markets

Was NEP a market economy? The two main indicators of market-resource allocation were the absence of an organized system of planning and the setting of most prices by markets. Although heavy industry was predominantly state owned, there were no real "planners" to instruct the managers of state enterprises. Attempts were made to set indicative targets for state enterprises, and the state assisted, using the limited means available, to link state enterprises in supply relationships. Most decisions appear to have been made on a decentralized basis. We do not know whether state enterprises were strongly motivated to maximize profits, but they apparently were motivated to cover their costs and to maintain their labor forces. In this sense, NEP state enterprises probably operated the way Soviet reformers in the late 1980s wished theirs would—namely, on an economic basis, free of budgetary subsidies.

The tendency to agglomerate into trusts meant that many supply and pricing decisions were made on a noncompetitive basis, but monopoly power does not mean the absence of market-resource allocation. We know too little about the degree of concentration of NEP industry and of cartel pricing arrangements to generalize about the degree of monopoly power. We would not be surprised, however, if especially in the absence of world trade, price-setting power was great.

During the early NEP period, the state tried to limit price increases of manufactured goods. These price-control actions were aimed at improving the terms of trade of agriculture. Insofar as private trade was legal during this early period, price controls were observed only in state retail establishments, not in private markets. Accordingly, one would expect that the major price-setting force in the economy was the market. Those who succeeded in buying at the lower state prices did so either through luck or through the process of administrative allocation.

The literature says relatively little about price-setting practices during the mid-NEP period, but there is little evidence of strong state intervention in price setting. Until the very late NEP period, the state did not appear to play a major role in price setting. Although state and cooperative organizations dominated wholesale trade, private traders dominated retail trade. The lack of state pricing intervention was evidenced by the fact that substantive divergences between state and private prices were not apparent from the mid- to the late 1920s, at which time the state started to intervene directly in pricing decisions, particularly in agriculture. The relatively small price differentials that did exist in agriculture in the mid-1920s could easily have been explained by the liquidity and ease offered by state trading organizations vis-à-vis private trading enterprises.

The monetary reform of the mid-1920s created a currency that appeared to be meaningful both for internal and external transactions. After the monetary reform, there is little evidence of the use of parallel currencies, and the chervonets was indeed a convertible currency from the mid- to the late 1920s.

The Soviet leadership appeared to recognize its inability to control resource allocation through administrative means, other than the limited controls that took place through the state budget. The most effective means of directing the economy in an environment of state ownership of heavy industry and market prices was through the control of credit. The "dictatorship of finance" was a recurring theme of the NEP period. Unable to control the economy directly, the state used its commanding heights control of the banking system to control the direction of economic activity.

One test of NEP economic decision making was whether NEP's industrial structure resembled that of a market economy. Statistical tests suggest that the NEP economy in 1928 closely resembled that of a market economy at a similar level of economic development. Despite changes in ownership and attempts on the part of the state to direct economic activity, the NEP economy was quite similar to that of the tsarist economy in 1913. It was not until the cataclysmic changes of the 1930s, when the administrative-command system was installed, that the structure of the economy came to differ significantly from that of comparable market economies.[34]

Soviet authorities experienced a number of difficulties during NEP when they attempted to intervene in markets. The ceiling prices set for manufactured goods in the early 1920s led to the "goods famine" of that period. Attempts to control agricultural prices during the late NEP period caused peasants to engage in what the Soviet leadership perceived to be marketing boycotts.

The level of literacy concerning market economics among the Soviet leadership was very low. Even the most well-trained Bolshevik economists, such as Bukharin and Preobrazhensky, were trained in the political economy of Marx and lacked an intuitive understanding of market forces. The middle-level leadership did not understand markets and tended to interpret natural economic actions as politically motivated. The key figure, Stalin, either failed to understand economics or used the common lack of understanding to interpret economic behavior to gain maximum political benefit.

The NEP period demonstrated to the Soviet leadership its inability to make policy in a market environment. First, the Soviet authorities failed to understand normal speculative behavior in a world of fluctuating prices. Particularly in agriculture, products will be withheld from the market when producers believe that prices are temporarily low. When Soviet pricing authorities set low agricultural prices, grain producers withheld their products from the market in expectation that the lower prices would not hold. It was primarily the more affluent agricultural producers who could afford to withhold grain from the market; therefore, most speculative grain stockpiling would was done by the upper peasants.

Second, Soviet authorities failed to appreciate fully the general inflationary pressures of the mid-1920s. Between 1924 and 1927 the money supply rose by 2,665 percent, which meant that there were strong inflationary pressures both in industry and in agriculture. Many pricing policies (both in agriculture and industry) were undertaken simply to hold down the rate of inflation. However, economic history tells us that, whenever price controls are introduced in tandem with excessive monetary growth, economic distortions of all sorts are bound to emerge.

Third, Soviet authorities failed to understand common notions of opportunity costs. There were several instances in the mid-1920s when the state prices for grains were set below the opportunity costs of production. One should not be surprised that peasants would reduce their production and marketings of grains with prices below opportunity cost.

Fourth, Soviet authorities appeared to be much more interested in grain collected by the *state* than in the total amount of grain offered to the *market*. Soviet authorities throughout the 1920s were more interested in how much grain they were able to obtain from the peasants than in total grain marketings (both to the state and to the population).[35]

The handling of the Scissors Crisis demonstrates the government's proclivity to intervene clumsily in the private economy. Although the price scissors probably would have closed by themselves, the government intervened directly in the hope of improving the peasants' terms of trade. First, maximum selling prices were set for industrial products and price cuts for selected products were ordered. Second, imports of cheaper industrial commodities were allowed to enter the country. Third, the state bank restricted the credit of the industrial trusts to force them to unload excess stocks. VSNKh even began to use quasi-antitrust measures against the syndicates, and some were abolished.[36] The substantial closing of the scissors (see Figure 5.1) by mid-1925 indicates the apparent success of these measures.

REJECTION OF THE MARKET

The setting of maximum industrial selling prices in a period of rising wage and price inflation had an important side effect: an excess demand for industrial products that could not be eliminated through price increases, because a ceiling had been set. Despite excess demand and its resulting shortages, no formal rationing system was in place. Lucrative profits could be made by the Nepmen by selling at prices in excess of ceiling prices. This general shortage of industrial commodities has been called the "goods famine," and the peasants, because of their isolation from the market, were hit especially hard.[37] Despite the efforts of the Peoples' Commissariat for Trade to sell in the village at the established ceiling prices, the peasants had to buy primarily from the Nepman, who sold at much higher prices. The peasants, despite the nominal closing of the scissors, still lacked incentives to market their surplus. In fact, there is some evidence to suggest that grain marketings were falling as the scissors were closing.[38] The net marketings of grain in 1926–27 were between 50 and 57 percent of prewar levels, although grain output was close to the prewar level.[39]

The state's pricing policy had another serious side effect that eventually destroyed the market orientation of NEP. Initially, two sets of industrial and agricultural prices coexisted side by side: the higher prices of the Nepmen, who sold to a great extent in the villages, and the official state ceiling price. In 1927 prices in private stores were 30 percent higher than in state stores. By the end of 1928 they were 63 percent above official state prices.[40] The Nepman soon came to be regarded as an enemy of the state. Beginning in late 1923, policies were adopted to systematically drive out the Nepman and widen the state's control over trade. This objective was pursued through the control of industrial raw materials and goods produced by state industry, surcharges on the rail transport of private goods, and taxes on profits of Nepmen. In 1926 making "evil-intentioned" increases in prices through speculation became a crime punishable by imprisonment and confiscation of property. Finally, in 1930 private trade was declared a crime of speculation.

Similar phenomena can be noted in agriculture. After 1926–27 the state lowered grain procurement prices (which eventually caused peasants to divert production to higher-priced crops and livestock), and the gap between state procurement prices and private purchase prices widened. Statistical studies undertaken during this period show that state procurement prices for the four major grains were below production costs in 1926 and 1927. Due to the higher production costs of small and middle peasants, the losses on sales to the state were highest for small and middle peasants.[41] The peasants responded by refusing to market their grain to state procurement agencies, creating the "grain procurement crisis" discussed in Chapter 6. Again, the private purchaser was systematically forced out of the agricultural market by the state. This trend culminated in 1929, when compulsory delivery quotas replaced the agricultural market system.

Such actions effectively signaled the end of NEP, for the market on which NEP primarily depended was no longer functioning. Prices were set by the state, and they no longer reflected supply and demand. The economy was without direction from either market or plan—a situation that was not to be tolerated long.

THE PRECEDENTS OF THE 1920S

During the 1920s the economic problem of resource allocation was dealt with by using two radically different economic systems. The first, War Communism, relied heavily on command elements, whereas the second,

NEP, attempted to combine market and command methods. The experiences of this early period established precedents that had a visible and lasting impact on the eventual organizational structure of the Soviet planned economy.

First, Soviet experiences with central planning during the 1920s indicated that the market cannot be eliminated by fiat, for unless an enforceable plan is introduced in its place, the economy will be without direction other than that provided by the "sleepless, leather-jacketed commissars working around the clock in vain effort to replace the market."[42] To use Trotsky's apt description: "Each factory resembled a telephone whose wires had been cut."[43] "Paper" planning was shown to be virtually no plan at all, and unless planners had detailed and coordinated information from the enterprise level and the political and economic muscle to ensure compliance, planning would be ineffective. To quote one expert: "War Communism cannot be considered a centrally planned economy in any meaningful sense."[44]

Second, the leadership's experiences with peasant agriculture during the 1920s also set important precedents. It was widely feared that peasant agriculture could be a thorn in the side of rapid industrialization, for the success of industrialization was seen as being dependent on peasant marketings to the state. The Soviet leaders' apprehension was the impetus for the introduction of force into the countryside with the collectivization of agriculture in 1929; it provides an explanation for the continuing reluctance of the leadership to reinstate individual peasant farming, despite the disappointing performance of collective agriculture.

The third precedent was the development of an ingrained mistrust of the market. Most experiences with the market during the late NEP period were perceived as negative. The predominant trusts used their monopoly power to restrict output and withhold stocks. The Nepmen sold at high market prices despite the efforts of state authorities to set price limits. The peasants withheld their output whenever they deemed market incentives insufficient. For these and other reasons, the market was virtually abolished after 1929, with only such minor exceptions as the collective farm market, the "second economy," and, in part, the labor market. It is in this context that one can better understand the Soviet leadership's inbred opposition to fluctuating prices, output and input decisions based on profit maximization, and other market phenomena. The 1920s convinced the Soviet leadership of the inevitability of an uneasy truce between the market and the central authorities. Throughout the 1920s, the bulk of consumer goods continued to be supplied by private markets, even during periods when market transactions of this type were proscribed. During War Communism, the Soviet state continued to print money, the use of which was proscribed in legal transactions, knowing full well it was destined for illegal private markets. During NEP, the Nepmen were tolerated because the state knew that it would be unable to supply populations living in remote areas.

The year 1928 found the Soviet Union on the eve of the Five Year Plan, about to embark on an ambitious program of forced industrialization. It was during the next few years that the Soviet command system evolved into the administrative-command system. War Communism and NEP represented a practical learning experience for the Soviet leadership. The result was the administrative-command economy, which endured from the late 1920s to the early 1990s.

NEP as a Model for Reform

Perestroika caused the Soviet leadership to reevaluate NEP's attempt to combine market and plan. The increased freedom of expression of the 1980s allowed Soviet scholars to question seriously whether NEP could have served as an alternative to the forced collectivization ordered by Stalin in 1929. Official Soviet writings on NEP represented a calculated attack on the remnants of Stalinism, but they also appeared to be a relatively sincere effort to learn more about combining market and plan in a setting of predominantly public ownership.

Official Soviet writings on this subject concluded that NEP was an unsuccessful attempt to find the optimal ratio between private initiative based on market relations and administrative allocation.[45] The use of market relations and private initiative in light industry and handicraft was viewed as a positive feature of NEP. The failure to find an appropriate formula for motivating the state-directed sector was criticized. Soviet writers saw in NEP a basic contradiction that caused it to carry the seeds of its own destruction. Essentially, the failure to find ways to channel initiative and risk in the state sector resulted in an expansion of the administrative-command system far beyond its necessary bounds.

On the matter of private ownership in agriculture, official Soviet writings maintained that private peasant agriculture was not a viable long-term alternative, but that Stalin's use of force to collectivize was premature. With continued private ownership, market allocation in agriculture would have resulted in a series of grain collection crises that could have been handled only by inflationary monetary expansion. The appropriate course of action, in the absence of crises, would have been to cultivate the natural cooperative tendencies of peasants as reflected in the continued strength of the village commune. By encouraging what Lenin called the "civilized cooperative" based on state ownership of land and high degrees of cooperation, Soviet agriculture would have evolved into sufficiently large-scale production units. Stalin's decision to collectivize was premature because it preceded the development of necessary cooperative tendencies.[46]

Although some Soviet writers saw NEP as an appropriate model for Soviet economic reform, official Soviet writers remained cautious and were willing to accept only selected parts of the NEP program. Private ownership of agricultural land was ruled out; cooperative tendencies were to be encouraged based on state ownership of capital; and more market allocation was to be used in place of the discredited administrative-command system. Most of all, appropriate incentive mechanisms needed to be found to guide the activities of state enterprises.

The collapse of the Soviet Union in late 1991 caused these initial stirrings of interest in NEP to be outpaced by the decision to attempt "radical" reform. Although interest in NEP remained alive, reformers saw the opportunity for a reform that went beyond the bounds defined by the NEP period.

Chapter 6

THE CRISES OF NEP

STALIN'S DECISION to collectivize agriculture was announced at the November 1929 plenum of the Communist party.[1] The all-out drive to collectivize began in January 1930. Collectivization can be rightly called the second socialist revolution. Its impact on Soviet life ranked in importance with the October Revolution and the Great Patriotic War. More than sixty years have passed since collectivization, and agriculture remains firmly in state hands in the former Soviet Union—an enduring legacy of a way of thinking born in the late 1920s.

This chapter deals with three separate issues. First, what caused the Soviet leadership to opt for collectivization? The various "crises" of Soviet agriculture in the 1920s are reexamined to consider the question of collectivization's inevitability. Second, what were the results of collectivization? Can a valid case be made that collectivization contributed in a positive and substantive way to Soviet economic development? Third, what would have happened had Soviet agriculture not been collectivized?

WAS STALIN NECESSARY?

Soviet ideology made some attempts to disentangle collectivization, socialism, and Stalinism in the late 1980s. With glasnost, collectivization raised the inevitable question of "Was Stalin really necessary?" This question can be rephrased in the contemporary context as "Was collectivization really necessary?"

Stalin's decision to abandon NEP was dictated by several considerations. First, it was generally felt that the NEP recovery had run its course. The New Economic Policy was viewed as a transitional system to promote recovery from civil war; once its task was complete, it was time to turn to a new economic system. Second, NEP's concessions to private ownership and to market allocation had rankled the left wing of the Party. The counterrevolutionary threats of NEP were perceived as extensive, especially the threat of a prosperous peasant and merchant class. Third, the Russian peasant, particularly the wealthier peasant, was perceived as a staunch enemy of socialism. Communist force remained weak in the countryside. The Soviet leadership needed to enhance its presence in the countryside, and collectivization offered such an opportunity. Fourth, the private economy, especially private agriculture, was perceived as an unreliable supplier of food products and agricultural raw materials. As long as agricultural marketing decisions remained in the hands of private individuals, any state industrialization effort would be subject to veto by private citizens.

Soviet ideology, even under glasnost, remained uncomfortable with collectivization. It emphasized that forced collectivization was motivated by Stalin's lust for power. Stalin prematurely forced collectivization, ignoring the advice of calmer heads like Lenin and Bukharin, who argued for a slower voluntary pace. The ultimate need for collectivization was not questioned but, rather, its pace and its forced nature were.

To reject collectivization as an integral part of the struggle to overcome Soviet industrial backwardness raised questions that remained too sensitive: If rapid industrialization could have been achieved without collectivization, why not return to private agriculture? Moreover the sensitivities of the Stalin generation had to be considered. If collectivization was not necessary, how could one justify its enormous material and human costs? As a party decision, the admission of a monumental mistake would be harmful to the continued existence of the Party. Such thoughts must have tortured the Party leadership prior to the demise of central Party authority in 1991.

Throughout the glasnost era Soviet writers continued to argue, often for bizarre reasons, that collectivization was inevitable in the circumstances of the late NEP period.[2] The official argument was that the Bolshevik leadership could not have survived in an environment of private peasant agriculture. The peasants would have been in a position to veto industrialization. The Bolshevik state had to amass political power in the countryside, which required some form of collectivization. Moreover, NEP's combination of market and plan meant that the state was bound to make pricing blunders that would threaten grain collections and hence industrialization.[3] Finally, private NEP peasant agriculture was not evolving in the appropriate direction of larger-scale units. Larger-scale production units were required to raise agricultural efficiency.

Western research has made a reassessment of collectivization timely.[4] R. W. Davies published a comprehensive political economy account of the early years of collectivization.[5] Prominent Western economic theorists have explored Preobrazhensky's model of nonequivalent exchange.[6] Considerable research has gone into the economics of NEP agriculture, including the publication of Soviet historian V. P. Danilov's study of NEP agriculture.[7] Holland Hunter's work on the counterfactuals of collectivization, a decade in the writing, is now available.[8] The ongoing debate on the agricultural surplus controversy continues.[9]

THE INEVITABILITY QUESTION

Soviet ideological writings emphasized the inevitability, the unavoidability, of the collectivization of agriculture. The outstanding issues were the timing, voluntariness, and scope of eventual collectivization—not the ultimate need for it.

Soviet writers made two economic arguments for collectivization: First, only through collectivization could economically scaled farm units be created. Without collectivization, Russian farming was doomed to be carried on by small, inefficient, family-operated units. Second, NEP agriculture was incapable of coexisting with and supporting industrialization. This incompatibility was evidenced by the various "crises" of NEP agriculture. Collectivization was a forced response to the failure of NEP agriculture.

The Scale of NEP Agriculture

New Economic Policy agriculture was not private peasant agriculture. It combined strong feudal elements with elements of market-resource allocation. Agricultural output was produced by communal institutions but distributed primarily through market allocation. The publication of Danilov's works on NEP agriculture sheds a great deal of light on the institutional setting of NEP and its relation to the collectivization decision.[10]

Although NEP agriculture has been loosely described as private agriculture, Danilov shows that Russian peasants reverted to the repartitional commune after the Land Decree of 1917. Throughout NEP, the repartitional commune accounted for over 95 percent of peasant families. The NEP commune had more restrictive communal arrangements than the mir on the eve of the revolution. Bolshevik decrees outlawed the hiring of labor, the selling of land, and interfamily rental agreements. Land distributions from the remaining estates, larger peasant holdings, and state land were based on the number of adult family members throughout the NEP period. There was close monitoring of landholdings to prevent them from exceeding one family's ability to cultivate, and violators were regularly reported by disgruntled neighbors.

Land redistributions were carried out on a regular basis throughout NEP—unlike the late tsarist period, during which land redistributions were rare. In fact, the Bolshevik government was forced to pass decrees resisting too frequent land redistributions because of their obvious disincentive effects.

The NEP redistributional commune retained the worst features of the prerevolutionary commune. Periodic redistributions reduced incentives to improve land; there were endless disputes about land distributions; strip farming wasted labor time in moving among strips (sometimes more than one hour per day). Compared to these arrangements, prerevolutionary communal agriculture was much more flexible. Estate agriculture offered economies of scale and employment opportunities for poor or non-entrepreneurial peasants. Land purchases were encouraged, and there was increasing differentiation of the peasantry. The Stolypin reforms of the early twentieth century entitled peasant families to leave the commune. It was possible to hire labor and lease land without violating prevailing laws.

Although insufficient research has been done on the relative performance of private peasant, communal, and estate agriculture in the prerevolutionary period, Russian agriculture, on the eve of the revolution, had a number of obvious advantages over NEP agriculture. The tsarist state did not act against peasant differentiation. Large estates offered opportunities for labor hiring and for mechanization. The lure of the frontier was ever present. The more adventurous farmers could extend the frontier of cultivated acreage free from communal restrictions.

The Stalinist literature attacked the prominent role played by NEP kulak farmers. In fact, Stalin claimed that the disruptive activities of the increasingly dominant kulaks made collectivization unavoidable and justified collectivization as a necessary move against a dangerous class enemy.

Danilov finds little statistical evidence of a strong and growing kulak class during the 1920s. He provides only vague hints of how kulaks were able to achieve their purported economic and political dominance over the peasant community in such a hostile environment.[11] The share of enclosed land grew very slowly throughout the 1920s prior to the enactment of restrictive laws against enclosures in the late 1920s. The kulaks, so maligned by Stalin, are hard to find in Danilov's research.

Restrictions on farm size and hired labor created a NEP agriculture of smaller average farm sizes than prior to the revolution. Average farm-size differences are impossible to calculate, but the average NEP farm was smaller than the average farm on the eve of the revolution. Moreover, restrictive laws and the strong egalitarianism of the repartitional commune made increased differentiation of the farm population difficult to achieve. If NEP farming was uneconomically scaled, its small scale was due more to legal restrictions than to the natural tendencies of Russian peasant agriculture.

Danilov provides conclusive evidence of the slow progress of collective agriculture during NEP. The share of farm families in collective farms rose imperceptibly despite state subsidies, tax incentives, and later legal sanctions against other forms of agriculture. Moreover, the collectives that were formed were not the "civilized" collectives (shared land and mechanized equipment) favored by Lenin, but primitive sharing arrangements.

A common technological justification was that collectivization was required to create economically scaled farms, following the model of large-scale farming in the United States. The technological case for forced collectivization, therefore, rests on the fact that civilized collectives were not being created spontaneously at a sufficient pace to support agricultural expansion. On the other hand, restrictive laws prevented differentiation and the spontaneous creation of economically scaled farm units. If collectivization was viewed as the only way to increase average farm size, it was because state policy made it the only solution.

The Soviet emphasis on the relative efficiency of large-scale farming was largely due to Lenin's avowed admiration for large-scale farms. Empirical evidence, however, fails to establish a significant and systematic link between farm size and productivity.[12] Hence, the Soviet policy of forcing gigantism in agriculture for technological reasons does not have a firm footing in world agricultural practice.

The Scissors Crisis

The literature has represented NEP as a series of agricultural crises. The first such crisis was the so-called Scissors Crisis of the early 1920s. As described in Chapter 5, Soviet authorities became alarmed when industrial prices rose sharply relative to agricultural prices in 1922 and 1923. Soviet authorities feared that private peasants would withdraw from the market as the terms of trade turned against them. The ensuing decline in agricultural sales would threaten the economic recovery and set off inflationary pressures.

An article of faith among the Soviet leadership of the time was that the terms of trade must necessarily turn against agriculture in the course of industrialization. Although industrialization elsewhere was not accompanied by a persistent deterioration in agriculture's terms of trade, the Soviet leadership believed that declining relative farm prices and industrialization went hand in hand. If industrialization indeed turned the terms of trade against agriculture, then it was feared that the lack of agricultural marketings would create problems in the form of inadequate agricultural raw materials and food products.

The seriousness with which Soviet writers accepted the argument that private agriculture would stymie industrialization is striking; it has not proven to be a problem in the course of industrialization elsewhere. Despite the lack of historical parallels, there was widespread agreement among Soviet writers that the terms of trade must inevitably turn against agriculture. When the two propositions are combined—industrialization causes agriculture's terms of trade to deteriorate and peasants market less under unfavorable terms of trade—Soviet writers could make a case against private agriculture. With agriculture's terms of trade inevitably falling, peasants would "withdraw from the market" and thwart any industrialization effort.[13] Thus, a form of command agriculture would be required to break the link between the terms of trade and peasant marketings.

The origins of this linkage theory are murky. They likely date to the historically brief Scissors Crisis of the early 1920s, which saw a remarkable short-term deterioration in agriculture's terms of trade—a shift that evoked a panic response from the Bolshevik leadership. The Scissors Crisis, however, was the result of short-term factors associated with the aftermath of the civil war and was not the consequence of long-term factors associated with industrialization. The belief in an inevitable deterioration of agriculture's terms of trade was not a part of Marx's economics; nor has it been demonstrated to be a regular empirical phenomenon of economic development. It is therefore remarkable that Soviet belief in the inevitability of decline in agriculture's terms of trade remained strong to the end of the Soviet state.[14]

If one examines the two propositions in a scientific context, one does indeed find that NEP agriculture tended to respond to a decline in its terms of trade by reducing marketings.[15] Agricultural marketings, however, were not extremely sensitive to the terms of trade.[16] This sensitivity was not sufficient to set off a crisis. There is no consistent long-term evidence that agriculture's terms of trade must inevitably decline in the course of modern economic growth.[17]

Elementary supply-and-demand analysis explains why a Scissors Crisis would not be self-perpetuating in a market-agriculture environment: If peasants indeed reduce their marketings when the terms of trade turn against them, withholding supplies from the market would eventually drive up relative agricultural prices. The Soviet leadership's mistrust (and lack of understanding) of market forces caused them to intervene with price controls rather than wait for "natural" market corrections to take place. The results of this intervention were the "goods hunger" and, in part, the procurement crises described in this chapter.

It is notable that the various models that call for a reduction in agriculture's terms of trade in support of industrial capital formation require nonmarket means (such as taxation or government price controls) to achieve this end. These models, therefore, implicitly recognize that nonmarket controls are required to bring about a permanent reduction in agriculture's terms of trade. Market forces per se cannot be counted on to turn the terms of trade against agriculture.

The Grain Collection Crises

That a temporary blip in agriculture's terms of trade could have had such a lasting effect on Soviet agricultural policy remains an astonishing part of the collectivization story and its aftermath. Yet it remains a pillar of the argument for collectivization's inevitability. The grain collection crises of the late 1920s represent another lasting pillar of the case for the inevitability of collectivization. The remarkable feature of the grain collection crises is the exclusive weight given to grain purchases by the state rather than to more comprehensive performance indicators such as grain sales or overall agricultural output.

The emphasis on state grain purchases can perhaps be explained in terms of a perceived power struggle between the Bolshevik state and the peasant class.

The Soviet leadership was schooled in a "balance mentality."[18] Balances of supplies and demands were to be brought about by administrative actions, not through automatic adjustments of relative prices. The Soviet leadership's actions in the late 1920s can be interpreted as motivated by fears of agricultural imbalances. In their view, the state was supposed to ensure adequate food supplies for urban dwellers and raw materials for industry. Agricultural balances, in their thinking, were assured as long as the state was the dominant purchaser of agricultural products. They were skeptical about the ability of private markets to supply the priority needs of the economy. Agricultural goods that disappeared into the private economy were regarded as lost to the economy.

This type of balance mentality remains strong even among contemporary reformers, who continue to worry about fuel and grain balances while arguing for a market economy.

Stalin used the grain procurement crises of 1927–28 and 1928–29 to justify forced collectivization of agriculture in 1929.[19] The grain procurement crises were evidenced by reductions in the amount of grain purchased by state grain procurement agencies.[20] According to official statistics of the period, state grain purchases fell from 10.6 million tons in 1926–27 to 10.1 million in 1927–28 to 9.35 million tons in 1928–29.[21] Reductions in state grain procurement forced the Soviet state to import grain for the first time in Russian economic history.[22]

The grain procurement crises provided Stalin with ammunition to move against the more prosperous peasants—the kulaks. Stalin, in a May 1928 report to the Communist Party, announced data showing that grain output had regained prewar levels by 1926–27 but that grain marketings were only half their prewar level.[23] Stalin blamed the decline in the marketed share of grain output on the kulaks, whose marketings had declined sharply while those of the lower and middle peasants had remained stable. Stalin used this information as proof that the kulaks were seeking to undermine Soviet power.

The party leadership's fear of an organized marketing boycott prompted the application of "extraordinary measures" (*chrezvychainye mery*) for procuring grain in October 1927. Party officials were dispatched to grain-producing regions to collect grain by administrative measures that included force. Regional and local Party authorities were made personally responsible for grain procurement, roadblocks were set up, grain sold on local markets was confiscated, and prison sentences were handed down for grain burning and private grain trading.[24] Stalin personally supervised the extraordinary measures applied in the Urals and Siberia and came away from this experience convinced that force was required to assure orderly deliveries of grain to the city.[25]

CAUSES OF THE PROCUREMENT CRISIS

Western thinking on the rationale for collectivization was initially influenced by the Stalinist version of the grain collection crises. Maurice Dobb (first published in the 1930s) accepted the Stalinist version of NEP agriculture as crisis-ridden and of the resulting inevitability of collectivization.[26]

Starting in the 1960s, Western economists began to question the Stalinist version of events. Jerzy Karcz argued that Stalin's figures on 1926–27 grain marketings (which appeared to show a peasant marketing boycott) were distorted.[27] In fact, Karcz disputed whether there had indeed been a decline in the grain marketing ratio between 1913 and the late 1920s. A more likely explanation, according to Karcz, was that Stalin simply doctored the data to bolster the case for forced collectivization and a movement against the kulak.

Karcz also argued that the procurement crisis—if it existed at all—was limited to government grain procurement and did not extend to agricultural marketings in general. In 1926–27 the government lowered the prices it was prepared to pay for grain. The lower official grain prices encouraged peasants to market grain through the private channels that still existed. Moreover, the low official grain prices encouraged peasants to shift production and sales to uncontrolled products, such as meat and technical crops. Karcz claims that, while peasant marketings of grain to the state may have declined, sales of agricultural products in general through all channels (state, cooperative, and private) remained healthy throughout the so-called procurement crises.

Karcz's analysis has been supported by a number of Western researchers. Stephan Merl determined that state grain procurement prices from 1926–27 on failed to cover average costs.[28] State prices were so low that many peasants chose to burn grain rather than turn it over to the state. Davies agrees that official grain procurement prices were set too low relative to industrial crops and meat and dairy products and that industrial goods were in such short supply that peasants had little to gain by marketing their grain.[29] Soviet writers conceded Karcz's contention that pricing mistakes contributed to the grain collection crises of the late 1920s.[30] Although Soviet writers continued to emphasize the deliberate sabotage of marketings by kulak households, low procurement prices were cited as one cause of the procurement crises. Soviet writers pointed out, however, that pricing mistakes were inevitable in the confusion of the late 1920s, and that the Bolshevik leadership would have had great difficulty in maintaining collections in a world in which decisions were based on relative prices.

Two versions of the grain procurement crises that preceded collectivization exist. According to the Stalinist version, the procurement crises were a deliberate political action, masterminded by the wealthier peasants, to sabotage the Soviet regime. By arbitrarily holding back grain supplies, the wealthier peasants sought to topple the Communist regime. According to the Western version, the so-called procurement crises were the result of economic mismanagement by a fledgling Bolshevik regime that poorly understood economic incentives. By setting state grain procurement prices below costs of production, grain sales were diverted to private markets, agricultural production was diverted to uncontrolled markets (such as technical crops and livestock), and peasant families substituted leisure or work in the city for grain production.

STATISTICS OF THE GRAIN COLLECTION CRISES

Official data on grain purchases and on state and private grain prices shed light on the grain collection crises. Table 6.1 shows that the decline in state grain procurement during the two grain collection crises was actually quite modest and was consistent with trends in grain production. The percentage of grain production finding its way into state purchases remained at about 15 percent from 1926 through 1929. Throughout the late 1920s most grain was consumed in the countryside.[31] Government purchase prices as a percentage of market prices declined sharply throughout the late

TABLE 6.1
Output, State Purchases, and Prices of Grain

Year	1926–27	1927–28	1928–29
Grain production (million tons)	74.6	72.8	72.5
Grain collection (million tons)	11.6	11.1	9.4
Price of wheat in private market (kopecks per centner)	861.0	892.0	1,120.0
State wheat prices (kopecks per centner)[a]	648.0	622.0	611.0
Ratio of state to private grain prices[b] (1913 = 100)	0.89	0.79	0.45

Sources: Davies, *The Socialist Offensive*, 427; Merl, *Der Agrarmarkt und die Neue Oekonomische Politik*, 366; *Statisticheski Spravochnik 1929*, sec. 6, Table 68.
   [a]Central USSR.
   [b]Consuming region (central and north central USSR).

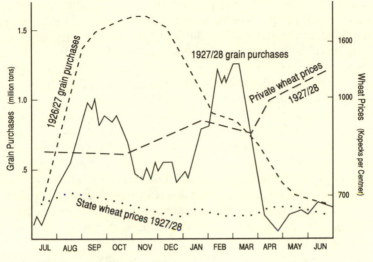

Figure 6.1: The Grain Collection Crisis
Source: Merl, *Der Agrarmarkt und die Neue Oekonomische Politik*, 321–22.

1920s. By the 1928–29 agricultural year, state grain procurement prices had fallen to less than half of prices offered in private markets. For the period as a whole, state grain procurement prices declined slightly in nominal terms, while inflationary forces pushed up nominal prices in private markets. The procurement figures in Table 6.1 do not provide direct evidence of grain procurement crises. In fact, given the growing disparity between state and private prices, it is surprising that state grain collections did not drop more sharply. In this context, one can understand the perceived need for extraordinary measures. With official prices falling relative to market prices, administrative force was required to stabilize state grain procurement.

Figure 6.1 shows the impact of extraordinary measures on state grain collections by contrasting the "normal" periodicity of state grain purchases in 1926–27 with the "crisis" collections of 1927–28. Grain procurements of 1926–27 show that, under normal circumstances, most grain was purchased between August and December. The state announced a reduction in nominal grain procurement prices in late August 1927, which widened the gap between state and market prices. These actions prompted a sharp drop in state procurement during the very period when grain purchasing was normally at its peak.

Extraordinary measures were adopted in late October to counter the decline in state procurement, and their effects began to be felt in January 1928. The result was a partial recoupment of grain procurements lost between September 1927 and January 1928. It is notable that Soviet authorities began to refer to state purchases as "campaigns" as state prices were set below private prices. What had been an economic activity (purchasing grain) now became a semimilitary operation.

Figure 6.1 shows a sensitivity of peasant grain sales to relative prices in state and private markets. The widening gap caused sales to be diverted from state to private purchasers. Although this price sensitivity was interpreted at the time as an effort to undermine Soviet power, it was a normal behavioral response to economic circumstances.

Figure 6.1 provides the chronology of the first grain collection crisis. The second grain collection crisis of the 1928–29 agricultural year is less well documented. By this time, the average state price had dropped to less than half of the private price. Strong administrative measures were required to bring in even smaller quantities of grain procurement.[32] Private economic activity was in the process of being strangled. Statistics on grain sales became even cloudier.

Econometric estimates (explained in the appendix to this chapter) show that the rising gap between state and private prices was the major cause of the drop in state grain procurements. The "crisis" of state grain procurement was induced by the growing gap between market prices and state prices. If the agricultural year 1925–26 is taken to represent "normal" behavior, the peasant economy reacted to every percentage point reduction in the relative state/private grain price by reducing its marketings to the state by thirteen percentage points. When the state determined in late 1927 to lower its nominal grain procurement price even further, it is no wonder that sales to state agencies dropped sharply. In fact, the econometric results show that administrative measures were already supplementing state grain procurement in the 1926–27 agricultural year.

By 1927–28 administrative measures dominated private economic decision making. The econometric model no longer shows "normal" responses to relative price incentives. By the 1928–29 agricultural year official grain prices were less than half of private prices, and extraordinary measures were required to extract grain from an unwilling peasantry. Command had replaced markets.

LESSONS FROM THE PROCUREMENT CRISES

The experiences of the late 1920s provide lessons for contemporary reform. They show the problems inherent in any economy in which state and private prices diverge. As private firms are legalized and accorded the right to buy and sell in private markets, competition for resources begins between the controlled state sector and the uncontrolled private sector. The prices offered by the state tend to be rigid for administrative or equity reasons; hence the private sector typically offers higher prices. These higher prices, unless restrained by "extraordinary measures," divert resources away from their "planned tasks" into the private economy outside the control of planners. The leadership, alarmed by the loss of resources, takes action to reduce the economic freedom of the private sector.

Opponents of market reform, to the present day, warn about the potential chaos of markets, particularly in agriculture, and doubt that markets can deliver reliable supplies of agricultural products to the city.

RATIONALES FOR COLLECTIVIZATION

Stalin gave a number of reasons for forced collectivization. Private agriculture was a threat to Soviet power. Private agriculture doomed Soviet farms to operate at inefficient scales of output. Private agriculture was a constant threat to industrialization. If the terms of trade moved against agriculture, there would be no supplies for the city. The grain procurement crises of the late 1920s demonstrated that any industrialization drive could be vetoed by private agriculture.

We have demonstrated above that the economic rationale for collectivization was weak and was the consequence of the Soviet leadership's failure (or lack of desire) to understand common economic principles. The actions of the late 1920s and early 1930s reflect an extreme distrust and lack of understanding of the workings of a market economy.

We have yet to examine the broader issue of collectivization: Whether collectivization was "necessary" to achieve the major goal of the Soviet leadership—namely, rapid economic development; whether collectivization contributed in a significant manner to the subsequent speed and scope of Soviet economic development. To answer this question, we must consider how collectivization might be used to accelerate capital formation.

The Stylized Facts

It has become standard practice to begin with the stylized facts that a particular theory or model is expected to explain. We are interested in looking at the stylized facts of Soviet economic development during the course of forced collectivization to determine what support they lend different views of collectivization. The most important stylized facts of economic development during the period 1928 to the late 1930s are:

1. The Soviet economy underwent unprecedented changes in its industrial structure in the form of declining product and labor force shares of agriculture and rising shares of heavy industry.
2. The investment rate approximately doubled in a short period of time.
3. Economic growth accelerated from slightly over 3 percent in the late tsarist

period to between 5 and 11 percent per annum depending on the choice of statistical methods.

4. Economic growth took place primarily in nonagricultural sectors. Agricultural output declined sharply in the mid-1930s and may have recovered 1928 levels by the late 1930s.

5. Grain marketings doubled by the mid-1930s and tripled by the late 1930s despite stagnant grain production.

6. Livestock herds halved by the mid-1930s, as did livestock production.

7. Private ownership in both agriculture and industry disappeared within a short period of time.

8. The terms of trade moved markedly against agriculture. Grain procurement prices fell relative to industrial prices.

9. Real wages fell in nonagricultural occupations. Presumably, real wages fell substantially in agriculture.

10. There was no substantial change in the net flow of saving from agriculture to industry between 1928 and 1937.[33]

Collectivization and the Stylized Facts

How did collectivization mold these stylized facts? Stated counterfactually: In what way would these stylized facts have been different if collectivization had not occurred? Some answers are immediately obvious. The swift elimination of private ownership in agriculture would not have occurred without forced collectivization. Although Soviet writers attempted at times to present collectivization as a voluntary movement, trends from 1917 to 1929 show that the voluntary movement into collectives was exceedingly slow.[34]

The halving of livestock herds is also, obviously, the direct consequence of forced collectivization. The doubling and then tripling of state grain procurements during a period of stagnant grain production is an obvious consequence of the institutional changes in grain procurement practice wrought by collectivization. Increasing sales during a period of declining relative prices is obviously contrary to normal economic behavior. It is the consequence of the application of force in the countryside.

The more difficult analytical questions have to do with the other stylized facts. To what extent did forced collectivization contribute to the unprecedented industrial transformation of the Soviet economy, to the doubling of the economywide investment rate, and to the decline in real wages?

Economic Theories and Collectivization

The most analytically challenging issue is collectivization's contribution to the doubling of the Soviet investment rate. Preobrazhensky, in his noted model of nonequivalent exchange, argued for (unspecified) institutional arrangements that would turn the sectoral terms of trade against agriculture. Declining agricultural terms of trade, Preobrazhensky contended, would raise the economywide investment rate.[35]

To Preobrazhensky's way of thinking, if the state could purchase grain at artificially low procurement prices, it would accomplish two things. First, it would lower agricultural incomes and hence lessen the farm population's claim on society's production. In effect, the lowering of peasant real incomes would create forced agricultural savings. Second, when the state resold grain at higher prices, the resulting budget surplus could be used for noninflationary budget finance. As a consequence of nonequivalent exchange, the state could raise the investment rate without setting off hyperinflation. Moreover, the burden of the rise in the investment rate would fall on the farm population in the form of reduced peasant real incomes.

Economic theorists offer two formal analytical models to assess Preobrazhensky's model. First, R. K. Sah and J. E. Stiglitz offer a two-sector analytical model to assess Preobrazhensky's main propositions.[36] Second, Nobel laureate W. Arthur Lewis's two-sector classical growth model examines conditions under which an institution such as collectivization could accelerate economywide accumulation and promote economic growth.[37]

THE SAH-STIGLITZ MODEL

Sah and Stiglitz deal directly with Preobrazhensky's question: Can a decline in agriculture's terms of trade raise the investment rate while cutting into rural real wages but not industrial real wages? In view of its importance to the field, Soviet specialists should analyze the Sah-Stiglitz model in some detail. As of yet, such an examination has not taken place.

Sah and Stiglitz find that Preobrazhensky's first proposition—that the state can increase the investment rate by moving the terms of trade against agriculture—is valid.[38] His second proposition—that the increase in the investment rate will be borne by the agricultural worker—depends on the supply elasticities of agriculture. The more elastic agriculture's supply response, the greater the burden borne by the industrial worker. The urban wage must decline in order to preserve the balance for the rural good (when agricultural marketings fall). Hence, the welfare of the urban worker may decline more than that of the rural worker if the price response of the rural surplus is large.

Sah and Stiglitz's analysis confirms that turning the terms of trade against agriculture can indeed raise the investment rate, but that both real industrial and real agricultural wages would be expected to decline. This finding backs the intuition of Abram Bergson, who wrote in 1961, "Contrary to a common supposition, the industrial worker fared no better than the peasants under Stalin's five year plans. Indeed he seemingly fared worse."[39]

The Sah-Stiglitz model provides unexpected insights into the stylized facts of Soviet economic development. Sah and Stiglitz show that the increase in the investment rate will be higher if the price responsiveness of the rural surplus (the marketed surplus) is large. This result appears at first counterintuitive, but it is explained by the fact that a decline in the rural surplus requires a reduction in the urban wage. The more the urban wage is depressed, the higher the rate of accumulation in industry.

Collectivization—as the stylized facts on grain collections show—eliminated the issue of the price responsiveness of the rural surplus. As the terms of trade deteriorated, marketings tripled—a clear sign that rural surpluses were being determined by administrative decree rather than by the market actions that the Sah-Stiglitz model studies. Thus, collectivization actually served to *hold down* the potential increase of the investment rate by administratively lowering price responsiveness. The reduction of price responsiveness meant that the industrial worker's burden was lessened. By placing more goods on urban markets, there was less pressure to reduce worker real wages.

The Sah-Stiglitz model shows that the stylized facts are consistent with the view that collectivization did indeed contribute to the increase in the Soviet investment rate by raising state accumulation. The advent of forced deliveries ensured that the main burden of the increase in the investment rate did not fall on urban workers.

THE LEWIS MODEL

The Lewis model of economic development with unlimited supplies of agricultural labor (elaborated by Fei and Ranis) was not formulated specifically to assess Soviet collectivization.[40] Unlike Preobrazhensky, the Lewis model does not require a change in agriculture's terms of trade to increase capital accumulation. Rather, the Lewis model utilizes surplus agricultural labor to generate industrial capital formation. Lewis considered a number of institutional ways to mobilize the hidden agricultural surplus, including Soviet-type collectivization and inflationary finance.

The Lewis model requires an agricultural labor surplus, which means that marginal productivity is zero in agriculture. With zero marginal productivity, rural wages must be determined by custom and tradition. Agriculture will settle on a constant agricultural wage based on agricultural labor's traditional average product.

If a device could be found to transfer surplus labor from agriculture (where marginal products are zero) to industry (where marginal products are positive), a surplus could be generated for industrial investment. The surplus would be assured because the increase in industrial employment does not drive up real industrial wages. With unlimited supplies of rural labor, the supply of labor to industry at the prevailing industrial real wage would be perfectly elastic. As the industrial surplus is invested in industry, the expansion of the industrial capital stock raises the demand for industrial workers and pulls more workers out of agriculture to generate further surpluses.

How well does the Lewis model apply to Soviet collectivization? For the investment rate to be raised, a number of conditions must be met. First, an unlimited supply of labor in agriculture is required, with the marginal worker producing a zero marginal product. Whether NEP agriculture was indeed characterized by zero marginal products will be discussed below, but the answer is by no means obvious. Second, agricultural output must not decline in response to the measures that draw surplus labor out of agriculture. In fact, agricultural output must remain constant (or even increase). Third, the existence of surplus agricultural labor must prevent real industrial wages from rising as industrialization proceeds. Fourth, as labor is drawn out of agriculture, those remaining do not raise their real incomes above the traditional agricultural wage.

How well does the Lewis model explain Soviet industrialization? First, as the stylized facts show, nonagricultural labor grew at unprecedented rates (both in absolute and relative terms) without driving up real industrial wages (which actually fell). This outcome does not prove that real industrial wages failed to rise because of surplus labor in agriculture. A more likely explanation is that real industrial wages were depressed by the peculiar residual compensation scheme of the collective farm rather than by the market forces of surplus agricultural labor. In fact, the zeal with which industrial managers recruited agricultural labor during the 1930s would have quickly depleted agricultural labor reserves.

There is little evidence that the transfer of "surplus" labor from agriculture to industry was accompanied by an intersectoral transfer of resources. Hidden surpluses are generated in the Lewis model as net intersectoral flows of saving. In the Lewis accounting scheme, the real surplus takes the form of a trade surplus on agriculture's balance on current account with the rest of the economy. In such a case, the flow of resources out of agriculture exceeds the flow of resources into agriculture—generating a flow of real saving. The transfer of labor out of agriculture finances industrial capital accumulation whenever the agricultural output freed up by the transfer of labor out of agriculture exceeds agriculture's consumption of industrial goods.[41]

Where Was the Surplus?

In his study of the surplus, James Millar failed to uncover evidence that collectivization created a change in the net intersectoral flow of saving (agriculture's surplus on current account) from agriculture to industry. In fact, the flow of saving may have gone the other way.[42] The more optimistic finding of Michael Ellman was that the agricultural surplus (if any) in the late NEP period was just as large as that of the collectivization era.[43] Millar and Ellman agree that collectivization did not raise the surplus.

There are a number of reasons why collectivized agriculture failed to deliver a hidden surplus of net saving to industry despite constant real wages and a substantial flow of labor out of agriculture into industry. First, the output of agriculture is not supposed to fall as labor resources are withdrawn. As the stylized facts show, agricultural output was disrupted by forced collectivization, and the initial declines in output, especially of the livestock sector, would have drawn down the agricultural surplus. Second, productivity differentials between industry and agriculture may not have been substantial in light of the low marginal productivity of untrained farm workers in industrial factories.

Holland Hunter has provided perhaps the most convincing explanation for the failure of the surplus transfer to materialize.[44] The slaughter of draft animals during the early years of collectivization destroyed approximately half of agriculture's draft power. To prevent agricultural output from falling precipitously, the Soviet state had little choice but to produce tractors and other heavy farm equipment to replace animal draft power. Collectivization forced Soviet industry to replace the agricultural capital stock lost during the first year of collectivization.

The failure of the hidden surplus to materialize meant that the increase in the investment rate could not take place with constant real wages. Real wages had to fall in both industry and agriculture. In effect, the Lewis model offers an explanation similar to that of Sah and Stiglitz. The increase in the Soviet investment rate took place at the expense of both urban and rural real wages. What the Lewis model highlights is the substantial cost of the drop in agricultural output, especially of draft animals, in the early years of collectivization.

The formal theoretical models of Soviet collectivization show that the doubling of the Soviet investment rate took place neither in a painless manner (the Lewis model) nor with the distributional effects desired by the leadership (Preobrazhensky). Preobrazhensky's plan to shift the burden to the peasant class failed because industrial real wages had to fall to compensate for the decline in wage goods. In fact, forced marketings prevented the burden from being shifted more to industrial workers. The Lewis plan to raise the investment rate in a costless manner by mobilizing hidden surpluses in agriculture failed due to declining agricultural output and the need to shift resources into mechanical power for agriculture.

Speed as a Justification

The Soviet industrial experience of the 1930s stands out in terms of the speed of the industrial transformation. Historical experience provides benchmarks for evaluating the speed of the shift of resources from the countryside to the city. Simon Kuznets documented the unprecedented nature of the shift of resources from agriculture to industry in the 1930s. Transformations of the magnitude of the USSR shift between 1928 and 1937 required more than a half century in other countries.[45] Unlike other countries, the Soviet Union experienced absolute rather than relative declines in its agricultural labor force during its period of rapid industrial transformation.

Collectivization accelerated the shift of resources out of agriculture and into industry. The disruptions and violence of collectivization caused people to flock to the cities for noneconomic reasons. Collectivization also facilitated administrative recruitment of labor. Compensation arrangements in collective agriculture shifted the risk of crop failures to the countryside and raised the attractiveness of industrial employment.

Whether collectivization was necessary to force this shift of labor resources has been seriously questioned.[46] The industrial economies had little difficulty attracting sufficient labor from agriculture through wage differentials to support industrialization. Other industrialized countries made do with more moderate and gradual shifts. Whether a shift so sharp and dramatic was really required is questionable. There may be noneconomic grounds for favoring dramatic change—such as preparation for war or encirclement by enemy nations—but the purely economic rationale is weak.

Long-run growth is the appropriate standard for judging the structural shifts wrought by significant institutional change. The deterioration of long-run Soviet economic performance after 1960 suggests that collectivization failed to place the Soviet economy on the path of sustainable long-term growth. It is clear that collectivization set back Soviet agriculture.

Could NEP Agriculture have Supported Sustained Growth?

What would have happened in the absence of collectivization? Holland Hunter has constructed the most serious counterfactual model of Soviet economic performance without collectivization.[47] He demonstrates what others long suspected: Soviet agriculture would have been much better off without collectivization. According to Hunter's calculations, at the high point of collectivization, crop output was 25 percent below and livestock herds were 50 percent below what they would have been without collectivization. Most striking, the 1940 population was 15 million below the expected population.[48]

Hunter's counterfactual research shows that procollectivization arguments must be based either on positive spillovers such as saving transfers or increased capital formation proportions. Collectivization's impact on agriculture was negative both in the short and the long run.

Hunter's broader projections of overall economic performance without collectivization (which have been subject to less scrutiny than his projections for agriculture alone) suggest that a noncollectivized Soviet economy could have approximately matched actual growth performance during the 1930s.[49] Accordingly, collectivization retarded agricultural growth and failed to accelerate economic growth during the 1930s industrialization drive.

The traditional economic argument for collectivization—proposed by Stalin and echoed by Dobb—was that NEP agriculture could not have sustained industrialization. There are two variants to this argument. The first is that NEP agriculture could not have supported an industrial transformation of the actual scope and magnitude of the 1930s. The second argues that NEP agriculture had reached its expansion limits and that even a relatively modest industrial expansion could not have been sustained by NEP agriculture.[50]

The various indexes of agricultural output show that the NEP economy had regained prewar output levels by the mid- or late 1920s. Although there is some disagreement on the exact magnitude, there is little disagreement that agricultural recovery was rapid during NEP. New Economic Policy agriculture, despite its limitations, had demonstrated its ability to support a rapid agricultural recovery. What it had not demonstrated was its ability to support long-run sustained industrial growth. By the late 1920s, therefore, the discussion had turned to NEP's potential for growth after the recovery had been completed. Stalin concluded that NEP agriculture was incompatible with rapid industrial growth and ordered collectivization.

Limiting Factors: Inputs

Let us consider the factors that could have limited NEP agriculture's ability to support sustained industrial growth. Holland Hunter concludes that NEP agriculture was characterized by surplus labor and unfavorable land-labor ratios, and that draft power was the limiting factor of production. Hunter therefore predicated his counterfactual projections of Soviet agriculture on projections of draft power without collectivization. Insofar as collectivization destroyed approximately half of the stock of draft animals, Hunter had little choice but to conclude that collectivization caused a substantial loss in output because of the decline of the limiting factor of production.

Hunter's notion that draft power was the key limiting factor of production requires closer examination. Hunter concludes that labor was not a limiting factor because labor inputs do not yield significant coefficients in his statistical estimates of production functions.

More conclusive evidence is required before one rules out labor as a limiting factor. For more than two centuries Russian agricultural growth had been extensive, with new cultivation on the periphery explaining most agricultural growth.[51] The Soviet Union did not suddenly lose its agricultural frontier in 1917. In economies with significant unexploited frontiers, it is likely that labor would be a limiting factor, especially after a lengthy experience of frontier expansion. Although Hunter's results may be correct, they are more likely explained by the fact that institutional changes limited incentives to take advantage of profit opportunities on the agricultural frontier.

Institutions as Limiting Factors

New Economic Policy agriculture retained communal features that, if continued, would have limited expansion opportunities. As noted at the beginning of this chapter, Soviet authorities reestablished the repartitional commune, limited the hiring of labor and the renting of land, and acted against the differentiation of the peasantry.

One has to consider how quickly these institutional restrictions would have disappeared if NEP agriculture had not been replaced by collective agriculture. The tsarist experience showed that the opening of agricultural markets caused feudal institutions to adapt. Repartitions occurred with less frequency; private deals allowed entrepreneurial peasants to accumulate large landholdings. We suspect that NEP agriculture would have adapted in the same manner to its maturing experience with market agriculture, particularly without Soviet force in the countryside to enforce restrictions that lowered farm agricultural productivity.

Indisputably, the Soviet industrial transformation of the 1930s was costly in both economic and human terms. The most convincing case for collectivization remains the political argument that the private peasantry represented a threat to the Bolshevik regime and that collectivization was the most efficient way to destroy their power. It is likely that the circuitous economic arguments cited to support collectivization (efficient scale, creation of surpluses, and the like) were only window dressing for the underlying political goal of collectivization.

Collectivization did not free hidden reserves. Both the Sah-Stiglitz model and the Lewis model confirm that the precipitous rise in the Soviet investment rate came at the expense of both urban and rural real wages—a result intensified by the stagnation of agricultural output. The slaughter of livestock prevented the expected net transfer of resources to industry. Industrial resources had to be devoted to stemming further calamities in agriculture. The institution of forced deliveries did serve to shift more of the burden to agriculture, but there is agreement that the industrial worker's burden was heavy as well.

If collectivization did speed up the Soviet industrial transformation, the long-term benefits of acceleration cannot be demonstrated, especially in view of the long-run deterioration in Soviet economic performance. Hunter's calculations of agricultural performance in the absence of collectivization chronicle the short-term output losses in agriculture.

The case for the inevitability of collectivization rests on the restrictions imposed on NEP agriculture by the Soviet regime, which prevented differentiation and the creation of efficiently scaled units. Moreover, Lenin's apparent belief in the gradual voluntary movement to "civilized" collectives was disappointed by NEP developments. The confused belief in the inevitability of a deterioration in agriculture's terms of trade (and the impending disasters to be caused thereby) provides, at best, shaky evidence for the inevitability of collectivization. Moreover, the practice of judging agricultural performance exclusively in terms of state grain purchases was remarkable. The relevant measure should have been overall agricultural performance.

Collectivization remains a puzzling phenomenon. Its economic rationale is weak, yet it continues to be defended in the former Soviet Union. If collectivization was instituted to achieve political goals, this point should be admitted. Economic arguments should not be applied to justify an action carried out for political reasons.

MODELING THE GRAIN COLLECTION CRISES

THIS APPENDIX reexamines the Soviet grain procurement crises that preceded the collectivization decision.[52] It uses regional cross-sectional data to study the effects of extraordinary measures and of relative state/private purchase prices on the "private grain surplus"—the amount of grain retained by peasants or sold to private markets. The empirical findings demonstrate that the peasant economy was extremely sensitive to relative state/private grain prices as long as marketing decisions were relatively free. This price sensitivity rendered the system of private agriculture, private markets, and administrative state pricing incompatible. The state could not set arbitrary grain prices below market without resorting to administrative resource allocation. The model identifies the growing force of administrative measures, which by 1927–28 dominated the agricultural economy.

The evidence in this appendix clearly supports the view that the grain collection crisis was induced by state pricing policy. In fact, strong administrative measures were required even before 1927–28 to prevent the decline in official procurement from being even greater. The experience of the late 1920s underscores the difficulties inherent in combining private market decision making with the planners' desire to administratively control the flow of resources. When private markets are asked to coexist with administrative resource direction, the private sector typically is able to divert resources away from planned activities.

Time series data do not offer sufficient degrees of freedom to model peasant marketings under the conditions that prevailed in the late 1920s. We must turn to regional evidence to obtain further answers.

If we define the "private surplus" of grain (S) as the difference between grain production (Q) and grain sales to state organizations (G), we are left with a residual that consists of the sum of private grain sales (P) and peasant retained consumption (R).

$$S = Q - G \tag{1}$$

$$= P + R. \tag{2}$$

S, or the private surplus, is an artificial construct. Under normal circumstances, it would make little difference whether grain is being sold to a private or state purchasing organization. In typical studies of peasant behavior, peasant demand (R) or marketings ($P + G$) are the subjects of analysis. The Soviet regime, for whatever reasons, used official grain purchases as a success criterion, rather than grain marketings to both public and private buyers. We use the notion of "private surplus" as the dependent variables simply because of its importance in official Soviet thinking.

In the absence of administrative grain collections, the relationship between S, the state procurement price of grain (p_s), and the market price of grain (p_m) would be as follows: A reduction in the state procurement price relative to the market price (p_s/p_m) diverts grain sales from the state (G) to the private market (P), thereby raising S. Peasants divert sales to the private market until transactions costs are equal to the price differential at the margin.[53] An increase in the market price (p_m), holding p_s/p_m constant, should increase the quantity of grain offered to both private and state purchasers. It also makes grain expensive relative to other goods and may reduce R through substitution effects. The sign of p_m, therefore, is ambiguous.[54]

Modeling the grain procurement crisis is complicated by one simple fact evident in Figure 6.1: Observed marketing behavior during the so-called procurement crises was the consequence of both market behavior and administrative actions. In the absence of administrative measures, peasant marketing reactions to prevailing state and private prices could be measured empirically. However, the state's use of coercive measures—in response to reduced procurement—to force grain deliveries muddies the waters considerably. If administrative measures fail to deliver results, the functional relationship between relative prices and the private surplus could be determined from empirical data. The more successful the administrative intervention, however, the more difficult it is to determine peasant market behavior.

In the absence of state intervention in grain marketings, the "notional" private surplus would be modeled as

$$S = f(p_s/p_m, p_m, X) \tag{3}$$

where X captures factors other than prices that affect the private surplus.

S, however, is not directly observable. It denotes the notional surplus that the private economy wishes to hold given the system of relative prices established by the state and by private markets. What is actually observed is

$$S^* = S + E, \tag{4}$$

where

   S^* denotes the observed private surplus,
   S denotes the notional private surplus in the absence of extraordinary measures; and
   E denotes grain gathered as a consequence of state intervention.

Hence, the model to be estimated is

$$S^* = S^*(p_s/p_m, p_m, X) + E. \tag{5}$$

E is an exogenous administrative variable determined by political decision makers, not by market forces.

Data and Estimation

We do not have enough time series observations to estimate equation 5. We can, however, apply cross-sectional data (three cross sections from the agricultural years 1925–26, 1926–27, and 1927–28 for thirteen regions of the USSR).[55] The cross-sectional data were gathered from official statistical publications of the period.[56] The dependent variable S^* is the difference between region i's production of grain and government purchases of grain from region i in time t (t = 1925–26, 1926–27, 1927–28). The market price of grain (p_m) is the unweighted average market (*bazarny*) price of wheat and rye in the ith region in year t. The ratio of the state procurement price to the market price (p_s/p_m) is for wheat.[57]

The three cross-section years include the grain-collection crisis of 1927–28 as well as two pre-grain-collection-crisis years—1925–26 and 1926–27. Regional data for the second grain-collection crisis (1928–29) are too incomplete to generate a fourth cross section.

The period 1925–26 to 1927–28 was characterized by a growing gap between state procurement and market wheat prices. The unweighted average ratio of state to market wheat prices for the thirteen regions was 0.76 in 1925–26, 0.68 in 1926–27, and 0.60 in 1927–28. Although extraordinary measures were not officially used prior to 1927–28, there was state pressure on peasants to sell grain to the state. The substantial price differentials that were present throughout the period would have required administrative inducements to market to state procurement agencies.[58]

We must add regional dummies (denoted by R_i) and time dummies (denoted by T_t) to the price variables to complete the specification of the model. The thirteen regional dummies hold constant regional differences in size, yield, density, and climate that affect the private surplus. Time dummies are included to capture the increasing use of administrative measures and the lesser role of market forces in each successive agricultural year. In effect, the time dummies capture the effect of E on the observed private surplus.

Results

Table 6.A provides an Ordinary-Least-Squares regression estimate of equation 5. The S^*, p_s/p_m, and p_m variables are in natural logs. The price coefficients are therefore elasticities. We assume that the effect of market

TABLE 6A.1
Soviet Peasants' Surplus Model, Dependent Variable: $1n\ S_{it}^*$

Variable	Parameter Estimates	Variable	Parameter Estimates
Price variables			
$1nP_{mit}$	0.74	R_1	−0.74
	(5.51)		(6.44)
$1n(P_s/P_m)_{i\,1925-26}$	−11.78	R_2	1.92
	(85.22)		(10.41)
$1n(P_s/P_m)_{i\,1926-27}$	−3.74	R_3	1.85
	(25.12)		(45.01)
$1n(P_s/P_m)_{i\,1927-28}$	0.69	R_4	−0.32
	(4.44)		(2.12)
		R_5	−0.58
			(3.66)
Time dummies			
$T_{1925-26}$	4.17	R_6	−0.66
	(56.04)		(5.77)
$T_{1926-27}$	−0.59	R_7	−1.53
	(7.61)		(9.29)
$T_{1927-28}$	−3.00	R_8	−1.16
	(4.00)		(9.65)
		R_9	−0.78
			(3.75)
		R_{10}	−0.19
			(4.32)
		R_{11}	−0.45
			(11.63)
		R_{12}	−0.82
			(4.49)
Adjusted-R^2	0.98		

Note: The t-tests in parentheses are White's heteroskedasticity-consistent t-tests.

prices on S^* is uniform throughout the sample period.[59] However, the effect of the ratio of state to market prices is allowed to vary in each successive cross section.

The regression results conform closely to expectations. The market price variable (p_m) shows that a ceteris paribus increase in the market price of grain raised the private surplus. For every percentage point increase in p_m, the peasant surplus increased by 3.2 percentage points. This result shows that the effect of higher prices on general grain marketings outweighs any substitution effects that cause peasant households to consume less grain.

For the 1925–26 cross section, a reduction in the state price relative to the market price raises the private surplus (diverting sales from the state into private markets as expected). In fact, the 1925–26 cross section shows the extreme sensitivity of peasant marketings to relative prices in state and private markets. A 1 percent change in the p_s/p_m induces an 11 percent change in the private surplus in the opposite direction. In the second cross section (1926–27), the private surplus is less sensitive to changes in relative prices: A 1 percent change in the relative price induced a 4 percent change in the opposite direction. By the 1927–28 agricultural year (the first grain-collection crisis), relative prices no longer move the private surplus in the expected direction. Administrative measures so dominated economic behavior by 1927–28 that a drop in the relative state price was accompanied by a reduction in the private surplus.

The time intercept dummies also show the growing role of administrative measures. The private surplus–market price function shifts down in each successive cross section. As administrative measures are applied with greater severity in each successive year, the private surplus falls for a given market price level.

Table 6.A shows that it no longer makes sense to use models of economic behavior after 1927–28. By this time, administrative measures outweighed economic behavior. Agricultural resources were being allocated by plan and not by market.

Chapter 7

COMPARISONS OF TSARIST AND SOVIET
ECONOMIC PERFORMANCE

THE RECORD of economic growth and structural change in the Soviet Union after 1928 is sufficiently well known.[1] This chapter compares the pattern of economic growth in the late tsarist era with that of the Soviet Union during the era of central planning. The main question being asked is: Did the industrialization drive "pay off" in terms of added growth during the Soviet period?

This chapter analyzes the era of central planning through 1985. In 1985 Gorbachev decided to change the economic system. Performance after 1985, therefore, reflects the combined effects of the administrative-command system and the costs of transition. Our analysis also concentrates on what is measurable. The administrative-command system was abandoned not for its inability to produce steel, trucks, and rockets but for its inability to produce goods and services that people wanted with a reasonable degree of efficiency.

Especially for the early Five-Year Plan period (1928–40), index number effects complicate growth comparisons, for the estimated economic growth and structure of the Soviet economy are markedly affected by whether "early" or "late" price weights are used. For example, the annual rate of growth of real output between 1928 and 1937 was approximately 5.5 percent in 1937 or 1950 (late) prices, but was almost 12 percent in 1928 (early) prices. The 1928 ratio of gross investment to GNP was 13–14 percent in late prices, but 25 percent in early prices.[2] Calculations of Soviet economic growth in early prices have not been made for the period after 1937, but Soviet growth over the entire plan era would be much more rapid if valued in early prices. The assessment of Soviet growth performance depends greatly on the choice of price weights.

The following comparisons use both early and late price weights to calculate Soviet growth rates, even though most observers would argue that the late-year weights provide more realistic measures of Soviet growth.

ECONOMIC GROWTH COMPARISONS

Table 7.1 provides the most widely accepted estimates of growth of real output for the tsarist and Soviet periods. The tsarist growth rates are in 1913 prices (late tsarist prices), and the Soviet indexes are in the ruble

TABLE 7.1
Annual Growth Rates, Tsarist and Soviet Periods (percent)

	(1) Total Product	(2) Product Per Capita	(3) Product Per Worker	(4) Incremental Capital Output Ratios (net)
A. Tsarist period, 1885–89 to 1909–13 (1913 prices)	3.3	1.7	1.7	3.1
B. Transitional period, 1913–28 (1913 prices)	−0.5 to −0.7	−1.1 to −1.5	— —	— —
C. Soviet period, central planning era				
1928–40 late prices	5.1	3.9	1.4	2.8
1928 prices	11.0[a]	9.8[a]	6.1[a]	—
1950–85 late prices	4.2	3.1	3.0	7.5
1950–60 late prices	5.9	4.3	4.8	3.7
1960–75 late prices	4.6	3.5	3.1	5.0
1975–85 late prices	2.1	1.2	1.2	14.8
1928–85 (1940–50 omitted)				
Late prices	4.5	3.3	2.6	6.0
Mixed index[b]	6.0	4.9	3.9	—
D. Transitional period plus Soviet period, central planning era (1913–85, period 1940–50 omitted)				
Mixed index 1913 prices and late Soviet prices	3.3	2.2	—	—

Source: Gregory, *Russian National Income,* Tables 5.3, 5.4, 6.1, 6.3; and *Handbook of Economic Statistics.*

Notes: Dash indicates data not available.

[a]Growth rate for 1928–37.

[b]Index for 1928–40 in 1928 prices; 1950–75 index in late prices averaged by number of years.

factor costs of a late period, principally those of 1937. The period 1940–50 has been deliberately omitted to eliminate the impact of World War II and its aftermath on Soviet economic growth. The 1913–28 growth rates are given as well for reasons to be considered below. Three types of price weights are presented: 1913 (late tsarist period) prices, 1928 (early Soviet period) prices, and late Soviet period prices. The late Soviet period prices are from the years 1937 (1928–40) and 1970 (1950–75). The choice of price weights after 1937 has little impact on calculated growth rates.[3]

The growth rates cited in Table 7.1 illustrate the importance of index number relativity in assessing Soviet growth: The figures in both late and early prices show an acceleration in the rate of economic growth above the long-term tsarist rate after 1928. In late-year prices, the pre–World War II and postwar growth rates are similar at 5.1 percent and 4.2 percent per annum respectively. The average postwar rate is a combination of the high rates between 1950 and 1960 and the increasingly slower rates after 1960. In early prices, the 1928–40 growth rate is roughly double that in late prices.

For the tsarist and Soviet periods as a whole, the Soviet period growth rate was higher than the tsarist period rate. The extent to which growth accelerated during the Soviet plan era strongly depends on price weights. However, a growth acceleration is shown by both sets of price weights.

The growth acceleration between the tsarist and Soviet eras is more prominent on a per capita basis because of the slower rate of growth of population after 1928 relative to the tsarist era. Even using the more conservative late-year index, the growth rate of per capita output almost doubled between the tsarist and Soviet plan eras (from 1.7 percent to 3.1 percent per annum).

On a per worker basis, the growth acceleration was also prominent, but only after 1950. During the early Five-Year Plan era (1928–40), the growth rate of product per worker was equivalent to that of the tsarist era. Thus, the initial growth acceleration of the early Soviet period was primarily a consequence of the more rapid expansion of the labor force.

Incremental capital-output ratios were higher in the Soviet era than in the tsarist era, although during the early Five-Year Plan era, incremental capital-output ratios were roughly comparable. The trend in incremental capital-output ratios is consistent with trends in labor force growth but more dismal: The Soviet labor force expanded most rapidly between 1928 and 1940, and this rapid growth had a beneficial effect on capital efficiency. The notable feature of the postwar Soviet era was the collapse of capital productivity. From 1975 to 1985 the incremental capital-output ratio was five times that of the tsarist period.

The 1.2 percent per annum difference between the Soviet long-term growth rate (1928–85) in late prices (4.5 percent) and the tsarist long-term rate (1885–1913) in 1913 prices (3.3 percent) provides a simple measure of the possible growth payoff of the system of centralized allocation. Cumulated over a fifty-year period, this acceleration factor yields a value of total Soviet output 80 percent above what would have prevailed had the long-term tsarist rate held over the Soviet plan era. We need not emphasize the highly speculative nature of this calculation; it assumes that the tsarist long-term growth rate was indicative of the hypothetical rate of growth of a capitalist Russia after 1928. A capitalist Russia would have participated in the world depression as well as in the general acceleration of economic growth after World War II, and the net balance is difficult to predict.

A different picture of long-term Soviet growth emerges if one assumes that the disruptions of the transition period (1913–28) were a necessary concomitant of the transition from capitalism to socialist central planning. According to available estimates (see Appendix B), the growth of total product was slightly negative during the 1913–28 transition period and was substantially negative on a per capita basis. If one therefore includes the transition period in long-term Soviet growth, the growth of total product for the entire Soviet era was equal to that of the tsarist era even omitting the years of World War II. Such a comparison understates the Soviet growth acceleration for two reasons. First, it includes the destruction of the Russian economy during World War I—a loss of output that cannot be attributed to the transition from capitalism to planned socialism. Second, it could be debated whether the disruptions that occurred after 1917 were indeed a necessary feature of the transition to planned socialism or whether they were historical accidents.

COMPARISONS OF ECONOMIC STRUCTURE

Table 7.2 compares the economic structures of the tsarist and Soviet economies. The tsarist period figures are in 1913 prices. The Soviet period figures are primarily in 1937 factor costs, but for 1928 alternate figures are given in 1913 and 1928 prices. The figures in 1913 prices are from Appendix A. The foreign trade proportions are in current year prices.

The tsarist economy began and ended the modern era with an investment rate that was high and a consumption rate that was low for the late nineteenth century. In this sense, a general similarity to the observed pattern of Soviet resource allocation was already present.

It now remains to contrast the tsarist and Soviet patterns of resource allocation. Concentrating first on the net domestic investment rate (panel 8), the transition period (1913–28) witnessed an increase in the investment rate. The most relevant figures are those in constant 1913 prices, which indicate a rise from 12 percent in 1913 from a low of 15 percent to a possible high of 17 percent 1928. The high figure is not that much different from that in current prices (at 18.6 percent).

The contrast of the 1928 investment rate in prevailing prices and in 1937 prices underscores the dramatic decline in the relative price of capital goods between 1928 and 1937, for the investment proportion in 1937 prices is half of the proportion in 1928 prices. A comparison of the 1928 investment proportion in 1913 and 1937 prices suggests that the 1937 relative price of capital was substantially below that of 1913, but less so than relative to 1928 prices. The relative price of capital appears to have risen between 1913 and 1928 and then to have fallen between 1928 and 1937. The industrialization drive of the 1930s drove down the relative costs of capital to a remarkable degree.

TABLE 7.2
Relative Shares of NNP, Russia and Soviet Union (percent)

	1885–89	1909–13	1928			1937		1955 (58)	1975
	1913 Prices	1913 Prices	1913 Prices	1928 Prices	1937 Prices	1928 Prices	1937 Prices	1937 Prices	1937 Prices
A. Sector shares of NNP									
Agriculture (A)	57.0	51.0	—	—	49.0	—	31.0	22[a]	19
Industry (I+) (broadly defined)	23.0	32.0	—	—	28.0	—	45.0	58[a]	62
Services S–	20.0	17.0	—	—	23.0	—	24.0	20[a]	19
B. End-use shares of NNP									
Personal consumption	83.5	79.6	76.0	70.2	83.0	36.9	55.4	52	51
Government	8.1	9.7	8.6	11.2	7.7	26.4	22.7	26	22
Net domestic investment	8.1	12.2	15.4	18.6	9.3	36.7	21.9	22	27
Net foreign investment	.3	-1.4	0	0	0	0	0.0	0	0
C. Foreign trade proportions									
(exports and imports divided by output)	17.0	15.0	6.0	—	—	—	1.0	5	—

Source: Gregory, *Russian National Income.*
Note: Dash indicates data not available.
[a]The figure is for 1958.

The 1913 tsarist investment proportion was relatively high for a low-income country. Since the Soviet investment proportion in 1928 was higher than in 1913 despite a decline in per capita income and then doubled between 1928 and 1937, the Soviet investment proportion was exceptionally high relative to per capita income by the mid-1930s. The positive deviation of the tsarist investment rate from the "normal" proportion was mild compared to the deviations of the Soviet plan era. The same can be said of the consumption ratio and government spending ratio after 1928; namely, any deviations from "normal" patterns observed for the tsarist era were mild relative to the enormous deviations of the Soviet plan era.

Long-term data on sector shares (panel A) are available only in 1913 prices for the tsarist era and in 1937 prices for the Soviet plan era; so the impact of price weights on the structure of output by producing sectors cannot be investigated. The switch from 1913 to 1937 prices would probably result in a lowering of the relative price of industrial goods and therefore in a lowering of the relative share of industry. Given the uncertainty surrounding these price effects, it is difficult to compare the structure of output during the tsarist and Soviet eras.

Chapter 2 noted that the changes in output shares that occurred between 1885 and 1913 were generally consistent with the early stages of modern economic growth, although the rate of decline of the agriculture share may have been slow for a country entering modern economic growth with a large share of agriculture. The Soviet Union began the Five-Year Plan era with an output structure much like that of the late tsarist period. Between 1928 and 1937, however, the Soviet economy experienced rapid change in the structure of output. Within one decade (1928–37), the decline in agriculture's and rise in industry's product shares dwarfed (by at least a factor of two) the structural changes of the entire 1885–1913 period.

The basic point of such comparisons is that any deviations from "normal" patterns observed in the late tsarist period were inconsequential when contrasted with the structural changes that took place during the early plan era. One further point of contrast was the shift from fairly normal reliance on world markets during the tsarist era to minimal (or zero reliance in the case of capital markets) reliance after 1928. Some 50 percent of the rise in domestic investment proportions between 1885 and 1913 was financed by net foreign investment, leaving the remainder to be covered out of domestic savings. During the Soviet plan era, the doubling of the investment rate within one decade was accomplished without the assistance of foreign savings. Thus, parallels between the "Asian" pattern of development of the tsarist era and under Stalin should not be overemphasized.

FACTOR PRODUCTIVITY

The rate of growth of factor inputs during the tsarist era is difficult to measure. Reliable estimates of labor inputs (either of employment or of hours worked) in a relatively backward economy where employment is concentrated in agriculture and handicraft are hard to find. We can, however, estimate the growth of the Russian capital stock.[4] From this data, we can draw some preliminary conclusions about tsarist period–Soviet period productivity performance.

Between 1928 and 1985 output grew at an annual rate of 4.1 percent, employment at 2 percent, and reproducible capital at 8 percent. Reproducible capital grew at approximately 3.5 percent per annum between 1885 and 1913, whereas output grew at 3.3 percent per annum. Although satisfactory estimates of labor force growth are not available, the best guess is a growth of aggregate employment of 1.6 percent per annum (the growth rate of the able-bodied population) for 1885 to 1913.

If one accepts these figures as depicting correct orders of magnitude and makes simplifying assumptions concerning the Soviet and tsarist production functions,[5] the following contrast is obvious: The aggregate rate of growth of factor inputs for the tsarist era was 2.1 percent per annum; for the Soviet plan era it was a higher 3.8 percent per annum. Thus, the principal force behind any Soviet period growth acceleration was the acceleration of the growth of factor inputs after 1928. This faster input growth "explains" the entire growth differential between the Soviet and tsarist eras. Subtracting the factor input growth from output growth yields annual growth rates of output per unit of factor input of 1.2 percent for the tsarist period and 0.7 percent for the Soviet plan era.

Both the tsarist and Soviet economies relied heavily on "extensive" growth, that is, growth based on the expansion of factor inputs. In the tsarist case, 70 percent of growth was accounted for by the expansion of factor inputs; in the Soviet case, a higher 84 percent was accounted for by factor inputs. Although the margin of error in these estimates could be substantial, tsarist productivity appears to have grown faster than Soviet productivity.

Evaluating Soviet Growth in Historical Perspective

Tables 7.1 and 7.2 use the most widely accepted estimates of Soviet economic growth. They are based on the famous estimates of Abram Bergson for the period 1928–60 and on extensions of Bergson's work carried out by individual researchers and later by analysts of the Central Intelligence Agency.

The "official" figures show that, for the plan-era period as a whole, long-term average growth was respectable, and if the 1913–28 "transition period" is omitted (along with World War II), Soviet growth was about 1 percent per annum higher than tsarist growth. Neither the tsarist nor the Soviet economies generated rapid technological progress; both relied on extensive growth. It appears that Soviet period growth relied more on the "expensive" growth pattern of input expansion. Table 7.2 clearly shows the tumultuous change in industrial structure that occurred during the 1930s—a period that compressed a century of change into one decade.

Table 7.1 shows why comparisons of average growth rates between the tsarist and Soviet eras may make little sense. The Soviet era average growth rate is a combination of rapid growth between 1928 and 1960 and steadily declining growth thereafter. The last fifteen years prior to Gorbachev's decision to begin abandoning the administrative-command economy saw growth rates decline to between 1 and 2 percent per annum.

The pattern of steady decline of growth and productivity performance caused Gorbachev and his associates to refer to the 1970s and early 1980s as the "period of stagnation" (*period zastoia*). Obviously, the Soviet leadership had reached the hard conclusion that the decline was irreversible. Hence, the decision to try radical reform can be viewed as official acceptance of the fact that the growth rates of the 1970s and early 1980s were indeed the rates expected to prevail if the administrative-command economy continued.

It may, therefore, make more sense to compare the tsarist period growth rate with the lower growth rate that prevailed during the final decade of the administrative-command economy. Such a comparison inevitably shows that the Soviet Union sacrificed growth by adopting the administrative-command system. With this scenario, the administrative-command system incurred only costs; it yielded no tangible benefits.

A second reason for not relying on the "official" figures for the Soviet era is that they measure production potential and not consumer welfare. When Abram Bergson pioneered the system of national income accounts for Soviet Russia, he clearly stated that it is only possible to calculate the growth of production potential, as measured by the factor costs of producing outputs. Values reflected the rates at which one product could be technologically transformed into another, not the rates at which consumers would be prepared to trade one product for another. If planners desired a mix of output (say, mostly military goods and products of heavy industry) that differs from the mix desired by consumers, the statistician, not knowing how to measure relative consumer valuations, has no choice but to accept these planners' preferences as the standard for evaluating Soviet growth performance.[6]

Although the rates of growth of output and productivity during the period of stagnation were abysmal compared to the earlier period, market economies have tolerated similar rates of growth for decades without social revolt—for example, Great Britain in the 1950s and 1960s. Why was the Soviet leadership and Soviet society unwilling to tolerate such performance in the mid-1980s? The likely answer is that the Soviet economy was producing goods that consumed scarce resources but that were valued by consumers at low or zero prices. The Soviet economy continued to produce the shoddy consumer goods and services for which it was noted and the unfinished construction, the ten-ton reinforced concrete blocks, and the randomly drilled oil wells that continued to consume scarce resources while generating little economic welfare for the population.

The clear discrepancy between production-potential measures of output and consumer-welfare measures of output had become so obvious by the mid-1980s that it challenged the credence of cost-based measures.[7] Glasnost, for the first time, permitted Soviet scholars to openly question the sacrosanct official estimates of economic performance and to suggest rates drastically lower than the official versions.[8] Although Soviet critics of the official estimates seemed to rely primarily on ad hoc adjustments to validate their lowering of Soviet growth, their estimates seemed to rest on the uneasy sense that the Soviet economy was producing goods that had little utility value for the Soviet population.[9] To this point, Western scholars themselves can only speculate about alternate ways to measure economic output during a period of transition from command to market.[10]

WHAT WOULD HAVE BEEN?

The decision to abandon the administrative-command economy in the late 1980s provides sufficient proof that both the Soviet leadership and its citizens had concluded that the administrative-command economy had failed. With this decision made, the remaining question was: What type of system should replace the administrative-command system—a market economy such as had prevailed in the last thirty years of tsarist reign, a NEP-type economy, or some other new type of economic system peculiarly compatible with the special circumstances of the former Soviet Union?

As this question is being asked, it makes sense to consider what would have occurred had the administrative-command system never been installed—if the tsarist economy had continued to develop after the conclusion of World War I on the foundations created during the final decades of the Russian empire. From a purely technical statistical analysis, it is hard to imagine that the result would have been inferior. Russia in 1913 was an enormous economy, of substantial potential, a magnet for Western investment, with many of the institutions of capitalism in place. Its natural wealth, astonishing to the contemporary observer, had become apparent to all. Russia, even in 1913, was the world's largest exporter of wheat and was a prime exporter of crude oil. Its coal resources exceeded those of western Europe, and it had a rail network that was impressive given the magnitude of territory it had to cover.

On the eve of World War I, Russian per capita income was about one-third that of France and Germany and about 60 percent that of Austria-Hungary. Agricultural producers, despite the well-publicized decline of the older central agricultural regions, were producing sufficient surpluses to provide a margin of subsistence for exports and for domestic consumption. By no means was Russia on the edge of economic subsistence, despite the continued presence of periodic famines. Russian industry produced about as much steel as Germany or France and more coal than any country but the United States.

It is hard to imagine a scenario in which the area of former imperial Russia would not today be a world economic power offering living standards to its citizens relatively close to those of Western Europe. Viewed in this perspective, the tragedy of the experiment of the administrative-command economy was the enormous loss of economic well-being that more than three generations have suffered.

The only scenario under which this conclusion would not hold would be one of permanent political turmoil. The 1905 revolution showed how political turmoil could disrupt the country. Political scientists and historians could answer with greater authority the probability of this scenario.

Appendix A

RUSSIAN ECONOMIC STATISTICS

THIS APPENDIX provides various Russian economic statistics for the period 1885–1913. These statistics serve as background for the material presented in the body of this book concerning the tsarist economy.

TABLE A.1: RUSSIAN NET NATIONAL PRODUCT (NNP), 1885–1913

Annual estimates of Russian net national product (NNP) are given in Tables A.1 and A.2. These figures are from my 1982 study of Russian national income. The major items are drawn primarily from annual, rather than interpolated, data. Interpolated figures are given in parentheses but should not have a significant effect on the overall figures. Net national product is in market prices with no adjustments for indirect taxes or subsidies. The investment series are net of depreciation. Government investment is included under investment outlays rather than under government expenditures. Real retail sales are in two variants, labeled the "Moscow-Petersburg" index and the "Podtiagin" index. These two variants correspond to retail sales deflated by the Moscow-Petersburg retail price index or by the Podtiagin all-Russian price index. For the period as a whole, the two variants yield very similar results.

TABLE A.3: COMPARISONS OF NATIONAL INCOME ESTIMATES

Table A.3 compares my 1913 figure with other national income estimates. The estimate that was accepted by Soviet officialdom for 1913 was by Gosplan. Table A.3 refers to this as the Gosplan-Strumilin estimate. An alternate measure, prepared by A. Nikitski in 1927 for Gosplan, differs only slightly from Gosplan-Strumilin. Two non-Soviet estimates of 1913 Russian national income are also available. The first, prepared in 1931 by the emigré S. N. Prokopovich, shows a much lower level of 1913 national income than Gosplan-Strumilin or Nikitski. The second estimate, by the English economist M. E. Falkus (published in 1968), is generally consistent with, but slightly higher than, the Gosplan-Strumilin estimate.

To render these various estimates comparable, indirect taxes must be subtracted and surpluses of government enterprises must be added in to obtain national income. These adjustments are shown in Table A.3. This

TABLE A.1
Net National Product, Russian Empire, 1885–1899 (millions of rubles, 1913 prices)

	1885	1886	1887	1888	1889	1890	1891	1892	1893	1894	1895	1896	1897	1898	1899
1. Retail sales															
Variant 1: Moscow-Petersburg price index	2,559	2,791	3,203	3,090	2,969	3,135	3,028	2,960	3,226	3,688	4,173	4,374	4,473	4,559	5,719
Variant 2: Podtiagin price index	2,722	2,869	3,251	3,135	3,185	3,358	2,763	2,731	3,283	4,232	4,870	5,021	4,511	4,450	5,697
2. Housing rents, total	639	649	643	676	698	720	724	736	732	726	760	776	772	803	814
a. urban	466	475	484	494	504	513	522	528	524	518	534	550	560	583	593
b. rural	173	174	158	182	194	207	202	208	108	208	226	226	212	220	221
3. Services, total	364	(377)	(390)	404	(410)	(417)	435	(431)	(437)	444	(461)	481	(484)	(491)	(497)
a. passenger rail	27			33			38			45		62			
b. communications	12			14			16			17		19			
c. utilities	72			80			86			88		96			
d. domestic service	209			218			230			225		228			
e. medical expenditures	44			59			65			69		76			
4. Consumption of farm products in kind, total	3,025	2,864	3,299	3,223	2,777	3,064	2,478	3,142	3,834	3,969	3,912	4,096	3,702	4,115	4,454
a. grain products	1,183	1,058	1,322	1,198	842	1,074	669	1,183	1,680	1,758	1,556	1,591	1,307	1,588	1,869
b. meat products	437	438	439	479	480	487	471	459	462	490	490	545	555	555	569
c. technical crops	108	100	125	149	138	133	110	131	172	195	195	223	187	213	164
d. dairy products	673	677	732	732	744	738	717	721	729	859	859	887	885	905	928
e. omitted products, forestry, hunting, fishing	624	591	681	665	573	632	511	648	791	819	812	850	768	854	924
5. Military subsistence	74	(72)	(69)	67	(62)	(57)	52	(66)	(80)	95	(101)	107	(104)	(101)	(99)
A. Personal consumption															
Variant 1 (1a + 2 + 3 + 4 + 5)	6,661	(6,753)	(7,604)	7,460	(6,916)	(7,393)	6,705	(7,335)	8,309	8,922	(9,407)	9,834	(9,535)	(10,069)	(11,583)
Variant 2 (1b + 2 + 3 + 4 + 5)	6,824	(6,931)	(7,652)	7,505	(7,132)	(7,616)	6,440	(7,106)	8,366	9,466	(10,104)	10,481	(9,573)	(9,960)	(11,561)
6. Imperial government expenditures, total	566	(593)	(592)	588	(601)	(652)	719	(704)	(705)	795	(910)	873	(836)	(965)	(946)
a. administration	249			262			329			342					
b. health and education	28			26			33			39		40			
c. defense	289			300			357			414		434			
7. Local government expenditures, total	145	(149)	(153)	157	(164)	(173)	180	(192)	(204)	217	(234)	250	(261)	(271)	(283)
a. administration	109			110			129			160		173			
b. health and education	31			41			45			51		69			
c. defense	5			3			6		6	8					

	47	(49)	(51)	54	(57)	(60)	64	(65)	(66)	68	(78)	88	(97)	(106)	(115)
8. Government capital expenditures, excluding defense capital															
B. Government															
Including government capital (6 + 7)	711	(742)	(745)	745	(765)	(825)	899	(896)	(909)	1,012	(1,144)	1,123	(1,097)	(1,236)	(1,229)
Excluding capital (6 + 7 + 8)	644	(693)	(694)	691	(708)	(765)	835	(831)	(843)	944	(1,066)	1,035	(1,000)	(1,130)	(1,114)
9. Investment in livestock	14	7	399	42	42	−161	−126	35	42	238	553	105	0	140	70
10. Net investment in equipment, total	52	53	56	66	69	62	61	63	89	105	120	168	191	237	248
a. agriculture	6	6	6	9	6	6	5	7	8	12	12	13	13	15	17
b. nonagriculture	46	47	50	57	63	56	56	56	81	93	108	155	178	222	231
11. Net investment, structures, total	344	235	242	256	217	353	143	147	41	265	403	197	400	430	424
a. industry	74	82	82	89	94	99	−7	60	84	25	119	77	198	87	181
b. agriculture	198	89	89	89	58	187	105	121	0	120	172	40	36	266	226
c. urban residential	72	64	71	78	65	67	45	−34	−43	120	112	80	166	77	17
12. Inventories, total	167	31	36	97	289	−57	47	257	553	1,053	−865	538	478	226	−72
a. industry	−4	53	40	62	−6	−20	34	80	102	117	−20	91	133	69	14
b. trade	171	−22	−4	35	295	−77	13	177	451	936	−845	447	345	157	−86
13. Net investment, transportation and communication	69	93	98	100	96	49	36	185	255	123	162	213	349	260	260
C. Net investment (8 + 9 + 10 + 11 + 12 + 13)	693	468	882	615	770	306	225	752	1,046	1,852	451	1,309	1,515	1,399	1,045
D. Net foreign investment	−114	−182	31	246	133	108	142	−179	−129	−185	−158	−228	−208	−242	−430
Net national product (A + B + C + D)															
Variant 1	7,904	7,732	9,210	9,012	8,527	8,572	7,917	8,739	10,069	11,533	10,766	11,950	11,842	12,356	13,312
Variant 2	8,067	7,810	9,258	9,057	8,743	8,795	7,654	8,510	10,126	12,077	11,463	12,597	11,880	12,247	13,290
Population (million)	109	111	113	115	117	118	119	120	122	123	124	125	126	128	130
Per capita income (rubles)															
Variant 1	72.5	69.7	81.5	78.4	72.9	72.6	66.5	72.8	82.5	93.8	86.8	95.6	94.0	96.5	102.4

TABLE A.1 (*cont.*)

Net National Product, Russian Empire, 1900–1913 (millions of rubles, 1913 prices)

	1900	1901	1902	1903	1904	1905	1906	1907	1908	1909	1910	1911	1912	1913
1. Retail sales														
Variant 1: Moscow-Petersburg price index	5,454	5,573	5,573	5,861	5,841	5,973	5,562	5,351	5,289	5,623	6,215	6,611	6,705	7,141
Variant 2: Podtiagin price index	5,647	5,644	5,622	5,951	5,899	5,881	5,391	4,851	5,002	5,492	6,209	6,576	6,567	7,141
2. Housing rents, total	830	868	939	982	1,008	1,081	1,127	1,154	1,185	1,220	1,285	1,354	1,412	1,465
a. urban	591	610	660	702	722	761	800	808	818	832	876	931	983	1,035
b. rural	239	258	279	280	286	320	327	346	367	388	409	423	429	430
3. Services, total	504	(519)	(534)	549	(573)	(597)	(623)	650	(677)	(706)	736	(756)	(776)	799
a. passenger rail	95			112				149			188			222
b. communications	25			29				38			52			65
c. utilities	83			94				118			125			118
d. domestic service	218			225				244			254			268
e. medical expenditures	83			89				101			117			126
4. Consumption of farm products in kind, total	4,444	4,058	4,857	4,704	5,258	4,675	4,096	4,494	4,881	5,392	5,658	4,908	6,209	6,726
a. grain products	1,885	1,588	2,143	2,079	2,437	1,979	1,517	1,830	2,014	2,327	2,479	1,914	2,821	3,228
b. meat products	576	567	579	578	569	603	587	572	570	657	688	701	679	720
c. technical crops	169	149	215	195	192	192	230	251	238	184	202	215	246	256
d. dairy products	891	912	912	876	968	931	912	908	1,046	1,105	1,115	1,059	1,174	1,126
e. omitted products, forestry, hunting, fishing														
5. Military subsistence	923	842	1,008	976	1,092	970	850	933	1,013	1,119	1,174	1,019	1,289	1,396
A. Personal consumption Variant 1	97	(100)	(102)	105	(111)	(117)	(123)	129	(139)	(149)	159	(164)	(169)	175
(1a + 2 + 3 + 4 + 5)	11,329	(11,118)	(12,005)	12,201	(12,791)	(12,443)	(11,531)	11,778	(12,171)	(13,090)	14,053	(13,793)	(15,721)	16,306
Variant 2														
(1b + 2 + 3 + 4 + 5)	11,522	(11,189)	(12,054)	12,291	(12,849)	(12,351)	(11,360)	11,278	(11,884)	(12,959)	14,047	(13,758)	(15,133)	16,306
6. Imperial government expenditures, total	991	(961)	(1,120)	1,147	(1,331)	(1,560)	(1,582)	1,139	(1,190)	(1,250)	1,293	(1,294)	(1,371)	1,707
a. administration	408			508				476			583			583
b. health and education	58			73				63			110			154
c. defense	525			566				600			600			970
7. Local government expenditures, total	294	(319)	347	375	(374)	(373)	(372)	370	(402)	(436)	475	(525)	(580)	643
a. administration	193			230				222			275			357
b. health and education	91			132				135			179			256
c. defense	10			13				13			21			30

8. Government capital expenditures, excluding defense capital	1,285	(1,280)	(1,467)	1,522	(1,705)	1,933	(1,954)	1,509	(1,592)	(1,686)	1,768	(1,819)	(1,951)	2,350
B. Government														
Including government capital (6 + 7)	1,160	(1,153)	(1,338)	1,391	(1,577)	1,807	(1,830)	1,387	(1,454)	(1,532)	1,597	(1,663)	(1,810)	2,224
Excluding capital (6 + 7 + 8)	-98	126	-7	-98	349	-161	-147	-34	881	322	125	-223	154	112
9. Investment in livestock	125	(127)	(129)	131	(128)	(126)	(124)	122	(138)	(154)	171	(156)	(141)	(126)
10. Net investment in equipment, total	222	224	210	226	244	255	248	226	235	247	286	321	360	454
a. agriculture	18	28	25	35	36	42	37	33	42	55	61	73	81	73
b. nonagriculture	204	196	185	191	208	213	211	193	193	192	225	248	279	381
11. Net investment, structures, total	682	771	556	483	719	865	224	429	580	786	1,246	1,018	976	1,043
a. industry	211	94	-77	-20	89	226	-151	37	112	87	139	320	285	248
b. agriculture	331	312	325	350	350	350	315	322	364	372	705	315	308	392
c. urban residential	140	365	308	153	280	289	61	70	104	327	402	383	383	403
12. Inventories, total	-127	281	940	—	110	-991	264	199	177	395	593	263	378	-371
a. industry	19	21	162	120	-125	130	77	57	85	122	274	96	177	152
b. trade	-146	260	778	-119	235	-1,121	187	142	92	273	319	167	201	219
13. Net investment, transportation and communication	361	268	192	138	260	257	262	177	209	67	337	320	185	208
C. Net investment (8 + 9 + 10 + 11 + 12 + 13)	1,165	1,797	2,020	881	1,810	351	976	1,119	2,220	1,971	2,758	1,855	2,194	2,314
D. Net foreign investment	-327	-199	-70	-35	18	35	-153	-369	-393	-30	-214	-185	-322	-578
Net national product (A + B + C + D)														
Variant 1	13,327	13,869	15,293	14,438	16,196	14,646	14,184	13,915	15,452	16,623	18,194	17,126	18,953	20,266
Variant 2	13,520	13,940	15,342	14,528	16,254	14,554	14,013	13,415	15,165	16,492	18,188	17,091	18,815	20,266
Population (million)	133	135	137	139	141	144	146	149	153	157	161	164	168	171
Per capita income (rubles)														
Variant 1	100.2	102.7	111.6	103.9	114.9	101.7	97.2	93.4	101.0	105.9	113.0	104.4	112.8	118.5

TABLE A.2
Net National Product, Russian Empire, 1885–1899 Current Year Prices (millions of rubles)

	1885	1886	1887	1888	1889	1890	1891	1892	1893	1894	1895	1896	1897	1898	1899
1. Retail sales	2,052	2,096	2,409	2,364	2,319	2,364	2,365	2,409	2,587	2,810	3,034	3,123	3,257	3,524	4,461
2. Housing rents, total	456	456	439	472	483	491	504	523	532	535	565	585	604	713	691
a. urban	313	312	309	318	326	328	336	351	360	358	381	400	417	517	482
b. rural	143	144	130	154	157	163	168	172	172	177	184	185	187	196	209
3. Services, total	266	(276)	(286)	297	(306)	(316)	326	(329)	(332)	336	(345)	353	(367)	(382)	(397)
a. passenger rail	42			47			51			57		66			
b. communications	12			14			16			17		19			
c. utilities	37			45			51			53		60			
d. domestic service	140			147			155			153		151			
e. medical expenditures	35			44			53			56		57			
4. Consumption of farm products in kind, total	2,477	2,219	2,699	2,932	2,471	2,573	2,364	2,991	3,151	2,715	2,679	2,696	2,779	3,594	3,875
a. grain products	1,100	899	1,084	1,138	790	913	829	1,336	1,411	1,037	825	834	954	1,525	1,663
b. meat products	310	315	360	431	418	395	405	381	402	388	333	343	411	511	484
c. technical crops	65	60	76	92	91	85	68	87	134	141	240	156	125	136	108
d. dairy products	491	487	622	666	662	649	574	570	554	589	696	674	637	670	761
e. omitted products	511	458	557	605	510	531	488	617	650	560	585	680	652	752	859
5. Military subsistence	65	(63)	(62)	60	(59)	(58)	57	(59)	(60)	62	(63)	64	(69)	(72)	(74)
A. Personal consumption (1 + 2 + 3 + 4 + 5)	5,316	(5,110)	(5,895)	6,125	(5,638)	(5,802)	5,616	(6,311)	(6,662)	(6,459)	(6,686)	6,821	(7,076)	(8,285)	(9,498)
6. Imperial government	457		569	477			569			611		673			
7. Local government	114			125			138			162		187			
8. Government capital expenditures, excluding defense capital	37	(39)	(42)	45	(47)	(49)	53	(54)	(58)	62	(66)	72	(77)	(85)	(93)
B. Government, excluding capital (6 + 7 + 8)	534	(541)	(548)	557	(587)	(620)	654	(674)	692	711	749	788	(838)	(887)	(939)

9. Investment in livestock	−8	4	225	243	27	−98	−76	19	26	143	331	61	0	83	43
10. Net investment equipment, total	49	55	55	66	70	65	64	65	89	111	120	170	182	223	234
a. agriculture	6	6	6	9	6	6	5	7	8	12	12	13	12	14	16
b. nonagriculture	43	49	49	57	64	59	59	58	81	99	108	157	170	209	218
11. Net investment, structures, total	285	189	193	210	176	279	118	122	34	225	326	162	352	386	396
a. industry	61	68	67	76	76	78	−6	50	70	21	96	63	174	78	168
b. agriculture	164	68	68	68	47	148	87	100	0	102	139	33	32	239	212
c. urban residential	60	53	58	66	53	53	37	−28	−36	102	91	66	146	69	16
12. Inventories, total	108	47	140	47	74	−45	−2	270	291	753	−582	458	497	329	86
a. industry	8	38	77	58	−23	−3	20	87	104	75	−36	81	118	109	60
b. trade	100	9	63	−11	97	−42	−22	183	187	678	−546	377	379	220	26
13. Net investment, transportation and communication	54	74	85	86	85	44	32	159	222	107	141	186	311	235	235
C. Net investment (8 + 9 + 10 + 11 + 12 + 13)	525	408	750	697	479	294	189	689	720	1,401	402	1,109	1,419	1,341	1,087
14. Net merchandise account	102	54	216	395	313	282	329	71	138	100	150	72	125	91	−56
15. Net dividend, interest payments and repatriated profits	−151	−155	−158	−162	−166	−162	−155	−161	−174	−177	−194	−184	−200	−212	−216
16. Net tourist expenditures and miscellaneous items	−40	−38	−34	−36	−48	−36	−59	−61	−65	−60	−68	−75	−86	−84	−89
D. Net foreign investment (14 + 15 + 16)	−89	−139	24	197	99	84	115	−151	−101	−137	−112	−187	−161	−205	−361
Net national product (A + B + C + D)	6,286	5,920	7,217	7,576	6,803	6,800	6,574	7,523	7,973	8,433	7,725	8,531	9,172	10,308	11,163

TABLE A.2 (cont.)
Net National Product, Russian Empire, 1900–1913 Current Year Prices (millions of rubles)

	1900	1901	1902	1903	1904	1905	1906	1907	1908	1909	1910	1911	1912	1913
1. Retail sales	4,292	4,397	4,441	4,630	4,725	4,975	4,906	4,982	5,167	5,415	5,861	6,221	6,665	7,141
2. Housing rents, total	707	735	790	849	854	914	975	1,003	1,031	1,057	1,130	1,232	1,362	1,465
a. urban	485	500	541	586	591	620	667	681	694	704	746	834	950	1,036
b. rural	222	235	249	263	263	294	208	322	337	353	384	398	412	430
3. Services, total	414	(436)	(460)	486	(511)	(537)	(564)	593	(625)	(659)	697	(732)	(768)	799
a. passenger rail	102			122				146			186			222
b. communications	22			29				38			52			65
c. utilities	66			76				97			111			118
d. domestic service	158			200				222			240			268
e. medical expenditures	35			59				90			108			126
4. Consumption of farm products in kind, total	3,776	3,519	4,189	3,937	4,323	4,118	3,810	4,666	5,252	5,655	5,448	5,076	6,769	6,726
a. grain products	1,376	1,239	1,736	1,580	1,852	1,742	1,456	2,196	2,538	2,606	2,281	2,086	3,272	3,228
b. meat products	518	533	533	457	461	567	581	549	570	696	743	743	788	720
c. technical crops	157	156	206	185	190	173	232	256	207	251	191	201	222	256
d. dairy products	802	766	766	710	794	782	793	844	1,046	1,061	1,059	1,027	1,198	1,126
e. omitted products	923	842	1,008	976	1,092	970	850	933	1,013	1,119	1,174	1,019	1,289	1,396
5. Military subsistence	76	(78)	(80)	82	(95)	(110)	(127)	147	(154)	(161)	169	(171)	(173)	175
A. Personal consumption (1 + 2 + 3 + 4 + 5)	9,265	(9,165)	(9,960)	9,984	(10,508)	(10,654)	(10,382)	11,391	(12,229)	(12,947)	13,305	(13,432)	(15,737)	16,306
6. Imperial government	855			879				1,070			1,195			1,707
7. Local government	236			283				341			437			643
8. Government capital expenditures, excluding defense capital	104	(104)	(104)	105	(105)	(105)	(105)	105	(117)	(133)	144	(138)	(132)	126
B. Government, excluding capital (6 + 7 + 8)	987	(1,009)	(1,032)	1,057	(1,112)	(1,171)	(1,235)	1,306	(1,351)	(1,402)	1,488	(1,682)	(1,934)	2,224

9. Investment in livestock	112	143	−187	109	280	749	−27	−104	−116	237	−66	−5	81	−63
10. Net investment, equipment, total	454	358	320	282	248	230	238	230	237	227	219	209	215	211
a. agriculture	73	77	72	60	54	42	35	32	38	32	33	33	27	17
b. nonagriculture	381	281	248	222	194	188	203	198	199	195	186	176	188	194
11. Net investment, structures, total	1,043	937	938	1,172	716	534	398	211	798	664	449	494	702	634
a. agriculture	248	273	282	131	79	103	34	−142	208	82	−19	−69	86	196
b. industry	392	296	296	663	339	335	299	296	324	324	324	289	284	308
c. urban residential	403	368	360	378	298	96	65	57	266	258	144	274	332	130
12. Inventories, total	371	506	526	607	315	47	157	522	−617	158	121	769	48	−225
a. industry	152	222	243	194	114	31	55	196	88	−114	95	137	−29	19
b. trade	219	284	283	413	201	16	102	326	−705	272	26	632	77	−244
13. Net investment, transportation and communication	208	188	291	300	60	186	161	241	232	229	123	173	233	317
C. Net investment (8 + 9 + 10 + 11 + 12 + 13)	2,314	2,264	2,026	2,614	1,752	1,863	1,032	1,205	639	1,620	951	1,744	1,383	978
14. Net merchandise account	128	329	416	353	510	77	198	285	425	371	314	261	164	71
15. Net dividend, interest payments and repatriated profits	−401	−394	−367	−345	−322	−309	−290	−232	−243	−230	−237	−230	−211	−220
16. Net tourist expenditures and miscellaneous items	−305	−267	−232	−211	−159	−149	−167	−191	−143	−126	−117	−99	−120	−119
D. Net foreign investment (14 + 15 + 16)	−578	−332	−183	−203	29	−381	−259	−138	39	15	−40	−58	−167	−268
Net national product (A + B + C + D)	20,266	19,603	16,957	17,204	16,130	15,062	13,470	12,684	12,603	13,255	11,952	12,678	11,390	10,962

TABLE A.3

1913 Russian Net National Product, National Income, Various Estimates
(empire and USSR pre-1939 territory)

	Million Rubles	
	USSR Pre-1939 Territory	Russian Empire
I. Gregory estimates (1982)		
A. Net national product	17,408	20,266
− Indirect business taxes	783	921
+ State subsidies to private sector	+83	+98
− Current surplus of government enterprises	631	742
National income	16,077	18,701
II. Omissions resulting from narrow Marxian national income concept	+1,058	+1,244
A. Product originating in rest of world	339	399
B. Net government product	+290	+341
C. Domestic and medical services	+335	+394
D. Net housing product	+772	+908
III. Alternate national income estimates Russia, 1913		
A. 1. Falkus 1968 original	14,987	18,476
2. Falkus 1968 expanded (original + II)	16,045	19,720
B. 1. Prokopovich 1931 original	13,896	14,700
2. Prokopovich 1931 expanded (original + II)	14,954	15,944
C. 1. GosplanStrumilin 1927 original	14,538	17,108
2. GosplanStrumilin 1927 expanded (original + II)	15,596	18,352
D. 1. Nikitski 1927 original	14,800	17,725
2. Nikitski 1927 expanded (original + II)	15,858	18,969

Source: Gregory, Russian National Income, 66.

comparison shows a surprising degree of agreement among the various estimates, with the exception of 1931 Prokopovich estimate.

TABLE A.4: TIME SERIES OF NATIONAL INCOME

The best-known and frequently cited time series study was by Raymond Goldsmith, for the period 1860–1913. Goldsmith measured aggregate Russian output in constant prices. Alternate price weights were used, but Goldsmith concluded that price weights had little impact on the outcome. Goldsmith's output index consists of a factory and a crop production index, which he expanded into an aggregate index by means of assumptions concerning omitted activities (livestock, services, and handicraft in-

TABLE A.4

Comparison of Growth Rates of Alternate National Income Studies

Period	Author/Pub. Date	Description	Annual Growth
1900–1913	Prokopovich (1918)	National income, Marxian concept, 1900 prices	2.6
	Falkus-Prokopovich (1968)	Upward revision of Prokopovich's 1913 estimate	3.1
	Goldsmith[a] (1961 & [1972])	GNP in 1900 prices, Goldsmith assumptions[b]	2.4
	Varzar (1929)	Aggregation of 35 physical production series, 1913 prices	3.1
	Gregory (1982)	NNP in 1913 prices	3.25
1885–1913	Goldsmith[c]		2.75
	Varzar[d]		3.25
	Gregory estimate (1982)		3.4

Sources: Prokopovich, Opyt ischisleniia narodnogo dokhoda 50 gubernii Evropeiskoi Rossii, 5; Falkus, "Russia's National Income, 1913," 58; Gregory, "Economic Growth and Structural Change in Tsarist Russia," 433; Goldsmith, "The Economic Growth of Tsarist Russia," 4,413. The Varzar index is given in Maslov, Kriticheski analiz burzhuaznykh statisticheskikh publikatsii, 459.

[a]1901–1903 to 1911–13.

[b]Service sector assumed to grow at the rate of employment in commerce. One percent annual growth of livestock used.

[c]1883–1913

[d]The Varzar figure is extrapolated from 1887 to 1885; margin of error = +0.25.

dustry). The Goldsmith figures cited in Table A.3 for the period 1900–1913 are from a recalculation prepared by the author in 1972 for the purpose of breaking Goldsmith's study down into subperiods.

The second major time series study of Russian national income was by S. N. Prokopovich (published in 1918), comparing 1900 and 1913 national income. Prokopovich applied 1900 prices to the physical outputs of 1900 and 1913 and then netted out intermediate expenditures. In this way, Prokopovich avoided the necessity of deflating with some type of national income deflator. A serious evaluation of Prokopovich's 1918 study was undertaken by Vainshtein.

M. E. Falkus's reevaluation of Prokopovich's estimate for 1913 provides a third index of the growth between 1900 and 1913. As Falkus noted, Prokopovich's estimate for 1913 in many instances used 1909–1913 averages rather than actual 1913 output. Insofar as 1913 was the best year for Russian agriculture of the entire tsarist period, Prokopovich understated

1913 national income by using 1909–13 averages. Falkus revised the 1913 Prokopovich estimate upward in light of this revision.

The fourth study is not national income per se but, rather, an ad hoc aggregation of thirty-five physical production series (both consumer and producer goods) in 1913 prices. This series was completed by the noted Russian statistician V. E. Varzar in the late 1920s but was never published. Although this is not a national income series, it provides an interesting check on the alternate series.

Table A.4 shows that my estimates are higher than those of Goldsmith and Prokopovich. For the entire period (1885–1913) my estimated annual growth rate is 3.25 percent, whereas Goldsmith's is 2.75 percent with a suggested error interval of +0.25 percent. For 1900 to 1913 Prokopovich and Goldsmith are in general agreement, with an annual growth rate of 2.5 percent. My own figure is 3.25 percent. My estimates are in general agreement with those of Varzar and Falkus. If my estimates are to be believed, Russian national income grew at a rate some 25 percent faster than the Prokopovich or Goldsmith series.

Three factors explain why my growth estimate is higher than Goldsmith's. The first is that the growth rate of omitted service sectors, which accounted for slightly less than 20 percent of 1913 national income, is much higher (2.8 percent) than Goldsmith's. Second, my calculated 1.5 percent annual growth rate of livestock production is substantially higher than Goldsmith's. Third, and most important, I calculate the growth rate of grain production at 3.1 percent annually, as compared with Goldsmith's rate of 2.5 percent. Because grain production accounted for some one-third of 1913 national income, this difference alone will yield an annual growth rate one-fifth of 1 percent higher than Goldsmith's. Although Goldsmith is not too specific about his method of calculating grain production, it appears that he employed *gross* output figures weighted by average grain prices near the turn of the century. Because of lack of better data, he used a series for the fifty provinces alone (which accounted for 78 percent of empire wheat production, 90 percent of rye production, and 82 percent of barley production in 1895) to calculate the growth of grain production prior to 1895.

According to my calculations, empire grain production grew at a slightly faster rate than production in the fifty provinces throughout the period. Moreover, my grain production figures are based (prior to 1898) on *net* production figures for sixty-three provinces, prepared by the Ministry of Interior. The ratios of net to gross grain output increased by some 10 percent between 1885–90 and 1909–13, and this alone accounts for almost half of the growth rate differential.

The official growth rates of grain production may be overstated because of better coverage for later periods, but I have no evidence to this effect. The

TABLE A.5
Russian National Income by Sector of Origin, 1883–87 to 1909–13
(1913 value added weights)

Indexes of Sector Growth	1883–87	1897–1901	1909–13	1913 Value Added (1913 Rubles) Million Rubles	%
1. Agriculture (including forestry and fishing)	49	70	100	10,294	50.7
2. Industry, factory	28	65	100	3,023	14.9
3. Industry, handicraft	42	74	100	1,311	6.5
4. Transport, communication	17	54	100	1,173	5.8
5. Construction	43	69	100	1,035	5.1
6. Trade	53	80	100	1,640	8.1
7. Net government product	33	63	100	565	2.8
8. Net housing product	52	61	100	743	3.7
9. Personal medical services	37	69	100	126	.6
10. Domestic service	78	81	100	264	1.3
11. Utilities	60	69	100	118	.6
National income	43.2	69.2	100	20,292	100

Source: Gregory, Russian National Income, 73.

adjustment that Goldsmith makes for increasing coverage is very small anyway. For other sectors, such as factory production and handicraft, I use Goldsmith's indexes and assumptions; so differences in growth rates of industrial production cannot explain the divergence between the two calculated national income growth rates.

Table A.5 shows the rates of growth by sectors and the composition of output in 1913.

Appendix B

THE ECONOMIC RECOVERY OF NEP

COMPARISONS OF the Soviet economy of the late 1920s with the Russian economy on the eve of revolution shed light on the relative starting point of Soviet forced industrialization and on structural and institutional differences between the late Russian and early Soviet economies.[1] This appendix poses a simple question and explains why an exact answer is hard to obtain: How much more or less national output (national income) did the Soviet economy produce in 1928 than in 1913? The ratio of 1928 to 1913 national income is the broadest measure of the economic recovery of the NEP economy from revolution and civil war. The two years chosen for comparing national income are 1928, the end of NEP (or alternatively the initial year of the Five-Year Plan era), and 1913, the peak year of the tsarist period.

If the Soviet industrialization drive began prior to recovery to prewar levels, some of the rapid growth of the 1930s should be attributed to the recovery process. Ultimately, the starting point of Soviet industrialization is more important in evaluating the early Five-Year Plan era than long-term Soviet economic performance. Since 1928 we have had more than a half century of Soviet economic growth. Whether the industrialization drive began slightly above or below prewar levels would not change any long-term assessment. Perhaps the main reason for interest in the relative starting point is that the monumental decisions of the late 1920s were based on contemporary assessments of the NEP recovery.

THE OFFICIAL SOVIET ESTIMATES

This appendix uses the various estimates of Russian and Soviet national income to evaluate relative 1928/1913 national income. The "official" Soviet series linking 1913 national income to the 1920s serves as our reference point.

It was during the late 1920s that the official Soviet estimates of relative 1928/1913 national income were prepared for Gosplan. The definitive estimate appears in the control figures for 1928/29, which were published in 1929.[2] The Gosplan calculation uses the Marxist material product concept, which omits many services and uses Prokopovich's calculation as its starting point for estimating 1913 national income.[3] Although Gosplan described its national income figures as only crude estimates at the time, the figures from 1929 continue to be cited without amendment by Soviet statistical handbooks to the present day.

The Gosplan estimate shows that the economic recovery was complete by the mid-1920s and that the Five-Year Plans began well above the pre-revolutionary peak in 1913. The Soviet national income in 1928 was 19 percent above the 1913 figure, and 1928 per capita income was 9 percent above that of 1913. According to the official figures, the Soviet economy regained the prewar national income level by 1926 and prewar per capita income by 1927. This represents a remarkable recovery, because official Soviet statistics placed 1920 national income at 40 percent of 1913 national income.[4]

Subsequent research has focused on the main finding of the official Soviet estimates of relative 1928/1913 national income; namely, that the recovery of national income to the prerevolutionary peak was completed by 1926. Research on this matter took place almost outside the Soviet Union. Once Soviet authorities settled on the official Gosplan figures, research on this subject ceased in the Soviet Union.

POTENTIAL ERRORS IN THE OFFICIAL SOVIET ESTIMATES

Gosplan calculated the ratio of 1928 to 1913 national income by converting 1928 national income into constant prices of 1913 and then dividing by 1913 national income. Table B.1 shows how Gosplan arrived at its result. The first row gives the Gosplan estimates of 1913 and 1928 national

TABLE B.1
Official Estimates of National Income, 1928 : 1913 (billions of rubles,
per capita income in rubles)

	1913	1928	1928 :1918
National income in current prices	14.5	27.2	1.88
National income in 1913 prices	14.5	17.2	1.19
Implicit price deflator			1.58
Per capita income in 1913 prices	10.4	11.3	1.09

Sources: The official Soviet series is taken from Gosplan SSSR, Kontrol'nye tsifry narodnogo khoviaistva, 71. We do not cite a nearly contemporaneous calculate in Katz, "Narodny dokhod SSSR i ego raspredelenie," which gives slightly different numbers for national income in 1913 prices: 1913 = 14.0 billion and 1928 = 16.5 billion. The growth indexes are nearly identical. Nikitskii's figure for 1913 was 14.8 billion and Gukhman's estimate was 15.1 billion according to Vainshtein, Narodny dokhod Rossii i SSSR, 66. The 14.5 billion figure cited above apparently uses the 1909–13 average harvest.

Note: The 1928 figures are calculated as the averages of 1927–28 and 1928–29. The underlying population figures are 137.2 million for 1913 and 152.2 million for 1928.

income in current prices. In current prices, 1928 national income was 1.88 times 1913 national income. The second row gives the Gosplan estimates in constant 1913 prices. The ratio of the 1928 figure in current to constant prices (27.2/17.2 = 1.58) is the implicit price deflator used to deflate 1928 national income. This 1.58 deflator will play a prominent role in subsequent discussions. Table B.1 shows that errors in the official estimates can enter in three ways:

1. The 1913 figure can be wrong.
2. The 1928 figure (in prevailing 1928 prices) can be wrong.
3. The deflator used to convert 1928 national income into 1913 prices can be wrong.

Controversy over Current Price Estimates

S. N. Prokopovich was a pioneer in studying the national income of tsarist Russia. His estimate of the national income of the fifty European Russian provinces in 1913 (published in 1918) served as the basis for Gosplan's own calculation of 1913 national income.[5] In 1931, as an emigrant in England, Prokopovich published the first critical assessment of the official Gosplan figures. Prokopovich argued that Gosplan had overstated the recovery by not adjusting for the considerable deterioration of product quality between 1913 and the 1920s. Prokopovich argued that this quality deterioration would not be reflected in the official industrial output statistics (which multiply the number of shoes in 1913 and 1928, for example, times the price of shoes in 1913 without adjusting for quality change). On the basis of scattered industry studies, Prokopovich concluded that product quality in industry in 1928 was some 20 percent below that in 1913. A 20 percent downward adjustment of industrial output yields a 5.5 percent reduction in 1928 national income. If one applies Gosplan's own implicit price deflator (1.58) to the Prokopovich figure, 1928 national income in 1913 prices drops to 112 percent of 1913 national income from Gosplan's 119 percent.

A second critic of the official series, M. E. Falkus, argues that Gosplan underestimated 1913 Russian national income.[6] Falkus finds that the original Prokopovich estimate for 1913 contained a number of averages for 1909–13 rather than 1913. Although Gosplan apparently corrected for some of this averaging in its 1929 calculations, Falkus concludes that 1913 national income was 3.5 percent above the Gosplan figure. Falkus's adjustment places 1928 national income at 115 percent of 1913 national income versus the Gosplan 119 percent.

If one accepts both the Prokopovich and Falkus adjustments, 1928 national income would have been 108 percent of 1913 national income versus Gosplan's 119 (see Table B.1, row 4). The two adjustments combined yield a 1928 national income 8 percent above the prewar peak and a per capita figure about equal to the prewar peak. The basic Gosplan conclusion remains intact: The recovery of both national income and per capita income was complete by 1928.

Both Prokopovich and Falkus use the Gosplan estimates for 1913 and 1928 as their starting point.[7] In retrospect, it would have been difficult for Gosplan to come up with conceptually comparable 1913 and 1928 national income figures in current prices. Property rights had changed; new ways of gathering statistics were employed; and new types of market relations had developed. It would thus come as no surprise if Gosplan had missed the mark by a wide margin. For this reason, it is important to have estimates of 1913 and 1928 national income in current prices that are independent of the official Gosplan figures.

An unplanned by-product of my 1982 study of Russian national income was a calculation of relative 1928/1913 national income.[8] I had deliberately patterned the prerevolutionary accounts after Abram Bergson's study of Soviet national income beginning with 1928.[9] Both studies employed Western concepts of national income by the "end-use" categories. Because of these common procedures, the 1913 and 1928 national income figures in current prices should be conceptually comparable. Table B.2 shows the official estimates for 1913 and 1928 and compares them with the estimates of other researchers.

Table B.3 compares the official Gosplan estimates of 1913 and 1928

TABLE B.2
Various Estimates of National Income, 1913 and 1928, in Current Prices and Constant 1913 Prices (using the official national income deflator billions of rubles)

		1913	1928	1928:1913
Official estimates	Current prices	14.5	27.2	1.88
	1913 prices	14.5	16.2	1.19
Prokopovich (1931)[a]	Current prices	14.5	25.7	1.77
	1913 prices	14.5	16.2	1.12
Falkus (1969)	Current prices	15.0	27.2	1.81
	1913 prices	15.0	17.2	1.15
Prokopovich-Falkus[a]	Current prices	15.0	25.7	1.71
	1913 prices	15.0	16.2	1.08

Sources: Falkus, "Russia's National Income, 1913," 55. For official estimates, see sources and note to Table B.1. Prokopovich (1931) is from his *National Income of the USSR,* Table 4, 12. Falkus (1969) is from "Russia's National Income, 1913," 55.

[a]I have reduced Prokopovich's average 1927–28 to 1928–29 industry figure by 20 percent (Prokopovich's suggested quality adjustment).

TABLE B.3
National Income, 1928 : 1913, in Current Prices, Various Estimates
(billions of rubles)

	1913	1928	1928 : 1913
A. Official Soviet estimates	14.5	27.2	1.88
B. Soviet estimates adjusted to include nonmaterial production (NNP)	15.5	28.9	1.87
C. Gregory-Bergson, NNP in factor cost	15.55	27.5	1.77
D. Gregory-Bergson, NNP market prices	16.5	30.2	1.83

Sources: On row A, see Table B.1. On rows B–D, see Gregory, Russian National Income, 110, 113.

Note: The nonmaterial product adjustment in row B is the ratio of adjusted to official Soviet national income in 1913 prices. The factor cost figures in row C are the averages of the two factor cost concepts.

national income in current prices (both in their original form and adjusted to conform to Western national income concepts) with Bergson's and mine. This comparison yields the startling conclusion that they are in remarkable agreement. The ruble figures are fairly close. The Gosplan ratios of 1928 to 1913 national income in current prices range from 1.88 to 1.87, and the Bergson-Gregory ratios range from 1.77 to 1.83, depending on whether factor costs or market prices are used. Using the Gosplan implicit price deflator on the Bergson-Gregory figures yields a 1928/1913 ratio of national income in constant 1913 prices of from 112 percent to 116 percent versus the Gosplan estimate of 119 percent. The substitution of the Gregory-Bergson figures does not alter the Gosplan conclusion of a completed recovery prior to 1928. By the standards of historical statistics, the differences between these figures are very small.

Tables B.1 to B.3 show that the various estimates of 1913 and 1928 national income in current prices are in basic agreement. The adjustments called for are relatively minor, especially in view of the wide error ranges in historical statistics.

Controversy over the Price Deflator

The agreement among the current-price estimates does not rule out substantial errors in the Gosplan estimates. In fact, the most substantial controversy surrounding the official Gosplan estimates centers on the measurement of price inflation between 1913 and 1928.

The noted Soviet authority on national income, A. L. Vainshtein, argued in his 1969 monograph that Gosplan grossly overstated 1928 national

TABLE B.4
Alternative Soviet Estimates of National Income, 1928 : 1913 (billions of rubles)

	1913	1928	1928 : 1913
A. Official national income estimates, Gosplan 1929 (1913 constant prices)	14.5	17.2	1.19
B. Same in 1913 prices with Vainshtein's implicit deflator (2.0)	14.5	13.6	.94
C. Control figures 1926–27 estimate (1913 constant prices)	14.5	13.3	.92
D. Gregory-Bergson, NNP market prices	16.5	30.2	1.83

Sources: For row A, see Table B.1. In row B, Vainshtein's deflator is from his *Narodny dokhod Rossii i SSSR*, 102–7. It is applied to the Gosplan 1929 estimate of 1928 national income in current prices. Row 3 is from Gosplan SSSR, *Kontrol'nye tsifry narodnogo khoziaistva SSSR*, 215. It gives a national income of 11.7 rubles (in 1913 prices) for 1926–27. This figure is updated to the average of 1927–28 and 1928–29 using the official growth indexes of Gosplan cited in the 1928–29 control figures. For 1913 the official Gosplan 1929 estimate of 1913 national income is used.

income (in 1913 prices) by understating the amount of price inflation between 1913 and 1928.[10] Gosplan converted 1928 national income into 1913 prices using an implicit deflator of 1.58. As an authority on the history of Soviet prices,[11] Vainshtein felt that this deflator was much too low because the various price indexes compiled during the 1920s generally found much higher price increases. Vainshtein believed (on the basis of evidence presented in Table B.5) that prices roughly doubled between 1913 and 1928. If Gosplan had used a doubling of prices instead of a 58 percent price increase, 1928 national income would have been at 94 percent of 1913 national income (instead of 119 percent) and per capita income at 86 percent of 1913 per capita income (instead of 109 percent). This result is shown in Table B.4. Because of this deflation error, Vainshtein recommended a recalculation of the historical series.

Vainshtein's conclusion that Gosplan's 1929 calculation grossly overstated the NEP recovery finds additional support in a study by Gosplan published in 1927. The national income figures cited in Gosplan's 1926–27 central figures show that 1926–27 national income and per capita income were respectively 20 and 25 percent below 1913 figures.[12] If one applies Gosplan's growth indexes in its 1929 publication to these 1926–27 figures, 1928 national income would have been 92 percent and per capita national income 83 percent of 1913 figures (see Table B.4, row 2). These figures are consistent with Vainshtein's conclusion that the recovery was far

TABLE B.5
Selected Price Indices (1913 = 100)

1. Price indices published in the 1920s	
A. Retail price indices	
Central Statistical Administration (TsSU)	
general index	214
state	177
cooperative	187
private	272
B. Producer price indices	
Producer price index	
general index	162
agriculture	148
industry	171
Producer price index, large-scale industry	
general	155
group A	176
group B	162
All-Union index: state industry transfer prices	185
C. Wholesale price indices	
Central Statistical Administration (Gosplan)	
general index	174
agriculture	160
industry	186
2. Implicit price indices from national income studies	
A. National deflator, official Soviet series	158
B. Industrial output deflator, official Soviet series	165
C. National income deflator, Gregory, "best estimate"	195
D. National income deflator, Gregory, "lowest estimate"	171

Sources: Part 1 is from Vainshtein, *Narodny dokhod Rossii i SSSR,* 83; Gosplan SSSR, *Kontrol'nye tsifry narodnogo khoziaistvo na 1928-1929,* Table XV-1, XV-2; Gosplan SSSR, *Kontrol'nye tsifry 1927-1928,* 479; *Promyshlennost' SSSR v 1927/28,* ii (Moscow: VSNKh, 1930). The weighing scheme for the TsSU-Gosplan wholesale price index is discussed in Bobrov, *Indeksy Gosplana,* 66–68. Part 2 is from Gosplan SSSR, *Kontrol'nye tsifry narodnogo khoziaistvo na 1928-1929,* 68, 71, 435, 436; and see Gregory, *Russian National Income,* 110.

from complete in 1928. Vainshtein and the control figures for 1926–27 agree closely that the major source of distortion in the official Gosplan figures is the understatement of price inflation between 1913 and 1928.

Vainshtein's criticism focuses attention on the key importance of price indexes. Table B.5 summarizes the various price indexes published during the 1920s. Gosplan, the Central Statistical Administration, the Kon'iunkturny' Institute, and the Supreme Council for the National Economy compiled price indexes at the factory, wholesale, and retail levels. By the late 1920s the pattern of pricing had become quite complex, a fact that greatly complicates comparisons of 1928 and 1913 price levels. Goods were changing hands in different markets at different prices. In retail trade, there were substantial differences among state, cooperative, and private market prices, with the highest prices being charged in private markets. Goods also sold for different prices in agricultural markets, with state procurement agencies purchasing agricultural goods at lower prices than private dealers. The published retail price indexes deal with multiple prices by averaging prices in the three types of markets according to market shares. The Central Statistical Administration (CSA) 1928 retail price index, for example, stood at 177 (1913 = 100) for state trade, at 187 for cooperative trade, and at 272 for private trade, with a weighted index of 214— implying an approximate 37 percent share for private trade.

The growing administrative allocation of industrial goods in the late 1920s raises a second pricing problem. Wholesale prices received by factories were becoming increasingly arbitrary. By the late 1920s, the gaps between factory transfer prices, wholesale prices, and retail prices were rising. Producer prices were 62 percent above 1913 in 1928; wholesale prices were 85 percent above 1913; and retail prices (even including the artificially low prices in state outlets) were more than double 1913 prices. Market linkages between producer, wholesale, and retail prices had been disrupted by 1928, and factory transfer prices of state-owned enterprises had increasingly come to serve an accounting function rather than an allocative function.

Vainshtein concluded that retail prices should be the standard for deflation.[13] Wholesale and factory transfer price indexes captured trends in artificial accounting prices. The two published retail price indexes showed prices at least doubling between 1913 and 1928, and this is the rationale for Vainshtein's choice of an implicit price deflator of 2.0.

The appropriate method of deflating 1928 national income is not to divide by one single price index, but rather to deflate each subcategory by an appropriate price index. As Table B.5 shows, one has a broad range of choice of price indexes relating 1913 to 1928. I constructed two national income deflators to determine whether Gosplan arrived at the "low" price deflator criticized by Vainshtein by systematically using the lowest available price deflators.[14] For the "best" deflator (see Table B.5), I selected from the published price indexes the one that appeared to be most appropriate for the subcategory. For retail trade, for example, we used the CSA weighted index of retail prices in state, cooperative, and private markets. For farm consumption in kind, we used the CSA weighted index of retail agricultural price. To calculate the lowest deflator, I used the lowest published price deflators for each subcategory. For retail trade, for example, we used the index of retail prices in state stores only. If my low national income price deflator duplicates the implicit deflator (1.58) used by Gosplan in its 1929 publication, then Vainshtein's mystery of the low deflator is resolved.

My experiment yielded the following results: The best implicit price deflator turned out to be 1.96 (slightly below Vainshtein's suggested 2.0), and the lowest deflator was 1.71 (about 8 percent above the Gosplan implicit deflator). If I apply the 1.96 deflator to Gosplan's own figures, 1928 national income would be 93 percent of 1913 national income and per capita income would be 85 percent of 1913. If I apply the low 1.72 deflator, 1928 national income would be 109 percent of 1913 and per capita income would equal that of 1913. The deliberate choice of the lowest possible price deflators explains why Gosplan found such a rapid recovery. When more reasonable price deflators are used, one finds that the recovery was still not complete in 1928.

Any results based on the lowest price deflators are implausible because they, in effect, assume that all 1928 transactions took place in state-controlled markets. If one accepts the official current-price figures as accurate, then one must conclude that the recovery of national income was not yet complete in 1928 and that per capita income was still more than 10 percent below the prewar peak. If one accepts the lower alternate estimates in current prices, then one must conclude that 1928 national income was more than 10 percent and per capita income 15 percent below figures for 1913.

More Criticism of the Current Price Estimates

The evidence presented in Tables B.1 to B.3 showed basic agreement among the competing estimates of national income in current prices. The fact that the various estimates agree does not conclusively establish their credibility, because they share the same basic statistical raw materials and they draw on each other in a number of cases. R. W. Davies and S. G. Wheatcroft raise important questions about the conceptual comparability of the 1913 and 1928 figures in current prices.[15] In comparing individual real expenditure categories in 1913 and 1928, Davies and Wheatcroft are perplexed by the steep drop in real consumption of farm income in kind indicated by my figures (1928 = 57 percent of 1913). Davies and Wheatcroft suggest that this result is caused by the failure to net out retained farm income agricultural shipments to local villages. If Bergson's 1928 estimate nets out such shipments (and includes them properly in retail sales), my 1913 figure is too high and understates the NEP recovery.

The proper calculation of consumption of farm income in kind is incredibly complex. For Russia in 1913, retained farm consumption is a major expenditure category accounting for almost one-third of net national product.[16] Although 82 percent of the Russian population was rural in 1913, the volume of retail trade in rural areas accounted for only 28 percent of total retail trade.[17] These figures suggest that most rural agricultural marketings do not show up in 1913 retail trade figures. As Davies and Wheatcroft point out, I estimated agricultural marketings in a way that would not capture deliveries by road to local markets. By understating total deliveries, the retained farm consumption (net output minus deliveries) would be overstated. This overstatement would be necessary, however, if the retail trade figures fail to capture transactions in local rural markets.

Retained farm income is inherently difficult to calculate. It would be foolhardy to argue that my figures for 1913 are accurate or conceptually the same as Bergson's. Because of the difficulty of sorting out retail sales and retained farm income, it may be more reasonable to rely on total personal consumption rather than to compare individual components. Table B.6 shows that total personal consumption in 1928 was 85 percent of 1913 consumption using market prices. It shows that retail sales in 1928 and 1913 were equal, providing some support for my suggestion that less rural sales found their way into retail sales in 1913 than in 1928. The decline to 85 percent of 1913 of personal consumption appears more

TABLE B.6
Gregory's Estimates of Net National Product, 1913 and 1928
(billions of rubles at 1913 market prices)

	1913	1928	1928 : 1913
Original version			
Net national product	16.5	15.3	0.93
Personal consumption	13.2	11.2	0.85
Consumption of farm products in kind	5.4	3.1	0.57
Retail sales	5.8	5.8	1.00
Maximum upward revision			
Net national product	16.5	17.6	1.07
Personal consumption	13.2	13.5	1.02
Consumption of farm products in kind[a]	5.4	5.4	1.00
Retail sales	5.8	5.8	1.00

Source: See Gregory, *Russian National Income*, Tables 5.3, 5.4.

Notes: The original figures have been amended according to a suggestion from R. W. Davies to raise the construction price deflator by including an index of construction wages in addition to an index of building material prices. This adjustment lowers 1928 NNP in 1913 prices by 0.3 billion rubles. The maximum upward adjustment is obtained by assuming that 1928 NNP by 2.3 billion rubles.

[a]Consumption of farm products in kind assumed to be equal in 1913 and 1928 to obtain maximum upward adjustment in 1928 NNP.

probable than the drop in retained farm consumption to 57 percent appears in isolation. It may indeed be the case that the total consumption figures are more comparable than the individual components of consumption.

If one assumes that farm consumption in kind in 1928 was equal to that in 1913 while making no offsetting reductions in retail sales, 1928 national income would have been about 4 percent greater than 1913 national income and 1928 per capita income would have been about 5 percent below 1913 per capita income (using the 1.95 price deflator). Such an adjustment may well overstate the recovery because much off-farm consumption in kind fails to enter the retail trade figures in 1913.

Physical Production Series

We can draw on one additional source of information to shed light on the NEP recovery. Rather than estimating 1913 and 1928 national income in current prices and then applying a price deflator, we could aggregate physical production series. Relatively little work has been devoted to aggregating physical production series into a national income series. The following discussion presents only some preliminary evidence.

Other scholars have calculated sector output indexes. The most reliable physical output series are for agriculture and transportation, because these sectors produce homogeneous products that can be tracked in physical terms over time. Yet even when products are homogeneous, such as in agriculture, great ingenuity and detective work are required to obtain reliable aggregated production series. Let us consider the various branch indexes. In Wheatcroft's study of agricultural output, 1928 net agricultural output is given as 98 percent of 1913 output. Westwood finds that the output of the transportation sector had recovered to 1913 levels by 1928. Gatrell and Davies argue that construction in 1928 was 15 percent below the 1913 peak and conclude that employment in trade in 1928 was probably less than in 1913, although the real volume of trade was about the same.[18] Agriculture, transportation, construction, and trade, which accounted for 70 percent of 1913 national income, had either just barely recovered to their prewar peak levels or were still slightly below peak levels in 1928.

Large-scale and small-scale industry accounted for another 20 percent of 1913 national income. Nutter compiled an index of industrial production from available physical production series and concluded that 1928 industrial output was essentially the same as 1913 output.[19] It is difficult to gauge the reliability of the Nutter series because of the sparse data on small-scale industry in both 1913 and 1928 and because of the difficulty of dealing with heterogeneous products such as machinery. If one further accepts Prokopovich's suggestion that a quality-deterioration adjustment is required, Nutter's series would show a decline in industrial output between 1913 and 1928.

If one adds Nutter's finding of a barely completed recovery of industrial output by 1928 to the other production series, one must conclude from the available physical production series (which account for some 90 percent of 1913 national income) that 1928 national income must have been approximately equal to 1913. There is no supporting evidence of a 1928 output level 19 percent above the 1913 level, as claimed by the official Gosplan figures. If one applies a quality-deterioration adjustment to industry, then 1928 national income would still have been slightly below the 1913 figure and per capita income would have been less than 90 percent of 1913 per capita income.

The alternate approach to estimating industrial production is to deflate the value of industrial output in 1928 into the prices of 1913 and then compare this figure with 1913 industrial output. Wheatcroft, Davies, and Cooper conclude that gross industrial production in 1928 was about 20 percent higher than in 1913.[20] Upon reviewing this and other studies of Soviet industrial output statistics,[21] I find that students of 1928/1913 industrial production indexes must grapple with the very same problems and puzzles as the student of national income. It appears just as difficult to determine comparable 1913 and 1928 figures in current prices and then to find appropriate price deflators. For both 1913 and 1928, it is difficult to determine the value of output of small-scale (noncensus) industries. For large-scale (census) industries, the value of output can be determined with greater precision, but it again appears that Soviet authorities used an unrealistically low price deflator (1.65) to convert 1928 industrial output into 1913 prices.[22] If we apply a more reasonable price deflator to Soviet industrial output, then one would have to conclude that 1928 industrial output was about 5 percent above 1913 output. This result is close to the physical output series of Nutter.

THE FEASIBLE RANGE

This appendix has reviewed the existing estimates of relative 1928/1913 national income. It has raised as many questions as it has answered, but we are in a position to define a feasible range within which the "true" figure falls. It is my conclusion that the official Soviet estimates showing 1928 national income at 19 percent and per capita income at 9 percent above 1913 figures can be dismissed as gross overstatements of the NEP recovery. They are based on a low implicit deflator that is not supported by contemporary price indexes. The evidence points to a national income deflator of between 1.9 and 2.0. With basic agreement among the different estimates of 1913 and 1928 national income in current prices, a price deflator of this magnitude would yield a 1928 national income at best equal to and likely below that of 1913. The lower bound would be a 1928 national income 93 percent of the 1913 figure, and this lower bound is supported not only by my study of national income but by Vainshtein and an earlier Gosplan calculation. In any case, 1928 *per capita* income would have been at least 10 percent below that of 1913. The available physical production series point to a 1928 national income about equal to that of 1913. The physical production series support the proposition that, at best, 1928 national income was equal to that of 1913, with a substantial per capita gap still to be recovered.

NOTES

CHAPTER 1

1. Simon Kuznets, "A Comparative Appraisal," In Abram Bergson and Simon Kuznets (eds.), *Economic Trends in the Soviet Union* (Cambridge, Mass.: Harvard University Press, 1963), 345–47.

2. See Alec Nove, *An Economic History of the USSR* (London: Penguin, 1969), chaps. 3–6; M. Lewin, *Russian Peasants and Soviet Power* (London: Allen & Unwin, 1968); and Stephan Merl, *Der Agrarmarkt und die Neue Oekonomische Politik* (Munich: Oldenbourg Verlag, 1981).

3. For a discussion of different assessments of NEP by Soviet reformers, see Yury P. Bokarev, "NEP i problemy perstroiki," presented at Soviet-American Conference on Soviet Economic Reform, Houston, Texas, December 1989. For an official assessment of the failures of NEP published shortly before the collapse of the Soviet Union, see G. L. Smirnov, "Vremiia trudnykh voprosov, Istoriia 20-30-x godov i sovremenaia obshchestvennaia mysl'," *Pravda*, September 30 and October 3, 1988.

4. Maurice Dobb, *Soviet Economic Development since 1917*, 5th ed. (London: Routledge & Kegan Paul, 1960), chaps. 4–9 (first published in the 1930s), left a lasting imprint on Western thinking about the NEP period, even though Dobb appeared to accept the Stalinist version of the NEP period.

5. V. I. Lenin, *The Development of Capitalism in Russia* (Moscow: Foreign Languages Publishing House, 1956).

6. Even the influential writings of Alexander Gerschenkron focus on Russian economic history as a means of explaining revolutionary events. See Alexander Gerschenkron, *Economic Backwardness in Historical Perspective* (Cambridge, Mass.: Harvard University Press, 1962), essay 1.

7. See Paul Gregory, *Russian National Income, 1885–1913* (London: Cambridge University Press, 1982), 11–17.

8. Ibid. chap. 6.

9. Z. M. and N. A. Svavitski, *Zemskie podvornye perepisi, 1880–1913* (Moscow: Izdanie Ts. S. U., 1926).

10. Consider, for example, the amount of scholarly attention devoted to the 1891–92 famine. See Richard Robbins, Jr., *Famine in Russia, 1891–1892* (New York: Columbia University Press, 1975).

11. For accounts, see Walther Kirchner, *Die Deutsche Industrie und die Industrialisierung Russlands, 1815–1914* (St. Katharinen: Scripta Mercaturae Verlag, 1986); and Urs Rauber, *Schweizer Industrie in Russland* (Zurich: Verlag Hans Rohr, 1985).

12. Quoted in Lazar Volin, *A Century of Russian Agriculture* (Cambridge, Mass.: Harvard University Press, 1970), 58.

13. Colin White, *Russia and America: The Roots of Economic Divergence* (London: Croom Helm, 1988).

14. The voluminous writings of R. W. Davies could be cited as an example, although Davies's works concentrate heavily on economic performance. Basically Davies is interested in explaining political events and employs the detailed statistics of the period to shed light on these events. See, for example, R. W. Davies, *The Socialist Offensive: The Collectivization of Soviet Agriculture, 1929–1930* (Cambridge, Mass.: Harvard University Press, 1980), and his *Soviet Economy in Turmoil, 1929–1930* (Cambridge, Mass.: Harvard University Press, 1989).

Chapter 2

1. Simon Kuznets, *Modern Economic Growth* (New Haven: Yale University Press, 1966), and *The Economic Growth of Nations* (Cambridge, Mass.: Harvard University Press, 1971).

2. Kuznets, *Modern Economic Growth* and *The Economic Growth of Nations*; Angus Maddison, *Economic Growth in the West* (New York: Norton, 1964); B. R. Mitchell, *European Historical Statistics, 1750–1970* (London: Macmillan, 1975); Paul Bairoch, *The Working Population and Its Structure* (New York: Gordon and Breach, 1969). For individual country studies, see Simon Kuznets, *Capital in the American Economy* (Princeton: Princeton University Press, 1961); Robert Gallman, "Gross National Product in the United States, 1834–1909," in National Bureau of Economic Research, *Output, Employment and Productivity in the United States after 1800*, vol. 30, *Studies in Income and Wealth* (New York: Columbia University Press, 1966); Walther Hoffmann, *Das Wachstum der Deutschen Wirtschaft seit der Mitte des 19. Jahrhunderts* (Berlin: Springer, 1965); Jan Marczewski, "Le Produit physique de l'economie française de 1789 à NB 1913 (comparaison avec la Grande-Bretagne)," *Histoire quantitative de l'economie française, Cahiers de l'I.S.E.A.*, AF, 4, 163 (July 1965); Charles Feinstein, *National Income, Expenditure and Output of the United Kingdom, 1855–1965* (Cambridge: Cambridge University Press, 1972); P. M. Deane and W. A. Cole, *British Economic Growth, 1688–1959* (Cambridge: Cambridge University Press, 1962); O. J. Firestone, *Canada's Economic Development, 1867–1953*, vol. 7, *Income and Wealth Series* (London: Bowes and Bowes, 1958); and Kazuchi Ohkawa and Henry Rosovsky, *Japanese Economic Growth* (Stanford: Stanford University Press, 1973).

3. Both Alexander Gerschenkron, "The Rate of Growth of Industrial Production in Russia since 1885," *Journal of Economic History* 7 (1947), and W. W. Rostow (ed.), *The Economics of Takeoff into Sustained Growth* (New York: St. Martin's Press, 1963), 152–54, have argued that Russia's industrial revolution began in the 1880s.

4. Gregory, *Russian National Income*.

5. Lenin, *The Development of Capitalism in Russia*.

6. Alexander Gerschenkron, "Russian Agrarian Policies and Industrialization, 1861–1917," in *Cambridge Economic History of Europe*, vol. 6 (Cambridge: Cambridge University Press, 1965), 706–800.

7. Olga Crisp, *Studies in the Russian Economy before 1914* (London: Macmillan Press, 1976), essay 1.

8. For a valuable comparison of Russia and the United States during this era, see White, *Russia and America*.

9. M. E. Falkus, *The Industrialization of Russia, 1700–1914* (London: Macmillan, 1972), 11–19; Crisp, *Studies in the Russian Economy.*

10. Paul Gregory, "Economic Growth and Structural Change in Tsarist Russia: A Case of Modern Economic Growth?" *Soviet Studies* 23, no. 3 (January 1972): 425.

11. This is contrary to Gerschenkron's conclusion that the pattern of Russian industrialization was biased in the direction of heavy industry. See Paul Gregory, "Some Empirical Comments on the Theory of Relative Backwardness: The Russian Case," *Economic Development and Cultural Change* 22, no. 4 (July 1974): 657–61.

12. For a breakdown of 1861–1913 growth rates by decade, see Gregory, "Economic Growth and Structural Change." According to Raymond Goldsmith, "The Economic Growth of Tsarist Russia, 1860–1913," *Economic Development and Cultural Change* 9, no. 3 (April 1961): 443, the growth rate from 1860 to the 1880s was about 2 percent per annum, about two-thirds the rate after 1880.

13. The cited series are reasonably comparable: They employ a fairly common methodology and use "late" year (postindustrialization) prices. It is, however, my suspicion that the more sophisticated series, such as those for the United States and Japan, avoid some of the systematic understatements of the other series. But because these biases apply primarily to capital goods and capital goods represent a relatively small share of total output, I would not expect the differential biases to be large. On the other hand, there are likely a whole series of unsystematic biases in the various national series that have escaped attention; one can only hope that these will be of a random character.

14. Kuznets, "A Comparative Appraisal," 338–39.

15. Maddison, *Economic Growth in the West,* 28.

16. Russian agricultural employment is assumed to grow at the same rate as agricultural population, and the data on employment in handicraft are grossly inadequate. Moreover, the part-time employment of agricultural workers in handicraft presents enormous difficulties. Similar weaknesses and ambiguities can be found in the labor force statistics of other countries.

17. Kuznets, *The Economic Growth of Nations,* 52–61, concludes that the labor force and population tended to grow at equal rates during this time period.

18. The conservative growth estimates of Goldsmith, "The Economic Growth of Tsarist Russia," are given in parentheses in Table 2.1.

19. Kuznets, *The Economic Growth of Nations,* 24.

20. The crude nature of these figures should be emphasized; some are in constant, others in current, prices; some are shares of GNP, others of national income. Moreover, rough adjustments have to be made to achieve comparable sector definitions. General conclusions can be drawn despite these shortcomings.

21. Lenin, *The Development of Capitalism in Russia*; Gerschenkron, "Russian Agrarian Policies.

22. The major problem in estimating Russian agriculture's labor productivity is the lack of agricultural labor force data. Hence, we must use the growth of agriculture's able-bodied population to represent the agricultural labor force. Substantial errors in the Russian estimates would be introduced only if the agricultural labor force grew at a rate substantially different from the able-bodied rural population, and I doubt that this occurred.

23. Kuznets, *Modern Economic Growth*, 86–126.

24. These figures must be handled with caution for several reasons. First, they are in most instances calculated from relative product and labor force shares, the former often in current prices. Thus the ratios can be affected by changes in relative prices between agriculture and industry. Second, the resulting ratios are often dependent on the period chosen. For example, the U.S. and Japanese ratios yield the typical pattern of agricultural productivity lagging behind that of industry, yet one can find subperiods where productivity grew at equal rates in the two major sectors.

25. Theodore von Laue, *Sergei Witte and the Industrialization of Russia* (New York: Columbia University Press, 1963), and "A Secret Memorandum of Sergei Witte on the Industrialization of Imperial Russia," *Journal of Modern History* 26, no. 1 (March 1954).

26. For an analysis of this question, see Paul Gregory, "1913 Russian National Income: Some Insights into Russian Economic Development," *Quarterly Journal of Economics* 90, no. 3 (August 1976): 445–60.

27. It is the contention of John McKay, *Pioneers for Profit: Foreign Entrepreneurship and Russian Industrialization* (Chicago: University of Chicago Press, 1970), that the truly unique feature of Russian industrialization was its reliance on the combination of private enterprise and foreign capital and foreign entrepreneurship. For a survey of the literature on the determinants of portfolio capital flows, see Erich Spitaller, "A Survey of Recent Quantitative Studies of Long-Term Capital Movements," *International Monetary Fund, Staff Papers* 18 (March 1971): 189–217. Evidence on the relationship between capital flows and economic development is summarized in Kuznets, *Modern Economic Growth*, 236–39.

28. Henry Rosovsky, *Capital Formation in Japan, 1868–1940* (New York: Free Press, 1961), 14.

29. *Opyt priblizitel'nogo ischisleniia narodnogo dokhoda po razlichnym istochnikam i po razmeram v Rossii* (Saint Petersburg: Ministerstvo finansov, 1906), xxxii.

Chapter 3

1. Nove, *An Economic History of the USSR*; Gerschenkron, "Russian Agrarian Policies."

2. For a survey of the historical literature, see Eberhard Mueller, "Der Beitrag der Bauern zur Industrialisierung Russlands 1885–1930," *Jahrbuecher fuer die Geschichte Osteuropas* 27, no. 2 (1979): 197–219.

3. R. Hennesy, *The Agrarian Question in Russia, 1905–1907* (Giessen: W. Schmitz, 1977), 22.

4. Volin, *A Century of Russian Agriculture*, 58.

5. I. D. Kovalchenko and L. V. Milov, *Vserosiiski agrarny rynok XVIII–nachalo XX veka* (Moscow: Nauka, 1974); B. N. Mironov, *Khlebnye tseny v Rossii za dva stoletiia (XVIII–XIX vv)* (Moscow: Nauka, 1985). See also V. I. Bovykin, *Rossiia nakanune velikikh svershenii* (Moscow: Nauka, 1988), chap. 2.

6. Volin, *A Century of Russian Agriculture*, 57.

7. Peter Gatrell, *The Tsarist Economy, 1850–1917* (New York: St. Martin's Press, 1986), chap. 4.

8. Arcadius Kahan, *The Plow, the Hammer, and the Knout: An Economic History of Eighteenth-Century Russia* (Chicago: University of Chicago Press, 1985), chap. 2.

9. Jacob Metzer, "Railroads in Tsarist Russia: Direct Gains and Implications," *Explorations in Economic History* 12 (1975) and "Railroad Development and Market Integration," *Journal of Economic History* 31 (1974); M. E. Falkus, "Russia and the International Wheat Trade, 1861–1914," *Economica* (November 1966).

10. The Gerschenkron model is enunciated in a number of articles: Gerschenkron, *Economic Backwardness in Historical Perspective*; and "The Early Phases of Industrialization in Russia: Afterthoughts and Counterthoughts," in Rostow, *The Economics of Takeoff*.

11. Gerschenkron's calculations of per capita domestic wheat and rye consumption are reported in Gerschenkron, "Russian Agrarian Policies and Industrialization," 778.

12. For a skeptical analysis of these Gerschenkron positions, see Gregory, "Some Empirical Comments."

13. For a survey of evidence in support of the agrarian crisis, see James Simms, "The Crisis in Russian Agriculture at the End of the 19th Century," *Slavic Review* 36, no. 3 (1977): 377–98.

14. For detailed discussions of tsarist agricultural statistics by Soviet and Russian authors, see V. I. Smirnsky, "Iz istorii zemskoi statistiki," in *Ocherki po istorii statistiki SSSR, Sbornik tretii* (Moscow: Gosstatizdat Ts. S. U., 1960), 130–45; A. I. Gozulov, *Istoriia otechestvennoi statistiki* (Moscow: Gosstatizdat, 1957), 1–81; P. I. Liashchenko, *Ocherki agrarnoi evolutsii Rossii* (Petersburg: n.p., 1908), 278–301. Detailed accounts of the various estimates of prerevolutionary agricultural output and marketings with analyses of their strengths and shortcomings are found in Jerzy Karcz, "Back on the Grain Front," *Soviet Studies* 22, no. 2 (1960): 262–94; S. G. Wheatcroft, "The Reliability of Russian Prewar Grain Output Statistics," *Soviet Studies* 26, no. 2 (1974): 157–80; R. W. Davies, "A Note on Grain Statistics," *Soviet Studies* 21, no. 3 (1970): 314–30.

15. For an analysis of the Russian grain market during this period, see Paul Gregory, "Grain Marketing and Peasant Consumption, Russia, 1885–1913," *Explorations in Economic History* 17, no. 2 (March 1979).

16. Gregory, *Russian National Income*, app. D.

17. Cited in S. G. Strumilin, *Problemy ekonomiki truda* (Moscow: Nauka, 1964), 279.

18. It is for this reason that restrictions on rural-urban migration play such a prominent role in the Gerschenkron model.

19. Goldsmith, "The Economic Growth of Tsarist Russia," 441–76.

20. See Kahan, *The Plow, the Hammer, and the Knout*, chap. 2.

21. These figures are from the Central Statistical Committee's land surveys for the years 1877–78 and 1905, cited in A. N. Antsiferov, *Russian Agriculture during the War* (New York: Greenwood Press, 1930), 19–20. During this period, the state was a major owner of land, but state ownership was primarily of forest and natural meadow land not used for grain cultivation.

22. Gatrell, *The Tsarist Economy*, 111–13.

23. Gregory, *Russian National Income*, 73–75.

24. The net production data are from *Bulletin Russe de statistique financiere et de legislation*, 5th ed. (1898), 222–31; *Ezhegodnik ministerstva finansov 1905*, 494–97; and *Statitischeski ezhegodnik Rossii* (1904–17 annual eds.).

25. Cited in P. P. Maslov, *Kriticheski analiz burzhuaznykh statisticheskikh publikatsii* (Moscow: Nauka, 1955), 459.

26. The real complication in evaluating the agricultural production series cited in Tables 3.1 and 3.2 is that no major study of intertemporal bias has ever been undertaken. It is always possible that improving coverage will impart an upward bias to any historical series, but so far the literature has failed to demonstrate that such a bias exists in the Russian series.

27. *Sbornik statistiko-ekonomicheskikh svedenii po sel'skomu khoziaistvu Rossii i inostrannykh gosudarstv*, vol. 7 (Petrograd: n.p., 1915).

28. Arcadius Kahan, "Capital Formation during the Period of Early industrialization in Russia, 1890–1913," in *Cambridge Economic History of Europe*, vol. 7, pt. 2 (Cambridge: Cambridge University Press, 1978), 265–307; Gregory, *Russian National Income*, table H-1.

29. Strumilin, *Problemy ekonomiki truda*, 275–317.

30. Gerschenkron, *Economic Backwardness in Historical Perspective*.

31. On this point, see Paul Gregory, "Rents, Land Prices and Economic Theory: The Russian Agrarian Crisis," in Linda Edmondson and Peter Waldron (eds.), *Economy and Society in Russia and the Soviet Union* (London: St. Martin's Press, 1992), 6–23.

32. A. V. Chayanov, *The Theory of Peasant Economy* (Homewood, Ill.: Irwin, 1966).

33. Gatrell, *The Tsarist Economy*, chaps. 3 and 4.

34. Gregory, "Some Empirical Comments."

35. Kahan, *The Plow, the Hammer, and the Knout*, chap. 2.

36. Crisp, *Studies in the Russian Economy*, essay 3.

37. Gatrell, *The Tsarist Economy*, 105–8.

38. I. D. Kovalchenko and L. V. Milov, *Vserossiiski agrarny rynok XVII– nachalo XX veka* (Moscow: Nauka, 1974), 257–82.

39. A. M. Anfimov, *Ekonomicheskoe polozhenie i klassovaia borba krestian Evropeiskoi Rossii, 1881–1904* (Moscow: Nauka, 1989), 110.

40. Gatrell, *The Tsarist Economy*, 197.

CHAPTER 4

1. This summary of the Witte system is based on Gerschenkron, "Russian Agrarian Policies," "The Early Phases of Industrialization in Russia," and *Economic Backwardness in Historical Perspective*; Theodore von Laue, "The State and the Economy," in Cyril E. Black (ed.), *The Transformation of Russian Society* (Cambridge, Mass.: Harvard University Press, 1960), 209–55, "A Secret Memorandum of Sergei Witte," and "The High Cost and Gamble of the Witte System: A Chapter in the Industrialization of Russia," *Journal of Economic History* 13 (Fall 1953): 425–44; Jurgen Nötzold, "Agrarfrage und Industrialisierung am Vorabend des Ersten Weltkrieges," *Saeculum, Jahrbuch fuer Universalgeschichte* 17 (1966): 170–90; Roger Portal, "The Industrialization of Russia," *Cambridge Economic History*, 6:801–74; McKay, *Pioneers for Profit*; Falkus, *The Industrialization of*

Russia; Bernd Bonwetsch, "Handelspolitik und Industrialisierung: Zur aussen-wirtschaftlichen Abhaengigkeit Russlands, 1890–1914," in D. Geyer (ed.), *Wirtschaft und Gesellschaft im vorrevolutionaren Russland* (Koeln: Kiepenheuer & Witsch, 1975), 277–301.

2. Soviet authors—in particular S. G. Strumilin, *Statistika i ekonomika, Izbrannye proizvedenia, I* (Moscow: Nauka, 1963), and *Ocherki ekonomicheskoi istorii Rossii* (Moscow: Nauka, 1960)—have stressed the mechanization of cotton textiles as the first "industrial revolution" of Russia. This claim has been disputed by Portal and Falkus. See Portal, "The Industrialization of Russia"; Falkus, *The Industrialization of Russia*. For a survey of the Soviet literature on this subject, see Valery Bovykin, "Probleme der industriellen Entwicklung Russlands," in Geyer, *Wirtschaft und Gesellschaft*, 188–209.

3. Gerschenkron, *Economic Backwardness in Historical Perspective*.

4. Surprisingly little information is available on the size and composition of the Russian bureaucracy. For the best source, see P. A. Zaionchkovski, *Pravitel'stvenny apparat samoderzhavnoi Rossii v XIX v* (Moscow: Mysl', 1978).

5. This framework for analysis of state actions is described in Paul Gregory, "The Role of the State in Promoting Economic Development: The Russian Case and Its General Implications," in Richard Sylla and Gianni Toniolo (eds.), *Patterns of European Industrialization: The Nineteenth Century* (London: Routledge, 1991), 64–79.

6. Michael Bordo and Anna Schwartz (eds.), *A Retrospective on the Classical Gold Standard* (Chicago: University of Chicago Press, 1984).

7. Von Laue, "A Secret Memorandum of Sergei Witte," and *Sergei Witte and the Industrialization of Russia*.

8. Arcadius Kahan, "Government Policies and the Industrialization of Russia," *Journal of Economic History* 27 (December 1967): 460–77.

9. Gregory, *Russian National Income*, app. F.

10. Crisp, in *Studies in the Russian Economy*, argues that the railroads were much more important to Russian industrialization than the peasant emancipation or other factors.

11. V. I. Pokrovsky (ed.), *Sbornik svedenii po istorii i statistike vneshnei torgovli Rossii* (Saint Petersburg: Departament tamozhennykh sborov, 1902); Gatrell, *The Tsarist Economy*, 165–67; Kahan, "Government Policies."

12. Kirchner, *Die Deutsche Industrie und Industrialisierung Russlands*.

13. McKay, *Pioneers for Profit*.

14. Gregory, "The Russian Balance of Payments, the Gold Standard, and Monetary Policy: A Historical Example of Foreign Capital Movements," *Journal of Economic History* 39, no. 2 (June 1979).

15. See, for example, Kirchner, *Die Deutsche Industrie und Industrialisierung Russlands*.

16. Ibid.

17. Thomas C. Owen, "Entrepreneurship and the Structure of Enterprise in Russia, 1800–1880," in Gregory Guroff and Fred C. Carstensen (eds.), *Entrepreneurship in Imperial Russia and the Soviet Union* (Princeton: Princeton University Press, 1983), 59–83; and *The Corporation under Russian Law, 1800–1917* (New York: Cambridge University Press, 1991).

18. Kahan, "Government Policies."

19. Haim Barkai, "The Macro-Economics of Tsarist Russia in the Industrialization Era: Monetary Developments, the Balance of Payments and the Gold Standard," *Journal of Economic History*, 33 (June 1973): 339–71.

20. Ibid., 351.

21. Barkai's reference is to P. I. Lyashchenko, *History of the National Economy of Russia*, trans. L. M. Herman (New York: n.p., 1949), 718, which comes from an earlier study by T. Engeev, "O platezhnom balanse dovoennoi Rossii," *Vestnik finansov* 5 (1928).

22. This analysis is based on Paul Gregory and Joel Sailors, "Russian Monetary Policy and Industrialization, 1861–1913," *Journal of Economic History* 36, no. 4 (December 1976).

23. I. M. Drummond, "The Russian Gold Standard, 1897–1914," *Journal of Economic History* 36 (September 1976): 633–88.

24. The "broad" money supply measure differs from the modern concept that includes time deposits. Our broad measure simply includes currency *and* current account deposits.

25. I do not include a calculated rate of growth of monetization as does Barkai because I think such estimates would be too crude. I note, however, that the inclusion even of extreme monetization rates would fail to effect my contrast of supply-demand balances during the 1880s and 1890s. Estimates of market economic activity (65 percent of NNP) suggest that Barkai's lower rates of monetization growth are the most reasonable, and they indicate a 2 percent annual difference in the 1880s and 1890s growth rates. See Gregory, "1913 Russian National Income."

26. Drummond, "The Russian Gold Standard," table 1.

27. For Soviet and Western references on this subject, see Valerii I. Bovykin, "K voprosu O roli inostrannogo kapitala v Rossii," *Vestnik Moskovskogo Universiteta* 1 (1964): 55–83; I. F. Gindin, *Russkie kommercheskie banki* (Moscow, 1948); A. L. Vainshtein, *Narodnoe bogatstvo narodnokhoziaistvennoe nakoplenie predrevoliutsionnoi Rossii* (Moscow, 1960); McKay, *Pioneers for Profit: Foreign Entrepreneurship and Russian Industrialization, 1885–1913*; Bernd Bonwetsch, "Das ausländische Kapital in Russland," *Jahrbuecher fuer die Geschichte Osteuropas* 22, no. 3 (1974): 412–25.

28. These calculations are summarized in Gregory, "The Russian Balance of Payments."

29. Parity (or above parity) with the new gold ruble rate was achieved in 1894. For a listing of the credit ruble–gold kopek exchange rate, see M. N. Sobolev, *Tamozhennaia politika Rossii vo vtoroi polovine 19 veka* (Tomsk: n.p., 1911), 1:411–12.

30. Apparently this was especially true during the tenure of Vyshnegradski as finance minister, when efforts were undertaken to extract "hunger exports" from agriculture. See Crisp, *Studies in the Russian Economy*, 100–104.

31. The positive current account balances in 1904 and 1905 were unexpected findings because in these years there was speculation that Russia would be forced to abandon convertibility. As the figures show, export surpluses were quite large in 1905 and 1906, so we would imagine that this speculation was due to political instability rather than to underlying economic factors.

32. To make this calculation we use a Harrod-Domar model with a capital-output ratio of 2.5. For an explanation of the calculation, see Gregory, "The Russian Balance of Payments."

33. This evidence of substantial increases in foreign savings after 1897 contradicts Barkai's assertion that the increase in net foreign investment after 1897 was patently small and short-lived. In making this judgment Barkai relied on the earlier Engeev estimates, which showed an annual growth rate of net foreign investment between 1881–97 and 1898–1913 of less than 5 percent, a rate less than half of the cited figure. Part of this difference—about one-third—is explained by Engeev's use of 1881 as a base year; but even if (using crude extrapolations) the current figures are extended back to the same base year, they are still 50 percent above Engeev's. If the current estimates are to be believed, the increase in foreign investment after 1897 was at least 50 percent more substantial than that indicated by Engeev. Comparisons of the current estimates with Engeev's reveal that the principal differences are due to his overstatement of both interest and dividend payments and net tourist expenditures for the pre-gold-standard era. We should stress that the early period comparison should not be taken too seriously because, prior to 1885, the data are very weak. Engeev's estimates are surprisingly close to the cited estimates for the gold-standard era, although there is disagreement about the separate accounts. Engeev's methodology was rather crude. Typically, he would estimate a particular item in one year and then assume that this amount held for the entire period. It is thus surprising that Engeev's figures were not farther off the mark.

34. Gregory, *Russian National Income*, 143.

35. After subtracting gold production net of industrial uses.

36. Comparing the results in Tables 4.2 and 4.3, we find that the indirect net foreign investment figures in Table 4.2 are in general accord with direct figures on foreign indebtedness and official reserves in Table 4.3. The direct figures yield an annual growth rate of 10 percent, as compared with the 11 percent figure of the indirect estimates. For both periods the statistical discrepancy is around +10 million rubles annually, indicating, if anything, a slight underestimate of net foreign investment for both periods. But due to the likelihood of measurement errors in Table 4.3, we would argue that the indirect net foreign investment figures are the more accurate. It should also be noted that Table 4.3 fails to reveal a gross understatement of the merchandise balance, the existence of which has been argued in the literature. On this point see John Sonntag, "Tsarist Debts and Tsarist Foreign Policy," *Slavic Review* 27 (December 1968): 529–41.

37. The figures in Table 4.3, columns 1–4, are subject to an unknown degree of measurement error, especially for the first period. First, the distribution of public debt between domestic and foreign owners is difficult to estimate for the period 1885–93. Second, it is difficult to obtain an accurate measure of the industrial uses of gold, because official estimates were not published. Third, early data on the foreign indebtedness of the Noble and Peasant Land Banks, municipalities, and nonincorporated enterprises are not available in sufficient detail. The measurement problems are not so important when estimating the current account balance, for relatively small interest payments will emerge at the beginning of the period for most conceivable indebtedness figures for these organizations. In sum, one must regard the 1885–97 foreign indebtedness figures as approximate. The figures for

1897–1913 should be much more accurate because the indebtedness data are much better for the gold-standard era.

38. For a Soviet attack on the policy of accumulating gold reserves, see A. I. Bukovetski, "Svobodnaia nalichnost' i zolotoi zapas tsarskogo pravitel'stva v kontse XIX-nachale XX v," in M. P. Viatkin (ed.), *Monopoly i inostranny kapital v Rossii* (Moscow: n.p., 1962), 359–76.

39. T. K. Engeev, "O platezhnom balanse dovoennoi Rossii," *Vestnik finansov* 5 (1928): 72–84.

40. See Arthur Bloomfield, *Monetary Policy under the International Gold Standard, 1880–1914* (New York: Federal Reserve Bank of New York, 1959), 19–20.

41. Finland had to maintain relatively large holdings of reserves since it had legal reserve requirements not only on note issues but also against other demand liabilities. England was the overwhelmingly dominant financial center, analogous to a world bank where all reserve drains are internal, in contrast to other nations where the drains were external, allowing England to keep a much lower reserve ratio than others.

42. Spitaller, "A Survey of Recent Quantitative Studies."

43. McKay, *Pioneers for Profit*.

44. This does not suggest that foreign capital inflows failed to affect the exchange rate. Obviously, if they had been less, the exchange rate would have dropped, all things being equal. What it does indicate is that variations in the exchange rate are explained (in a statistical sense) by variations in the excess demand for money.

45. Leland B. Yeager, *International Monetary Relations* (New York: Harper & Row, 1966), chap. 14.

46. For a discussion of this issue, see M. I. Tugan-Baranovsky, *Statisticheskie itogi promyshlennago razvitiia Rossii* (Saint Petersburg: Tsepov, 1898).

47. A. A. Mendel'son, *Teoriia i istorii ekonomicheskikh krizisov i tsiklov*, 3 vols. (Moscow: Sotsekizdat, 1959); A. F. Iakovlev, *Ekonomicheskie krizisy v Rossii* (Moscow: Gosizpolit, 1955); I. A. Trakhtenberg, *Denezhnye krizisy* (Moscow: Nauka, 1963).

CHAPTER 5

1. M. I. Tugan-Baranovsky, *The Russian Factory in the 19th Century*, trans. Gloria S. Levin (Homewood, Ill.: Irwin, 1970).

2. Chayanov, *The Theory of Peasant Economy*.

3. Gerschenkron, *Economic Backwardness in Historical Perspective*.

4. These results are summarized from Gregory, "The Role of the State in Promoting Economic Development."

5. McKay, *Pioneers for Profit*.

6. Owen, *The Corporation under Russian Law*.

7. Mironov, *Khlebnye tseny v Rossii za dva stoletiia*; Kovalchenko and Milov, *Vserossiiski agrarny rynok XVIII–Nachalo XX veka*.

8. Paul Gregory, "A Note on Relative Backwardness and Industrial Structure," *Quarterly Journal of Economics* 78 (August 1974): 520–27.

9. The discussions of War Communism and NEP are largely based on Nove, *An*

Economic History of the USSR, chaps. 3 and 4; E. Zaleski, *Planning for Economic Growth in the Soviet Union, 1918–1932* (Chapel Hill: University of North Carolina Press, 1971), chap. 2; Dobb, *Soviet Economic Development*, chaps. 4–9; E. H. Carr and R. W. Davies, *Foundations of a Planned Economy, 1926–1929*, vol. 1, pt. 2 (London: Macmillan, 1969), chaps. 33–35; Lewin, *Russian Peasants and Soviet Power*, chaps. 1–15; Y. Avdakov and V. Borodin, *USSR State Industry during the Transition Period* (Moscow: Progress Publishers, 1977); L. Szamuely, *First Models of the Socialist Economic Systems* (Budapest: Akademiai Kiado, 1974); V. A. Vinogradov et al. (eds.), *Istoriia sotsialisticheskoi ekonomiki SSSR* (Moscow: Nauka, 1976), vols. 1 and 2; V. P. Diachenko, *Istoriia finansov SSSR* (Moscow: Nauka, 1978), chaps. 2–4; and Merl, *Der Agrarmarkt und die Neue Oekonomische Politik*.

10. The history of the 1920s is discussed in detail in Paul Gregory and Robert Stuart, *Soviet Economic Structure and Performance*, 5th ed. (New York: Harper Collins, 1993), chaps. 3 and 4. The next two sections of this chapter are adapted from this work.

11. See V. P. Danilov, *Rural Russia under the New Regime*, trans. Orlando Figes (Bloomington: Indiana University Press, 1988), chap. 7.

12. Lewin, *Russian Peasants and Soviet Power*, 26–28.

13. Dobb, *Soviet Economic Development*, 98; Vinogradov *Istoriia sotsialisticheskoi ekonomiki SSSR*, 1:236.

14. Szamuely, *First Models of the Socialist Economic Systems*, 21; Diachenko, *Istoriia finansov SSSR*, 54–55.

15. A statement of E. Preobrazhenzy quoted in Zaleski, *Planning for Economic Growth*, 20. For further discussion of hyperinflation as a means of destroying a money exchange system, see Malle, *The Economic Organization of War Communism*, 174.

16. Quoted in Dobb, *Soviet Economic Development*, 130. According to P. C. Roberts, *Alienation and the Soviet Economy* (Albuquerque: University of New Mexico Press, 1971), 36–41, this quote is not reflective of Lenin's true position during War Communism. Instead, Lenin tended to view War Communism as a basically correct movement in the direction of revolutionary socialism, which he was forced to back away from by the strikes and civil unrest of 1920. Roberts points out the pains taken by Lenin during this period to justify the abandonment of War Communism on ideological grounds, which would have been unnecessary if War Communism had simply been a temporary wartime measure.

17. Vinogradov, *Istoriia sotsialisticheskoi ekonomiki SSSR*, 2:37–38; and Merl, *Der Agrarmarkt und die Neue Oekonomische Politik*, 303–8.

18. Dobb, *Soviet Economic Development*, 143; and Merl, *Der Agrarmarkt und die Neue Oekonomische Politik*, 56.

19. Dobb, *Soviet Economic Development*, 142. Census establishments were those employing sixteen or more persons along with mechanical power, or thirty or more without it. G. W. Nutter, *The Growth of Industrial Production in the Soviet Union* (Princeton: Princeton University Press, 1962), 187–88.

20. Dobb, *Soviet Economic Development*, 135. See also W. Conyngham, *Industrial Management in the Soviet Union* (Stanford: Hoover Institution Press, 1973), 17–24.

21. Avdakov and Borodin, *USSR State Industry*, chaps. 3 and 4.

22. For discussions of NEP trade policy, see M. R. Dohan, "Soviet Foreign Trade in the NEP Economy and Soviet Industrialization Strategy" (Ph.D. diss., Massachusetts Institute of Technology, 1969); L. M. Herman, "The Promise of Economic Self-Sufficiency under Soviet Socialism," in M. Bornstein and D. Fusfeld, *The Soviet Economy: A Book of Readings*, 3d ed. (Homewood, Ill.: Irwin, 1970), 260–90; and W. Beitel and J. Notzold, *Deutsch-Sowjetische Wirtschaftsbeziehungen in der Zeit der Weimarer Republik* (Ebenhausen: Stiftung Wissenschaft and Politik, 1977).

23. Nove, *An Economic History of the USSR*, 137.

24. Ibid., 138.

25. Cited in Dobb, *Soviet Economic Development*, 161–62.

26. Merl, *Der Agrarmarkt und die Neue Oekonomische Politik*, 40–43.

27. J. R. Millar, "A Reformulation of A. V. Chayanov's Theory of Peasant Economy," *Economic Development and Cultural Change* 18, no. 2 (January 1970): 225–27.

28. Paul Gregory, "Grain Marketings and Peasant Consumption, Russia, 1885–1913," *Explorations in Economic History* 17, no. 2 (April 1980): 135–64.

29. Jerzy F. Karcz, "Thoughts on the Grain Problem," *Soviet Studies* 18, no. 4 (April 1967): 407. The one effort to test Russian peasant behavior in response to changing relative prices using modern econometrics shows that peasants in the 1920s did indeed reduce marketings when the terms of trade fell. Paul Gregory and John Antel, "Agricultural Surplus Models and Peasant Behavior: Soviet Agriculture in the 1920s" *Economic Development and Cultural Change*, forthcoming 1993.

30. Erlich, *The Soviet Industrialization Debate*, 105–6; Paul R. Gregory, *Socialist and Nonsocialist Industrialization Patterns* (New York: Praeger, 1970), 28.

31. L. M. Danilov and I. I. Matrozova, "Trudovye resursy i ikh ispol'zovanie," in A. P. Volkova et al. (eds.), *Trud i zarabotnaia plata v SSSR* (Moscow: Nauka, 1968), 245–48.

32. M. Reiman, *Die Geburt des Stalinismus* (Frankfurt/Main: EVA, 1979), chap. 2.

33. Carr and Davies, *Foundations of a Planned Economy*, 787–836.

34. On this, see Gregory, *Socialist and Nonsocialist Industrialization Patterns*.

35. For an account of the thinking of Soviet authorities on these points, see Merl, *Der Agrarmarkt und die Neue Oekonomische Politik*, 50–140. The monetary growth figures cited above are from *Statisticheski spravochnik SSR za 1928* (Moscow: Ts. S. U, 1929), 600.

36. Avdakow and Borodin, *USSR State Industry*, 196–98.

37. Karcz, "Thoughts on the Grain Problem," *Soviet Studies*, 419.

38. The marketed share of grain for the Ukraine between 1923 and 1926 was: 1923–24, 26 percent; 1924–25, 15 percent; 1925–26, 21 percent.

39. R. W. Davies, "A Note on Grain Statistics," *Soviet Studies* 21, no. 3 (January 1970): 328. The controversy over grain marketings during the late 1920s was discussed in Chapter 4.

40. *Statisticheski spravochnik SSR za 1928* (The USSR Statistical Handbook 1928) (Moscow; Ts. S. U, 1929), 727.

41. These studies are cites by Merl, *Der Agrarmarkt und die Neue Oekonomische Politik*, 104.

42. Nove, *An Economic History of the USSR*, 74.

43. Quoted in Szamuely, *First Models of the Socialist Economic Systems*, 97.

44. Malle, *The Economic Organization of War Communism*, 318.

45. Official statements on the NEP economy are published in G. L. Smirnov (ed.), "Vremiia trudnykh voprosov, Istoriia 20–30-x godov i sovremennaia obschestvennaia mysl," *Pravda*, September 30 and October 3, 1988.

46. It is understandable that Soviet authorities have encouraged the publication of V. P. Danilov's classic studies of Russian agriculture during the NEP period. Danilov emphasizes the natural cooperative tendencies of the NEP peasant and objects to the premature forced collectivization move. See Danilov, *Rural Russia under the New Regime*.

CHAPTER 6

1. R. W. Davies, *The Socialist Offensive: The Collectivization of Soviet Agriculture, 1929–1930* (Cambridge, Mass.: Harvard University Press, 1980), chap. 4–5.

2. The definitive official Party version of collectivization was published in *Pravda* in article form. See "Vremiia trudnykh voprosov, Istoriia 20–30-kh godov i sovremennaia obshchestvennaia mysl'," *Pravda*, September 30 and October 3, 1988.

3. The *Pravda* article does recognize the harm done by setting low grain procurement prices in the late 1920s. It argues, however, that procurement prices could not have been raised without setting off rapid inflation.

4. Lynne Viola , "Back on the Economic Front of Collectivization or Soviet Agriculture without Soviet Power," *Slavic Review* 47, no. 2 (Summer 1988): 217–32.

5. Ibid. See R. W. Davies, *The Soviet Collective Farm, 1929–1930* (Cambridge, Mass.: Harvard University Press, 1980).

6. Raj Kumar Sah and Joseph E. Stiglitz, "The Economics of the Scissors Crisis," *American Economic Review* 74, no. 1 (March 1984): 125–38.

7. Danilov, *Rural Russia under the New Regime*. Another significant work on NEP agriculture is Merl, *Der Agrarmarkt und die Neue Oekonomische Politik*.

8. Holland Hunter, "Soviet Agriculture with and without Collectivization, 1928–1940," *Slavic Review* 47, no. 2 (Summer 1988): 203–16.

9. James Millar, "Views on the Economics of Soviet Collectivization of Agriculture: The State of the Revisionist Debate," in Robert Stuart (ed.), *The Soviet Rural Economy* (Totowa, N.J.: Rowman & Allanheld, 1984), 109–17; James Millar, "Collectivization and Its Consequences," *Russian Review* 41, no. 1 (January 1982); Michael Ellman, "Did the Agricultural Surplus Provide the Resources for the Increase in Investment during the First Five Year Plan?" *Economic Journal* 85, no. 4 (December 1975): 844–64.

10. Danilov, *Rural Russia under the New Regime*.

11. For example, Danilov writes about how the more prosperous farmers could dominate politically the repartitional commune and about how kulaks struck private deals that allowed them to farm larger units. It appears that the major source of kulakism was the existence of large families that gave the large family a greater claim to plots at the next redistribution.

12. For a survey of this literature, see Frederic Pryor, "The Plantation Economy

as an Economic System," *Journal of Comparative Economics* 6, no. 3 (September 1982): 301–7.

13. On this, see G. Bogomazov, *Formirovanie osnov sotsialisticheskogo khoziaistvennogo mekhanizma v SSSR v 20–30-e gody* (Leningrad: Izdatel'stvo Leningradskogo Universiteta, 1983), chaps. 3 and 4.

14. Smirnov, "Vremiia trudnykh voprosov.".

15. Paul Gregory and John Antel, "Agricultural Marketings and the Terms of Trade: The Case of NEP agriculture," *Economic Development and Cultural Change* (forthcoming, 1993).

16. The lack of sensitivity is explained by the fact that a decline in the terms of trade sets off two countervailing effects: The income effect lowers agriculture's own consumption of farm products, while the substitution effect tends to reduce farm output.

17. Kuznets, *Modern Economic Growth*, chap. 3.

18. Paul Gregory, *Reforming the Soviet Economic Bureaucracy* (London: Cambridge University Press, 1990), 156–58.

19. In this period, Soviet statistical authorities used the agricultural year concept. An agricultural year spanned the two agricultural growing seasons.

20. The main state purchasing agency was Tsentrosoiuz.

21. Davies, *The Socialist Offensive*, 427.

22. Lewin, *Russian Peasants and Soviet Power*, 214–44.

23. Karcz, "Thoughts on the Grain Problem," 399–402.

24. Merl, *Der Agrarmarkt und die Neue Oekonomische Politik*, 313–67.

25. Davies, *The Socialist Offensive, chaps. 1 and 2*.

26. *Dobb, Soviet Economic Development*.

27. Karcz, "Thoughts on the Grain Problem," 399–402.

28. Merl, *Der Agrarmarkt und die Neue Oekonomische Politik*, 137–39.

29. Davies, *The Socialist Offensive*, 39–41.

30. See Karcz, "Thoughts on the Grain Problem"; and Smirnov, "Vremiia trudnykh voprosov."

31. This phenomenon is to be expected in a country more than 75 percent rural.

32. The most detailed account of the 1928–29 crisis is provided by Davies, *The Socialist Offensive*, chap. 2.

33. These stylized facts are taken from Paul R. Gregory and Robert C. Stuart, *Soviet Economic Structure and Performance*, 3d ed. (New York: Harper and Row, 1986), chaps. 3 and 4; D. Gale Johnson, "Agricultural Production," in Bergson and Kuznets, *Economic Trends in the Soviet Union*, 203–34; Janet G. Chapman, "Consumption," in Bergson and Kuznets, *Economic Trends in the Soviet Union*, 235–82. The fact that the net flow of saving between agriculture and industry did not increase appears to be shown by both the Millar and Ellman studies cited in note 9. Hence it is included as a stylized fact.

34. Danilov, *Rural Russia under the New Regime*, chap. 2.

35. Preobrazhensky's views are summarized in Alexander Erlich, *The Soviet Industrialization Debate, 1924–1928* (Cambridge, Mass.: Harvard University Press, 1960).

36. Sah and Stiglitz, "The Economics of the Price Scissors."

37. W. Arthur Lewis, "Development with Unlimited Supplies of Labor," *The*

Manchester School, May 1954; John Fei and Gustav Ranis, *Development of the Labor Surplus Economy* (Homewood, Ill.: Irwin, 1964).

38. This outcome depends on agricultural supply elasticities being positive. If agricultural marketings behave perversely with respect to agriculture's terms of trade, the outcome is ambiguous. Sah and Stiglitz cite empirical studies to support their assumption of positive supply elasticities. Millar and Chayanov have offered arguments that question the assumption of positive supply elasticities of Russian peasant agriculture. On this, see Millar, "A Reformulation of A. V. Chayanov's Theory of Peasant Economy."

39. Abram Bergson, *The Real National Income of Soviet Russia since 1928* (Cambridge, Mass.: Harvard University Press, 1961), 257.

40. Fei and Ranis, *Development of the Labor Surplus Economy*.

41. The return to landowners is ignored because of the socialization of land ownership in the Soviet case.

42. James R. Millar, "Soviet Rapid Development and the Agricultural Surplus Hypothesis," *Soviet Studies* 22, no. 1 (July 1970); A. A. Barsov, "Sel'skoe khoziaistvo i istochniki sotsialisticheskogo nakopleniia v gody pervoi piatiletki (1928–1933)," *Istoriia SSSR* no. 3 (1968).

43. Ellman, "Did the Agricultural Surplus.".

44. Hunter, "Soviet Agriculture with and without Collectivization."

45. Simon Kuznets, "A Comparative Appraisal," 345–47.

46. James R. Millar, *The Soviet Economic Experiment*, ed. Susan Linz (Urbana: University of Illinois Press, 1990), chap. 5.

47. Hunter, "Soviet Agriculture with and without Collectivization."

48. Ibid., 210–11.

49. For Holland Hunter's broader intersectoral and overall growth projections without collectivization, see Holland Hunter and Everett Rutan, "Modelling Structural Change Using Early Soviet Data," *Journal of Development Economics* 9, no. 1 (August 1981): 65–87.

50. See Mark Harrison, "Why Was NEP Abandoned?" in Stuart, *The Soviet Rural Economy*, 63–78.

51. White, *Russia and America*, chaps. 3–5; Kahan, *The Plow, the Hammer, and the Knout*, chap. 2.

52. This appendix is based on Paul Gregory and Manoucher Mokhtari, "State Grain Prices, Relative Prices, and the Soviet Grain Procurement Crisis," in *Explorations in Economic History* 30 (1993): 182–94.

53. Transaction costs include transportation costs, fines and penalties imposed for selling to private traders, and the loss of credits.

54. As noted above, the dependent variable—the private surplus—is an artificial construct. This fact is seen in the modeling of the S, p_m relationship. One can make theoretically sound predictions about the effect of p_m on R or on $P + G$, but not about its effect on S. The effect on S depends on how peasants distribute their sales to state or to private buyers. In normal economic models, this would be an uninteresting question because both would pay the same price.

55. The regions are Ukraine, Belorussia, consumer region, black earth region, middle Volga, lower Volga, Crimea, northern Kazakhstan, Kazakstan-Kirgizia, Urals, Siberia, far north, Mongolia.

56. *Statisticheski spravochnik za 1928*, sec. 3, Tables 5 and 24; sec. 6, Tables 68 and 71; T.S.U., *Indeks roznlichnykh tsen za vremiia 1. Okt. 1925 po 1. Apreliia 1926*, (Moscow: n.p., 1926), Tables 2 and 3.

57. These price ratios are available only for six of the thirteen regions. Rather than using average values for the available regions, we constructed an instrumental variable estimation where rural population and the prices of meat, wheat, and barley were utilized as instruments. This allows consistent coefficient estimates of the price ratio.

58. See Merl, *Der Agrarmarkt und die Neue Okonomische Politik*, chaps. 2, 4, and 5.

59. Testing this restriction by a Chow-test (at a .05 confidence interval) yields a 0.9 value, supporting the uniform response of S^* to the effect of market prices.

CHAPTER 7

1. For discussions of Soviet economic growth and a structural change during the Soviet era, see Bergson, *The Real National Income of Soviet Russia since 1928*; Kuznets, "A Comparative Appraisal"; Gur Ofer, *The Service Sector in Soviet Economic Growth* (Cambridge, Mass.: Harvard University Press, 1936); Gregory, *Socialist and Nonsocialist Industrialization Patterns*; Gregory and Stuart, *Soviet Economic Structure and Performance*, chap. 12; and Rush Greenslade, "The Real Gross National Product of the USSR, 1950–1975," in Joint Economic Committee, *Soviet Economy in a New Perspective* (Washington, D.C.: U.S. Government Printing Office, 1976), 269–300. This chapter is based on Gregory, *Russian National Income*.

2. Bergson, *Real National Income of Soviet Russia since 1928*, 217, 237.

3. Ibid., 217.

4. Gregory, *Russian National Income*, app. 6.

5. I apply fixed weights of 0.7 and 0.3 for labor and capital, respectively; thus I implicitly assume that the tsarist and Russian aggregate production functions were of the Cobb-Douglass type with a unitary elasticity of substitutions between capital and labor. This assumption may not be accurate for the Soviet economy in the postwar period according to M.I. Weizman, "Soviet Postwar Economic Growth and Capital-Labor Substitutions, *American Economic Review* 60, no. 4 (September 1970): 676–92.

6. Bergson, *Real National Income of Soviet Russia since 1928*, chap. 3.

7. Interviews with former Soviet citizens reporting about their lives during the period of stagnation confirm the desparate state they considered the Soviet economy to be in. The majority of respondents felt that their living standards were falling and that economywide productivity was falling. On this, see Paul Gregory, "Productivity, Slack, and Time Theft in the Soviet Economy," James Millar (ed.), *Politics, Work, and Daily Life in the USSR: A Survey of Former Soviet Citizens* (New York: Cambridge University Press, 1987), 241–78.

8. For a survey of the estimates of Selyunin, Khanin, and Aganbegyan, see Directorate of Intelligence, *Revisiting Soviet Economic Performance under Glasnost: Implications for CIA Estimates* (Washington, D.C.: Central Intelligence Agency, 1988).

9. G. I. Khanin estimates long-term Soviet growth for the period 1928 to 1987 at 85 perent of the Western estimates used in this chapter. See Mark Harrison, "Soviet Economic Growth Since 1928: The Alternative Statistics of G. I. Khanin," *Europe-Asia Studies* 45, no. 1 (1993): 141–67.

10. Paul Marer, "Conceptual and Practical Problems of Comparative Economic Performance of the East European Economies in Transition," Bureau of Labor Statistics Conference on Economic Statistics for Economies in Transition, Washington, D.C., February 14–16, 1991.

Appendix B

1. This appendix is adapted from Paul Gregory, "National Income," in R. W. Davies (ed.), *From Tsarism to the New Economic Policy* (London: Macmillan, 1990), 237–47.

2. Gosplan SSSR, *Kontrol'nye tsifry narodnogo khoziaistva na 1928–1929 g.* (Moscow: Izdatel'stvo Planovoe Khoziaistvo, 1929), 68–72.

3. Prokopovich's 1918 study is *Opyt ischisleniya narodnogo dokhoda 50 gubernii evropeiskoi Rossii v 1900–1913 gg.* (Moscow: Sovet Vserossiiskikh Koopertivnykh Sezdov, 1918).

4. A. L. Vainshtein, *Narodnyi dokhod Rossii i SSSR* (Moscow: Nauka, 1969), 102.

5. S. N. Prokopovich, *The National Income of the USSR*, memorandum 3, Birmingham Bureau of Research on Russian Economic Conditions, November 1931. Prokopovich's 1918 study of 1913 national income is summarized in Prokopovich, *Opyt ischisleniya narodnogo dokhoda 50 gubernii evropeiskoi Rossii v 1900–1913 gg.*

6. Falkus, "Russia's National Income, 1913: A Revaluation," *Economica* 35, no. 137 (Feb. 1968): 52–73.

7. Actually Falkus compares his results with the original Prokopovich calculation of 1918 and Prokopovich's 1931 calculation.

8. Gregory, *Russian National Income.*

9. Bergson, *The Real National Income of Soviet Russia since 1928.*

10. Vainshtein, *Narodnyi dokhod Rossii i SSSR*, 102–7.

11. See A. L. Vainshtein, *Tseny i tsenoobrazovanie v SSSR v vostannovitel'nyi period, 1921–1928 gg.* (Moscow: Nauka, 1972).

12. Gosplan SSSR, *Kontrol'nye tsifry narodnogo khoziaistva na 1926–1927 g.,* 215.

13. Vainshtein, *Tseny i tsenoobrazovanie v SSSR v vostannovitel'nyi period, 1921–1928 gg.,* 14–16.

14. Gregory, *Russian National Income*, 108–15.

15. The Davies-Wheatcroft comment on retained farm products was transmitted via personal correspondence. It is published in S. G. Wheatcroft, R. W. Davies, and J. M. Cooper, "Soviet Industrialisation Reconsidered: Some Preliminary Conclusions about Economic Development between 1926 and 1941," *Economic History Review* (1986): 267–68.

16. Gregory, *Russian National Income*, Table 3.6.

17. G. A. Dikhtyar, *Vnutrenniaia torgovlia v dorevoliutsionnoi Rossii* (Moscow: Nauka, 1960), 83.

18. These studies are all published in Davies, *From Tsarism to the New Economic Policy.*

19. Nutter's results are summarized in his chapter "The Soviet Economy: Retrospect and Prospect," in Abshire and Allen (eds.), *National Security: Political, Military and Economic Strategies in the Decade Ahead* (New York: 1963), 165.

20. See Wheatcroft, Davies, and Cooper, "Soviet Industrialisation Reconsidered," 267.

21. See R. W. Davies, "Soviet Industrial Production, 1928–1937: The Rival Estimates," *Centre for Russian and East European Studies Discussion Papers*, no. 18 (Birmingham: University of Birmingham, 1978).

22. Gosplan SSSR, *Kontrol'nye tsifry narodnogo khoziaistva na 1928–1929 g.,* Tables 6.1 and 6.2.

INDEX